Making Poetry Matter

Also available from Bloomsbury

Literacy on the Left, Andrew Lambirth

Making Poetry Happen, edited by Sue Dymoke, Myra Barrs, Andrew Lambirth and Anthony Wilson

MasterClass in English Education, edited by Sue Brindley and Bethan Marshall

Teaching English Texts 11-18, Sue Dymoke

The Poetry Toolkit, Rhian Williams

Making Poetry Matter

International Research on Poetry Pedagogy

Edited by Sue Dymoke, Andrew Lambirth and
Anthony Wilson

Bloomsbury Academic
An imprint of Bloomsbury Publishing Plc

B L O O M S B U R Y
LONDON • NEW DELHI • NEW YORK • SYDNEY

Bloomsbury Academic
An imprint of Bloomsbury Publishing Plc

50 Bedford Square	1385 Broadway
London	New York
WC1B 3DP	NY 10018
UK	USA

www.bloomsbury.com

BLOOMSBURY and the Diana logo are trademarks of Bloomsbury Publishing Plc

First published 2013
Paperback edition first published 2015
Reprinted 2015

© Sue Dymoke, Andrew Lambirth, Anthony Wilson and Contributors, 2013

Sue Dymoke, Andrew Lambirth, Anthony Wilson and Contributors have asserted their right under the Copyright, Designs and Patents Act, 1988, to be identified as Author of this work.

All rights reserved. No part of this publication may be reproduced or transmitted in any form or by any means, electronic or mechanical, including photocopying, recording, or any information storage or retrieval system, without prior permission in writing from the publishers.

No responsibility for loss caused to any individual or organization acting on or refraining from action as a result of the material in this publication can be accepted by Bloomsbury or the author.

British Library Cataloguing-in-Publication Data
A catalogue record for this book is available from the British Library.

ISBN: HB: 978-1-4411-0147-1
PB: 978-1-4725-1505-6
ePUB: 978-1-4411-6353-0
ePDF: 978-1-4411-0568-4

Library of Congress Cataloging-in-Publication Data
Making poetry matter: international research on poetry pedagogy/edited by Sue Dymoke, Andrew Lambirth and Anthony Wilson.
   pages cm
Includes bibliographical references and index.
ISBN 978-1-4411-0147-1 (hardcover) – ISBN 978-1-4411-6353-0 (epub) –
ISBN 978-1-4411-0568-4 (pdf) – ISBN 978-1-4725-1505-6 (pbk.) 1. Poetry–Study and teaching. I. Dymoke, Sue, 1962- II. Lambirth, Andrew, 1959- III. Wilson, Anthony, 1964-
PN1101.M27 2013
808.1'071–dc23
2013005998

Typeset by Deanta Global Publishing Services, Chennai, India
Printed and bound in Great Britain

Contents

Acknowledgements   vii
Publisher's Acknowledgements   viii
List of Figures   ix
List of Tables   x
About the Contributors   xi

1   Introduction   *Sue Dymoke, Andrew Lambirth and Anthony Wilson*   1

Part 1   Reading Poetry

2   Exploring Teachers' Positions and Practices   *Teresa Cremin*   9
3   Primary Student Teachers' Attitudes Towards Poetry and Poetry Teaching   *Fiona M. Collins and Alison Kelly*   20
4   Exploring Resistance to Poetry in Advanced English Studies   *Gary Snapper*   31
5   Commentary: Confidence and Resilience in Poetry Teaching   *David Whitley*   42

Part 2   Writing Poetry

6   Students' Metalinguistic Understanding of Poetry Writing   *Debra Myhill*   49
7   Teachers' Metaphors of Teaching Poetry Writing   *Anthony Wilson*   61
8   Ecocritical Approaches to Writing Nature Poetry   *Sasha Matthewman*   71
9   Responding to Children's Poetry   *Andrew Lambirth, Sarah Smith and Susanna Steele*   84
10   Commentary: Writing Poetry, Teaching Poetry   *Jane Spiro*   96

Part 3   Speaking Poetry and Listening to Poetry

11   Preadolescents Writing and Performing Poetry   *Janine L. Certo*   105

List of Tables

7.1	Summary of codes: Metaphors of 'freedom' in teachers' responses about poetry writing instruction	65
9.1	Interviewee profile	90
11.1	Demographic Summary of Student Participants	108
17.1	Chart used to explore how each mode offers a different layer of meaning	178

About the Contributors

Joy Alexander was a secondary school teacher for 20 years, mainly in Northern Ireland, and lectures in the School of Education, Queen's University, Belfast, UK, where she shares responsibility for the PGCE English course. Her recent research and publications focus on the synergies between English and science education.

Myra Barrs is Visiting Professor at the University of East London, UK, a former co-director of the Centre for Primary Literacy Education and an elected member of the International Reading Association's Reading Hall of Fame. Publications include *The Reader in the Writer* (with Valerie Cork, 2001).

Julie Blake is education manager of *The Poetry Archive* in the UK and a research associate at the University of Bristol, UK. Publications include *The Full English* (2006).

Janine L. Certo is associate professor of language and literacy in the Department of Teacher Education and a principal investigator for the Literacy Achievement Research Center (LARC) at Michigan State University, USA.

Fiona M. Collins is principal lecturer in English education at Roehampton University, UK. She is the MA convener for English education and co-ordinates the suite of MA programmes in the Department of Education.

Teresa Cremin is Professor of Education (literacy) at the Open University, UK, a trustee and past president of UKLA and board member of Booktrust and the Poetry Archive. She is also a joint coordinator of the BERA Special Interest Group on Creativity and chair of the IRA's Outstanding Dissertation Award Committee.

Sue Dymoke is a poet, senior lecturer and national teaching fellow at the School of Education, University of Leicester, UK, where she co-leads the Secondary PGCE course. She was a co-convenor of the ESRC *Poetry Matters* seminar series. Publications include: *Teaching English Texts 11–18* (2009) and *Moon at the Park and Ride* (2012).

John Gordon is Senior Lecturer in the School of Education and Lifelong Learning at the University of East Anglia, UK, where he leads the English 11–18 PGCE/Masters course and co-directs the full PGCE(M) programme. His doctoral research focused on children's responses to heard poetry.

Janette Hughes is Associate Professor in language and literacy education at The University of Ontario Institute of Technology, Canada. In 2011, she was a recipient of the Early Researcher's Award, sponsored by the Ontario Ministry of Research and Innovation, the first educational researcher to receive this honour.

Alison Kelly is Principal Lecturer in English education at Roehampton University, UK. She coordinates the English education team. She is a co-editor (with Judith Graham) of *Reading Under Control* and *Writing Under Control*.

Andrew Lambirth is Professor of Education in the School of Education at the University of Greenwich, UK. Publications include *Teaching Early Reading and Phonics: Creative Approaches to Early Literacy*. (2011). He was a co-convenor of the ESRC *Poetry Matters* seminar series.

Sasha Matthewman is Senior Lecturer in the School of Curriculum and Pedagogy at the University of Auckland, New Zealand. Her book, *Teaching Secondary English as if the Planet Matters*, was published in 2010.

Debra Myhill is a professor in the College of Social Sciences and International Studies at the University of Exeter, UK, where she also leads the PGCE Secondary English with Media programme. Her research projects include *Grammar for Writing?* – an ESRC-funded study of the effectiveness of contextualized grammar teaching.

Vicky Obied is a lecturer in the Department of Educational Studies at Goldsmiths, University of London, UK, where she works on the PGCE secondary English with Media and Drama programme. Her expertise is in language development and she has published widely in this field.

Andrey Rosowsky is Director of Initial Teacher Education at the University of Sheffield, UK, and leads the PGCE course. Publications include *Heavenly*

Readings: Liturgical Literacy in a Multilingual Context (Multilingual Matters, 2008).

Sarah Smith is Senior Lecturer in the School of Education at the University of Greenwich, UK, where she leads the literacy team in the Primary Education Department.

Gary Snapper specializes in teaching literature at post-16 level. He is a research associate at Brunel University, editor of NATE's professional journal *Teaching English* and co-author *of Teaching English Literature 16–19* (2013).

Jane Spiro is Principal Lecturer in education and TESOL/Student Experience and a national teaching fellow at the Oxford Brookes University, UK. Her book, *New Methodologies for TESOL*, is published in 2013.

Susanna Steele is Senior Lecturer in primary education (English and literacy) at the School of Education at the University of Greenwich, UK. She is also education associate in learning and participation at The Unicorn Theatre for Children, UK.

Morag Styles is Professor of Poetry in the Faculty of Education, University of Cambridge, UK, where she currently leads an international project on the teaching of Caribbean poetry, working with partners at the University of the West Indies. Publications include *From the Garden to the Street: Three Hundred Years of Poetry for Children* (1998).

David Whitley is a university lecturer in the Faculty of Education, University of Cambridge, UK. He co-edited *Poetry and Childhood* (2010), with Morag Styles and Louise Joy and leads a British Academy-funded project on the teaching of poetry across institutional phases.

Anthony Wilson is a lecturer, poet and writing tutor. He leads the primary English PGCE course at the Graduate School of Education, University of Exeter, UK, and was a co-convener of the ESRC *Poetry Matters* seminar series. Publications include *The Poetry Book for Primary Schools* (1998) and *Riddance* (2012).

1

Introduction

Sue Dymoke, Andrew Lambirth and Anthony Wilson

This book has two key purposes. Primarily, it places on record the significant international research perspectives on poetry pedagogy that were first presented and debated at the *Poetry Matters* seminar series (2011–2012) funded by the Economic and Social Research Council (ESRC). Secondly, the book gives an international audience of English teachers, teacher educators, poets, researchers and other interested parties the opportunity to reflect on these perspectives and their implications for research and practice in 5–19 classrooms in a range of contexts. The *Poetry Matters* seminar series was the first of its kind. It drew on the research and experience of both established and new researchers in the field together with contributions from teachers, practising poets and writers in schools and other educational settings. This book mirrors the highly distinctive nature of the series.

We believe there has been a woeful neglect of the enormous contribution poetry can make to young people's knowledge and intellectual development. Poetry creates opportunities to enrich an awareness and knowledge of language through both its reading and writing. Andrews (1991) reminds us of how contemplation of poetry can create a 'margin of silence' allowing us to consider the relationship between words and their features – the rhythmic, auditory and visual. These intellectual benefits of reading poetry are further confirmed by poetry's ability to challenge young people's comprehension skills through the problematic nature of many texts with their 'hints and clues and silences' (Dias and Hayhoe 1988:86). Poetry presents unique stimulating challenges that the seminar series sought to address.

Some evidence suggests that poetry is the least well-taught part of English curricula in the United Kingdom and abroad (Thompson 1996; Ofsted 2007; Locke 2009, 2010) and is indeed disappearing from the curriculum in some schools in England, due to the pressure of National Testing and league tables (Henry 2001; Ofsted 2007).This situation is in stark contrast to the wider interest in poetry of society at large where it is currently finding new audiences through rap music, the slam movement, festivals, open mic readings and online. In addition, learning how to teach poetry has long been identified as an aspect of the English curriculum that presents specific pedagogic challenges for both trainee and experienced teachers working in many different international contexts, many of whom appear to lack confidence in the genre (see Benton 1984; Ray 1999; Dymoke and Hughes 2009; Lambirth et al. 2012). Although these challenges are being recognized, non-rhetorical, systematic research on poetry pedagogy is scant compared with other genres (Wilson 2005a).There is also a gap within the literature of writing theory where poetry is concerned. Poetry does not feature in paradigms of writing development established by Hayes and Flower (1980), Bereiter and Scardamalia (1987), Kellogg (1994) or Sharples (1999). There remains an urgent need to address these key pedagogical issues. The ESRC *Poetry Matters* seminar series initiated debate on many of the issues above. It provided opportunities for in-depth reflection on poetry pedagogy and planning for further research on a seriously neglected aspect of the English curriculum. We hope that the publication of *Making Poetry Matter* will enable this debate to move on to the next stage and lead to new understandings about the challenges and pleasures of teaching poetry.

Organization of this book

Making Poetry Matter is organized in four main sections that reflect the structure of the four seminars and feature a number of papers from each seminar strand. Each section is accompanied by a short commentary from another contributor to the seminar series. In shaping this book and striving to convey a sense of the dialogue that developed across the four seminars, we are indebted to Viv Ellis, Carol Fox and Brian Street's *Rethinking English in Schools* (2007) for providing us with such an appropriate model to stimulate discussion.

The first section of *Making Poetry Matter* focuses on the demands that reading poetry and responding to poetry present to learners and teachers and how these demands are addressed in different contexts and with different types of learners. In 'Exploring teachers' positions and practices: a case study of one poetry teacher', Teresa Cremin maps the interplay between one teacher's developing knowledge and enthusiasm for poetry, and the subtle shifts in her positioning and practices as a teacher of poetry. Cremin points to the growing sense of agency and responsibility for poetry embedded within these practices when a teacher recognizes what counts as poetry in school and shares a developing love of poetry with younger learners. In a complementary vein, Fiona Collins and Alison Kelly's chapter 'Primary Student Teachers' Attitudes towards Poetry and Poetry teaching' focuses on primary student teachers' poetry learning journeys from childhood through to teacher training and the impact of these on their developing practice in school. Their chapter reports on a research project carried out by a large UK provider of initial teacher education and is contextualized by a review of curriculum developments in relation to the teaching of poetry and research perspectives about teacher and student teacher subject knowledge and attitudes. Gary Snapper's chapter 'Exploring Resistance to Poetry in Advanced English Studies' takes us to the other end of the 5–19 continuum. It examines some of the ways in which this resistance to poetry manifests itself in high school and university English, and reflects on the ways in which it might be related to broader issues pertaining to literary study in schools and universities.

In the second section, we focus on writing poetry and the demands it presents to learners and teachers. We investigate how the writing process is conceptualized and taught. Debra Myhill's chapter 'Weaving words: students' metalinguistic understanding of poetry writing' analyses how what young people's thinking about poetry and their responses to discussing specific poems reveal about their conceptualization of poetry and poetry writing. She explores this within the paradigm of writing as design and argues that young people need to see beyond the words on a page to be able to experience the full range of meanings, associations and connotations that those words evoke. Anthony Wilson's chapter 'Teachers' metaphors of teaching poetry writing' examines the conceptualizations of teachers for whom poetry writing is a 'lifeline in a target driven job'. In a high-stakes context which does not explicitly reward poetry writing, these teachers are found to view poetry as simultaneously marginalized and a unique space where they have freedom to utilize, deepen and enjoy their own and learners' creativity.

In their chapter, 'Responding to Children's Poetry: Primary School Subject Leaders give their Views', Lambirth, Smith and Steele investigate some of the debates and tensions over the assessment of children's poetry and how this may provide the drive and motivations behind how poetry writing is being assessed in primary schools. The authors investigate what a small group of subject leaders said about responding to children's poetry in their schools. Top-down prescription and pressure to assess other forms of writing have led to its neglect in classrooms. Yet, the authors' conclusions are more positive and point to how teachers can take genuine delight in teaching poetry and responding to what children have written in sensitive and formative ways. Even those teachers who declared that they did not take a real interest in poetry themselves, in the context of the pedagogy, could galvanize their professional knowledge to make important interventions.

Continuing this section of the book's theme of encouraging children to write poetry, Sasha Matthewman's chapter 'Ecocritical Approaches to Writing Nature Poetry' asks 'Can poetry save the earth?' She outlines the 'ecocritical' moves involved in reading a selection of nature poems before exploring the implications of these ecocritical moves in relation to established methods for teaching children to write poetry in a case study located in a place with deep poetic connections – Tintern Abbey. Matthewman argues that an ecocritical approach to the teaching of poetry can forge strong links between learning about poetry and learning about locality.

The third section explores the challenges that teaching speaking and listening and poetry present to learners and teachers. In 'Poetic Voices: Preadolescents Writing and Performing Poetry', Janine Certo draws on a study of classroom and school-based poetry writing and performance among US children to ask 'What do fifth graders' poems, their discourse about their poems, and their discourse about their performances reveal about their poetry writing and performance practices?' Certo, like several other authors published here, is a poet who uses both her skills as a writer and a researcher to analyse the impact that the performances had on students' identity as writers and their understandings of the genre. Her work emphasizes the symbiotic relationship between who we are and what we write. In contrast, John Gordon's chapter focuses on listening to poetry. In 'Listening for echoes: heard poetry and oral response', he uses transcripts of recorded classroom discussion to consider how students experience poems through listening and use additional resources such as volume, intonation, pace and silences to develop their distinctive responses. Gordon's findings suggest that the pedagogy of poetry needs to recognize the unique nature of this process and to acknowledge 'the new effort of attention' (Lawrence 1929: 255) that is an integral part of the poetic experience. Joy Alexander argues that a large part of the 'attention' poems require in the classroom is in fact aural: for learners to experience a poem it needs at the very least to be heard. Too often, like Coleridge's Wedding Guest, we 'domesticate the sublime' by paying lip service to poems and anatomizing their meanings before we listen to them as living literature.

In the final section, the chapters investigate the transformative and creative potential of poetry teaching to support the intellectual and aesthetic development of all learners across the 5–19 age range. This section also considers the assessment challenges presented to teachers by shifting constructions of curricula as they endeavour to work with learners in a range of contexts.

In her chapter 'Developing poetry pedagogy for EAL learners within inclusive intercultural practices', Vicky Obied explores the development of poetry pedagogy for EAL learners and examines how trainee teachers of English approach poetry in diverse multilingual school settings. She investigates pressing questions that arise when teaching poetry in inner city schools in London, England and contests existing relationships between language, power and pedagogies. In doing so, she argues that poetry uses language in aesthetic, imaginative and engaging ways that have considerable potential to extend the learning of EAL pupils. In 'Teaching poetry in New Zealand secondary schools at a time of curriculum change', Sue Dymoke takes us to the Southern hemisphere to focus on the pressures on poetry pedagogy felt by teachers there. These issues are explored with an eye to the opportunities in New Zealand classrooms for reading and composing poetry that represents a range of cultural perspectives and embraces the specific contexts in which students live and learn. Janette Hughes's chapter 'Digital Poetry, Power and Social Justice' gives a remarkable insight into the lives of adolescent learners in Canada who merge digital technology with poetry to literally find a voice and speak about their identity. Giving learners access to 'worlds of fantasy and reality' in this way is found to foster and strengthen their self-image as agents of change.

The Poetry Matters seminar series also included highly successful themed workshops. Materials from the workshops, teacher case studies and the poetry subsequently created by school students will be included in a companion volume *Making Poetry Happen*. The paperback edition of *Making Poetry Matter* will be published in tandem with *Making Poetry Happen*. The latter text will showcase the immediate and, we hope, lasting impact of the seminar series and look beyond it to consider how practices in poetry teaching can be developed. It will revisit learners' and teachers' perceptions of what poetry teaching is like within a variety of contexts (including initial teacher education) and provide support for the development of creative practices across the age phases.

The *Afterword* for this book has been written by two of the staunchest defenders and champions of poetry in schools. In this skilfully written piece, Myra Barrs and Morag Styles offer their wisdom on the state of poetry in schools now and for its prospects in the future. They also provide insights on what the current research and scholarship in this collection of essays tells us about poetry. They argue eloquently that poetry teaching can create change and can provide people with a unique way of perceiving everything. We are proud to have Myra Barrs and Morag Styles contribute to this book as they have given so much time and effort to supporting the teaching of poetry in schools over many years.

The editors of this book recognized the urgency of forcing the subject of teaching poetry in schools back to the centre of professional and academic debates about education. For too long poetry has been the area of English teaching that attracts only the sympathetic and guilty sighs of many teachers, advisors and education academics who have arguably had their attention distracted by the demands of targets, tests and league tables. We believe that it is a moral duty of policy makers and those involved in education to champion poetry. All those teachers, poets and academics who joined us on the ESRC *Poetry Matters* seminars have begun the process of bringing poetry back to children in schools. The objective of the seminar series and these new poetry books is to rekindle a love for poetry and to regenerate the passion for introducing poems to young people. This is a fascinating area of education practice and research, and we have much to do to develop our understanding of how best to ensure that poetry is taught well in schools in the United Kingdom and internationally.

Sue Dymoke, Andrew Lambirth and Anthony Wilson
Leicester, Greenwich and Exeter
October 2012

Part One

Reading Poetry

2

Exploring Teachers' Positions and Practices

Teresa Cremin

Drawing upon research into teachers' reading habits, practices and identities, and data from a United Kingdom Literacy Association (UKLA) project which sought to widen teachers' repertoires and practice with regard to reading for pleasure, this chapter explores the interplay between one teacher's developing knowledge and enthusiasm for poetry, and the subtle shifts in her positions and practices as a teacher of poetry. In tune with US studies which show that 'Reading Teachers; teachers who read and readers who teach' (Commeyras et al. 2003) offer significant support to child readers, it focuses on a single 'Poetry Teacher' – who both reads poetry for her own pleasure and teaches poetry to young learners. In the project, this primary phase professional sought to document her own reading habits and practices as she read poetry and also scrutinized the reading practices and positions enacted in her classroom. As a consequence, she sought to widen these and came to share more explicitly her own enthusiasm and engagement as an adult reader of poetry with the children.

The chapter highlights the significance of considering the relationship between teachers' positions and practices and those selected and enacted in the literacy classroom in relation to poetry. It reveals the advantages that can accrue when teachers recognize they are responsible for framing what counts as poetry in school and share a developing love of poetry with younger learners.

Teachers' reading habits and practices

There is evidence to indicate that teachers are adult readers (Cremin et al. 2008a) and that student teachers come to teach English due to a love of literature (Peel

2000; Gannon and Davies 2007). However, while a UKLA *Teachers as Readers: Phase I* survey of 1200 primary practitioners found that three quarters of the sample had read a book in the last 3 months, less than 2 per cent of the respondents had read any poetry over this period and only 1.5 per cent noted poetry as their favourite childhood reading (Cremin et al. 2008a). In relation to these teachers' knowledge and use of poetry in the classroom, there was even more cause for concern. It was evident that they had extremely weak subject knowledge in relation to poetry: 22 per cent did not name a single poet, 58 per cent named two, one or no poets and only 10 per cent named six (Cremin et al. 2008b). Overall, there was considerable reliance upon the work of poets and particularly named poems by authors that the teachers were likely to have known since childhood. The English inspectorate survey also noted that teachers tend to lean upon a limited range of poets and poems in school, relying upon those presented in publishers' resources or from childhood (Ofsted 2007). There is a strikingly similar 'canon' of children's poetry noted in their list of the most well-used 'primary poems' –' poems regularly used for study in literacy lessons' such as Stevenson's 'From A Railway Carriage' and Milligan's 'On the Ning Nang Nong' (Ofsted 2007).

In the UKLA survey, the highest number of mentions was for Michael Rosen (452) with only five others gaining over a hundred mentions, namely: Allan Ahlberg (207), Roger McGough (197), Roald Dahl (165), Spike Milligan (159) and Benjamin Zephaniah (131). After these, only three poets were mentioned more than 50 times: Edward Lear (85), Ted Hughes (58) and A. A. Milne (57). Only 13 women poets were mentioned: Grace Nicholls received the most mentions (16), followed by Christina Rossetti (11) and Eleanor Farjeon (9), Carol Ann Duffy (not then English Poet Laureate) received 3 mentions, and Jackie Kay and Valerie Bloom 2 each, while Wendy Cope received just one. Although this gender imbalance may reflect wider ideological, cultural or publishing practices, it has potential consequence for the classroom. In addition to this lack of knowledge, and Ofsted's perception that many primary and secondary teachers are neither keen nor regular readers of poetry, concerns have also been voiced about a perceived overemphasis on the study and imitation of poetry's forms and features (Wilson 2005: Grainger et al. 2005) and the relative infrequency with which teachers read poetry aloud. For example in the UKLA survey, less than 2 per cent of the teachers who had read aloud to their classes for pleasure in the preceding 6 months mentioned reading any poetry (Cremin et al. 2008b).

Teachers' reading identities

In relation to research exploring teachers' reading identities and positioning in the classroom, there is evidence to suggest that teachers' practice may be morally compromised in the context of high-stakes testing (Assaf 2008; Dooley 2005; English et al. 2002). Also that home, peer and institutional practices shape children's identities as readers (Hall 2002) and that teachers' conceptions of reading identities can frame and limit children's identities as readers (Hall et al. 2010). In addition, in the United States, autobiographical work suggests that an apparent continuity exists between teachers and children as motivated and engaged readers (e.g. Bisplinghoff 2002; Dreher 2003). Some of this work claims that teachers' pleasure in literature influences both their personal lives and their classroom practice (Rummel and Quintero 1997; Commeyras et al. 2003). Nonetheless, it is noteworthy that the US studies which foreground the conception of a Reading Teacher tend to rely on autobiographical self-reports from teachers on credit-bearing courses. There is almost no observation in context, little or no attention to children's perspectives and a lack documentation of the consequences of this stance for learners.

The Phase II study, on which this chapter draws, chose to focus not just on teachers, but also on learners. Children's development as readers was also tracked, and observations were used to document some of the ways in which connections between the teachers' personal reading insights and their classroom practice were made manifest.

The project *teachers as readers phase II*

The UKLA project *Teachers as Readers: Building Communities of Readers (2007–8) Phase II* was planned as a response to the above concerns about teachers' habits and practices as readers of poetry, and to the recognition that teachers' identities and conceptions of reading can frame and constrain children's literate identities. It sought to develop children's reading for pleasure through expanding teachers' knowledge and use of children's literature and to interrogate the concept of Reading Teachers. Forty-three primary teachers were involved from five Local Authorities (LAs) in England; nine of these were from Medway (three KS1 and six KS2). This LA chose to focus on poetry.

In their local group as well as through National Days, the Medway teachers were challenged and supported to widen their working repertoires of adult and children's poetry. In local sessions in particular, poetry was read aloud, the teachers were invited to share their forays into the work of self-selected poets and they borrowed from a newly constituted collection of poetry anthologies. The first term of this year-long project was almost exclusively devoted to teachers' own reading and sharing of texts; individually and collaboratively, they engaged in explorations of poetry through art, drama, dance, discussion and writing. The teachers as co-participant researchers were also invited to document their learning journeys, to reflect upon their attitudes, choices, habits, practices and preferences as readers of adult and children's poetry and to record their thoughts in reflective journals.

In terms two and three, while the teachers continued to read poetry, the core focus shifted to the classroom; they were encouraged both to consider their positions/stances as readers *and* as teachers of poetry and to explore any opportunities which emerged as a result of either stance influencing the other. The teachers also tracked the responses of three 'disaffected and reluctant' child readers to their changing pedagogic practice, and Moss's (2000) category of 'can but don't' readers was employed for this purpose. In addition, Medway organized an end-of-year poetry festival for all the teachers and children involved (Wells and Swain 2008).

In sum, the project involved considerable reflection on learning; the teachers were invited to

- participate personally as well as professionally as readers
- develop their reflective awareness of themselves as readers' –their metacognitive knowledge about the social processes of reading
- explore the pedagogic consequences of their personal /professional engagement and reflection.

In order to document any teacher knowledge expansion and changes to pedagogic practice, as well as to understand any dispositional shifts on the part of the practitioners, the research team identified a random sub-sample of two schools per LA for case study enquiries. Baseline, mid-phase and end-of-project data about these teachers' knowledge and practices was gathered (through surveys, interviews and observations in school), and three interviews were undertaken across the year with each of these practitioners as well as three with their head teachers and the disaffected readers, respectively. The case study teachers' professional learning portfolios were additionally subject to meta-analysis; these large files included common project prompts, the teachers' own documentation about their reading and their observations and assessments of the focus children. One of the Medway case studies, Brenda, (a pseudonym) represents the focus of this chapter.

Project data analysis

A mixed methods approach was used for data analysis. Initially, the data was analysed inductively, with the Medway assigned researcher working independently to draw out themes from her case studies, one of which was Brenda. Subsequently, data were categorized under the project's themes/aims and new themes that emerged in the analytical process. The selection and segmentation of this data was undertaken through purposive sampling (Strauss and Corbin 1990) and was analysed for thematic content using the iterative process of categorical analysis (Coffey and Atkinson 1996). The multiple sources of data supported the reliability and validity of the findings and helped with the triangulation of the data. All data were analysed by more than one team member and were cross-checked with an independent researcher.

Across the period of the project, an increase in all the Medway teachers' personal pleasure in, and breadth of knowledge of, poetry was noted, alongside shifts in pedagogy and new relationships with children (Cremin et al. 2009). Although some of the teachers expressed reservations about taking time to share something of their own poetry reading in school and perceived this might be time wasting, often commenting that such practice was neither recognized nor expected by the Primary National Strategy (DfES 2006). Brenda, however, sought to explore the transformative potential of this personal/professional identity shift and over time came to adopt a new stance – that of a Poetry Teacher. Four main threads emerged through analysis of the dataset which related to this teacher. These included

- increased pleasure in reading poetry and widening repertoire
- increased sharing of own poetry reading in school
- increased awareness of her own reading strategies while reading poetry and
- influence upon the children

It is to an examination of the themes that this chapter now turns, seeking to illuminate the synergies between Brenda's own rekindled knowledge and pleasure in poetry, her sharing of this and the development of her pedagogic practice which was reshaped in response to a new meta-cognitive awareness of the social practice of reading poetry.

A case study of an emerging Poetry Teacher

Through the project, Brenda, who had been teaching for 31 years, was challenged to develop knowledge of poetry and share this with the 6–7-year olds she taught in a large two-form entry infant school in Medway. In an early interview, this teacher, who worked as the literacy consultant in her school, acknowledged that she had never thought of sharing her own reading habits and interests; she thought 'the children would 'be far too young . . . I just don't think they'll be interested in what I read'. However, her journey as a Poetry Teacher was to indicate to Brenda that this was a misconception.

Increased pleasure in reading poetry and widening repertoire

In talking about her reading history, Brenda revealed that when she had learnt to read she had struggled and had felt labelled because she needed additional help. Many years later as a young teacher a pile of flashcards had fallen out of a cupboard and involuntarily her stomach had dropped, and the memories of her early difficulties returned. Yet, somewhere on her journey (she was unsure when), she had found a deep satisfaction in reading. She perceived this was influenced in part because of her father's love of the sound and savour of words, and in part was prompted by friends who swapped books and shared their preparedness to read. From the first interview, Brenda framed herself as a keen reader, listing historical novels, texts about China (her new daughter-in-law was Chinese), newspapers and specialist magazines about making scrapbooks as her current reading interests. She observed though that she had not read much poetry in years and set herself the challenge of getting to know the work of two contemporary poets each term. In the early phase interview, she observed that she had selected Gervase Phinn, (as she had not appreciated he wrote poetry) and Sheree Fitch, a Canadian poet whose work she had found in one of the Medway book boxes as her first pair to get to know. Brenda also found considerable pleasure in revisiting some of her old school favourites, as she noted:

> I'm finding again how much I love the old fashioned poets like Christina Rossetti and Robert Louis Stevenson. I'd forgotten how much music and pleasure there

is in their work- I'm reading a biography of Rossetti at the moment. (Written reflection, Dec)

By the Spring term, Brenda was immersed in reading poetry and other texts and displayed increased interest in poetry, initiating conversations about particular poems and poets, making recommendations to colleagues on the project and borrowing regularly from the box. This enthusiasm began to be transferred into the classroom, as she noted 'This project has given me the freedom to revisit texts that I'm more passionate about myself . . . . . It has allowed me into my teaching again- to share something of my own love of literature and particularly poetry' (Interview, Spring). It appeared that in being offered both time and texts, and being encouraged to read, research and share, her expanding repertoire had rekindled her pleasure in the music of poetry.

Increased sharing of own poetry reading in school

When Brenda engaged her class in discussing their own reading histories, memories and favourite books from home and the nursery, she also chose to share her own childhood difficulties and noted they seemed 'frankly amazed' and 'genuinely interested'(Researcher notes after an interview, Spring). This may have prompted her to share more in school of her own self-set challenges and current focus on poetry, which had immediate consequences, as she noted:

> I told them that I'm trying to get to know new poets and three children brought in collections from home for me to read- so I've lent them some of my books too. (Interview, mid-phase)

While Brenda perceived she read regularly, several times a week to her class, this was nearly always picture fiction and very rarely poetry; however, with a wider repertoire to draw upon, from the spring term she sought to read poetry aloud at least three times a week. She set up her own class poetry book box (she had borrowed a collection from the local library) and was observed reading and recommending particular books from this to individual children. In one case, her suggestion to Gurjit to read Claire Bevan's *Mermaid Poems* was to prove pivotal.

In addition, Brenda talked to the class about the frustrations and pleasure of reading and how she had 'fallen in love with words' when listening to the radio and as a consequence of her father reading aloud to her. She brought in some of her adult poetry reading, a Rossetti biography and scrapbook magazines as well as multiple other texts over time.

Heightened awareness of own reading/comprehension strategies in relation to poetry

Brenda, now read poetry outside school and talked to other project teachers about her favourite poets from childhood as well as new writers. She also sought to document her own reading habits, preferences and practices. She kept a reading journal in which she reflected upon her own reading of fiction, poetry and multiple other forms and in this way began to develop an increased awareness of the strategies she employed when reading. In relation to poetry, she noted, for example, that she engaged in an extensive re-reading of whole poems, verses and lines, in visualizing elements of poems and also in revisiting her own life through creating connecting visuals prompted by poems. Her journal also included multiple references to subvocalizing and a sense of felt/physical engagement with some poetry as well as frequent questioning of, and pondering on, the text and subtext. Recognizing that these were ways of her making sense of the poetry she was reading, Brenda came to reconsider her practice and the extent to which she was affording opportunities for the children to ponder and wonder, ask questions, engage physically with poems and represent the musical tenor of words.

As a consequence, Brenda began to share her personal feel for the pattern and rhythm in poetry and her love of classic verse in particular with the young children in her class. She noticed that her enthusiasm and pleasure in reading and re-reading child and adult texts had consequences in relation to the children's attitudes and this encouraged her. For example, she observed: 'I had been repeatedly reading R. L. Stevenson's "From a Railway Carriage" and was delighted when I heard Harry during ERIC time quietly reading it out loud, with the same rhythm and evident pleasure. It spurred me on' (Interview, early stage). She described offering much more time for reading poetry aloud and responding to the children's requests for particular poems, such that re-repeated readings became the norm. For example, she commented: 'They love My Cat Cuddles- It feels like I'm reading it nearly every day- "Again" they say- "Cuddles again!"' (Interview, mid-phase). In addition, she felt there was 'more time to ponder and wonder' . . . you know just read them, hear them and then NOT discuss them'. The observational notes evidence considerable informal discussion about poetry developed as well as peer-to-peer and child-to-teacher, teacher-to-child recommendations.

Other pedagogical consequences included a more integrated focus on art craft and display relating to poetry, and opportunities to re-read and add percussion and drama as well as dance. They also performed poems and wrote poetry together in the playground, on school trips and at the poetry festival. Much of this work involved the children selecting ways to represent their poems, though there was also teacher modelling. Additionally, appreciating that at home she would often read poetry in the comfort of an armchair or in the bath, Brenda set up an undersea role play /reading area based upon Claire Bevan's *Mermaid* collections and encouraged the children to read poetry in class reading time, and she too read alongside them. As she commented in the final interview:

> It is surprising how you think the children would obviously know you are a reader and enjoy reading – they don't necessarily – unless you explicitly tell them and give examples and show them the adult books you are reading . . . . I now teach from a reader's point of view. (Interview, Summer)

Influence upon the children

There was evidence that Brenda's increased knowledge, pleasure and use of poetry widened the children's repertoires and experience of poetry, and made a particular positive impact upon the case study readers' attitudes. As the year progressed, children were observed choosing to read poetry aloud to one another, choosing to perform poetry in 'golden time', writing poetry from choice and swapping poetry books. This was a significant change from the early observations in which poetry was 'on the shelf' and no child was observed choosing to access it in these ways.

In a final interview, the three initially reluctant readers offered an extensive list of their favourite poets, including Eleanor Farjeon, Robert Louis Stevenson, Wes Magee, Edward Lear, Tony Mitton, John Agard, Christina Rossetti, Sheree Fitch and Gervase Phinn. It was clear that the opportunities to read, re-read, hear, perform and write poetry had created a rich set of 'texts in common' for these children, who spontaneously quoted from some of their favourite poems in interview.

> Gurjit: I still love poetry best, though I like Anne Fine too.
> Jonah: My favourite reading is poetry too.
> Interviewer: Why do you think that is?
> Jonah: Well it's kind of short- though not all poems are short and it's enjoyable. You can choose what you like in a poetry book you don't have to read it all -you just read the ones that interest you- like My Cat Jack and the Boneyard Rap- who's that one –you remember?

> Toby: Wes Magee I think.
> Gurjit: Yeah it is.
> Gurjit and Jonah and Toby: (together)
> It's a boneyard rap and it's a scare
> Give your bones a shake up if you dare
> Rattle your teeth and waggle your jaw
> And let's do the boneyard rap once more.
> (Interview, final phase)

This practice of spontaneously quoting extracts and talking about their reading with ease and interest was a noticeable change from the autumn; it often had a performative element about it and reflected the children's new pleasure in word play and poetry, shaped perhaps by her intonation and engagement during reading aloud. As Toby, commented: 'When she reads some poems she slows down and kind of does actions and descriptions - so when the people turned into stone in the haunted house one she kind of did this (he imitates his teacher going into slow motion) and made it slow and we could see them turning into stone and it was brilliant . . . I love her reading aloud'.

Additionally, the children's perception of their teacher as a fellow reader shifted considerably; in the autumn, they were unable to offer information about her reading habits or preferences. As Brenda shared more of her reading life and pleasure in the sense, sounds and savour in poetry, her passion and practice was mirrored by the children and they developed an increased awareness of her as a reader. When asked what their teacher was reading, their responses were revealing.

> Jonah: 'Silver' by Walter de la Mare – we've heard it on a tape too, she remembers her dad reading it to her when she was a child.
> Troy: She's also reading Christina Rossetti's poems – like 'Hurt no living thing' – it's about animals and Mrs. Longing has been talking about how Christina Rossetti likes nature so she writes about it. You can choose what you write about if you are a poet.
> Jonah: She's doing a scrapbook and she chose this William Wordsworth poem and she's made the page with his poem – but she didn't know all of it – so we found it for her . . . the scrapbook is hers to hold onto stuff that's important to her.
> Gurjit: Also she's been reading Sheree Fitch, she's a new poet and she's still alive although lots of poets are dead.
> (Interview, mid phase, Y2, MBB)

Overall, the data suggest there was a complex interplay between Brenda's enhanced repertoire, her pedagogic practice and her positioning as an adult reader. She was socially interactive about what she read and this influenced what was available to be learnt about poetry and being a reader of poetry in her classroom.

Conclusion

This study highlights the crucial role of subject and pedagogical content knowledge, as well as personal passion and teachers' positioning. Brenda's stance strongly influenced the children's knowledge about, and pleasure in, poetry, and this contributed to the children's development as motivated and developing readers (Cremin et al. 2009). Teachers such as Brenda, for whom reading is significant in their own lives, who read more than the texts they teach and explicitly share their reading practices and preferences with children, appear to have the confidence to teach both effectively and affectively and draw in reluctant readers. Such teachers recognize, as Martin (2003: 16) acknowledges, that 'a poem is worth reading for its own sake not simply in order to teach something about poetry'.

If we are to alter the challenging poetry landscape in the primary years, then teachers and student teachers need to consider their identities and attitudes as poetry readers and as teachers of poetry, and more research needs to explore the dynamic between teachers' and children's reading practices and identities.

Acknowledgements

The author wishes to acknowledge the funders: the Esmée Fairbairn Foundation and UKLA and the research team: Marilyn Mottram, Fiona Collins, Sacha Powell and Kimberley Safford.

3

Primary Student Teachers' Attitudes Towards Poetry and Poetry Teaching

Fiona M. Collins and Alison Kelly

Introduction

The intention of this chapter is to explore primary student teachers' poetry learning journeys from childhood through to teacher training and the impact of these on their developing practice in school. The chapter reports on a research project carried out by a large provider of initial teacher education in the United Kingdom. The study is contextualized by a review of curriculum developments in relation to the teaching of poetry and research perspectives about teacher and student teacher subject knowledge and attitudes. Findings included differences between the students' personal experiences at primary and secondary school, with more positive responses noted in the primary phase. In addition, once on school experience, the confluence between the student teacher's learning journey and that of her class teacher is revealed as significant.

Journeys: Primary student teachers' attitudes towards poetry and poetry teaching

> I used to love writing poetry as a child, loved writing little poems about how I felt. I used it as form of expression so I thought I wanted to do that with children . . .
> (Memories from BA Primary Education student teacher)

Early encounters with poetry, whether positive or negative, are often mediated by teachers whose dispositions can create lasting impressions. Carol Ann Duffy memorably recalls the 'brilliant, enthusiastic' Miss Scriven, her secondary school teacher, who

> introduced us to Shakespeare, naturally, and to poetry, her particular interest. Keats 'Ode to a Nightingale' and, later, John Donne's 'The Flea' and Yeats' 'The Song of Wandering Aengus' inspired my first, imitative poems. All 'thou' and 'dost', but I was lost forever to prose, for which service Miss Scriven should be thanked. (Duffy as cited in Fraser 1992: 227)

This chapter explores the impact of childhood memories on student teachers' attitudes towards poetry and poetry teaching. These poetry learning journeys are significant because their professional identities (Day et al. 2006) are still evolving and are potentially vulnerable. The focus of the chapter is a study carried out with a group of primary education students who reflected on their attitudes towards poetry and their experiences of it: at home, at primary and secondary schools and, currently, as teachers to be.

Curriculum developments

Poetry and the teaching of poetry have always been a significant part of the English curriculum. In 1975, *A Language for Life* (DES 1975), also known as *The Bullock Report*, noted the challenges faced by teachers who are tasked with 'showing that poetry is not some inaccessible form of utterance, but that it speaks directly to children, as to everyone else, and has something to say which is relevant to their living here and now'(135).

It is hardly surprising, given these challenges, that Bullock found an uneven national picture across all age-phases in which poetry received a 'wide range of treatment' with some children rarely encountering it in school at all. He noted that 'in many schools it [poetry teaching] suffers from lack of commitment, misunderstanding, and the wrong kind of orientation; above all it lacks adequate resources' (DES 1975: 137). In addition, the report raised the importance of teachers' subject knowledge and sounded a warning note about anthologies which, while they may be a significant resource for teaching, should not be 'a substitute for the extensive reading of poetry by the teacher himself [sic]' (DES 1975: 136). It is through such extensive reading that teachers come to a greater understanding of the uniqueness of poetry and its way with words: 'Poetry is about individual poets: about what they have to say to us through the artifice of language used in the special ways poetry allows' (Chambers 1979: 73).

The *National Curriculum* (DES 1989) included poetry in the English curriculum as statutory. A later version (DfEE 1999) made requirements more explicit stating, for example, that pupils should experience a range of literature which should include 'good-quality modern' and 'classic' poems as well as those 'drawn from different cultures and traditions'. In addition, consideration of poetic forms and their effects was highlighted.

The *National Literacy Strategy* (*NLS*) (DfES 1998), a pedagogically prescriptive framework for primary pupils, expanded these requirements, placing a strong emphasis on the teaching of poetic forms at particular ages. This meant that form came to dominate the teaching of poetry at the expense of response and engagement as well as poetry's other, more elusive, characteristics. Despite Bullock's earlier warning, anthologies such as *The Works* (Cookson 2000) were published as a direct result of the *NLS*. Designed specifically to present a neat package of the relevant poetic forms required by the *NLS*, such anthologizing militated against the teachers' own reading and research. In addition, an emphasis on form can lead to a model of teaching that harks back to behaviourism as there is a risk that it is reduced to the recycling of form, rather than active engagement with either the form or the 'special ways' of poetic language. The subsequent *National Strategy* (DfEE 2006) for Key Stages 1 to 3 took a more enlightened approach and offered literature-based planning units which ensured that poetry was taught on a regular basis. In addition, the welcome inclusion of objectives for speaking and listening (combined with two strands of objectives which focused entirely on response and engagement in reading) opened up possibilities for more creative approaches to poetry teaching. The following year, OFSTED endorsed these possibilities:

> The most effective teaching . . . made good use of strategies such as: drama and role play; cloze, sequencing and other activities that encourage pupils to play with and deconstruct poems; prepared readings of poems; setting poems to music; and choosing images, including moving images, to match poems. . . . The best teaching also provided pupils with opportunities to read and share a wide range of poems. (2007: 9)

However, as pupils progress through secondary school into the era of examinations, Snapper has shown how clearly the assessment agenda dominates and encroaches on such approaches, noting

> an almost exclusive emphasis on written literary analysis of poetry under exam conditions which dominates GCSE onwards, along with a significant reduction

in time spent on other modes of response (such as performance), and on creative writing. (Snapper 2009a: 2)

From the 1990s, anthologies were specifically created by the different examination boards that were tailored to teach to the GCSE examination. Many teachers welcomed the broad range of poems offered by these anthologies, rather than being restricted to the works of just one poet or one type of poetry. In addition, the anthologies did open the door for events such as *Poetry Live!* in which GCSE pupils were able to experience live performances of the poems being studied (Powell 2009). On the other hand, as already noted, an issue remains about the possible disempowerment that comes with bespoke anthologies created solely to serve the curriculum. Furthermore, the need to teach to the examination and to cover a prescribed number of poems may close down the creative pedagogical possibilities of what teachers actually choose to do with the anthology (Snapper 2009b).

It can be seen then that an increasingly prescriptive curriculum agenda has had two major outcomes: for some primary teachers, it has meant a reductionist privileging of form and, for secondary teachers, the domination of assessment has led to a narrowing of pedagogical approaches. In both cases, important affective, 'special', dimensions of poetry may have been sidelined.

Research perspectives

In addition to these curriculum pressures, teachers' personal attitudes and dispositions towards poetry are important because, as Andrew Motion noted,

> we are producing a lot of teachers who remember being anxious around the reading and writing of poetry when they were children themselves, and who are therefore very likely to end up communicating that anxiety, rather than anything else . . . (2010)

There have been a number of significant research studies about the attitudes of secondary and primary school teachers towards poetry, both as an object of interest in its own right and also about its place in the curriculum. However, there is less written about student teachers. What follows here is a brief overview of the research landscape within which this study is situated.

In the secondary field, two seminal research studies were carried out by Peter Benton (1984; 1999). The first found that many teachers perceived poetry to be unpopular but 'important'. Referring back to Bullock's criticisms of a lack of resources for poetry teaching, Benton made the point that it is not resources *per se* that matter but 'personal experience of poetry and sympathy towards it' (1984: 326). Limitations of teacher subject knowledge and teaching skill were noted. In the later, post-National Curriculum study, Benton did find a rise in teacher confidence, but worries about assessment and getting the right answer were turning children into 'trainspotting fanatics eagerly looking for assonance, sibilance etc. and ignoring the taste of it [poetry]' (1999: 530).

In the primary phase, the findings of the *Teachers as Readers* project (Cremin et al. 2008) chime with Benton's work in their revelations about the impoverished nature of teacher knowledge about poems and poets. An OFSTED report revealed similar concerns, noting that many primary school teachers 'do not know enough about poetry and . . . this was reflected in the limited range of poems studied' (2007: 5). In particular, they noted that poems from other cultures and classic poems are rarely studied. Most recently, OFSTED reported inspection findings in which over half the cohort of teachers interviewed could name only 'one, two or no poets at all' (2012: 31).

The case of student teachers is not so well documented. For those studying to become secondary teachers, along the same lines as the restraints identified by Snapper, Dymoke notes the tension between what she describes as the 'tentacles of assessment' (2007: 7) and the creative approaches students were being encouraged to adopt as part of their university training. Of particular significance for this study is her observation about the vulnerable status of student teachers who are encouraged to develop a particular poetry pedagogy at university but may encounter difficulties in enacting this in school, where there may be a very different, performance-driven culture. Working with primary student teachers, Ray noted that the *NLS's* insistence on form, already discussed in this chapter, had become an overwhelming pedagogy, thus obstructing any kind of 'deeper knowledge' about poetry (1999: 404). It is this lack of deeper, more embedded personalized knowledge that has implications for students in school trying to enact pedagogical principles taken from university courses.

Primary student teachers' attitudes and journeys

This study is framed by the research outlined above which suggests that primary teachers' subject knowledge about poetry is fragmentary and that this is compounded by an uncertain grasp of pedagogy around all aspects of teaching poetry. This can be set against the wider cultural anxiety about poetry that Motion observed.

The research was carried out with undergraduate students training to be primary school teachers at a city university which is one of the largest providers of teacher education in the United Kingdom. Poetry is a strong feature of the university's provision. Modules include sessions focusing on response to, and engagement with, texts and regularly feature poetry; students are expected to include poetry in the literature logs they develop across their programme. In addition, the university has been running a project – *A Poem a Day* – for the last 6 years whereby each teaching session is prefaced with the reading of a poem and exploring ways of bringing it to life for children.

A small pilot evaluation of the *Poem a Day*, carried out in 2009 with PGCE students (Collins and Kelly), showed a significant increase in the number of children's poets the students could name by the end of the project. However, it was a question about the students' earlier experiences of poetry – at home, primary and then secondary school – that triggered an interest in their poetry learning journeys thus far. Very broadly, the pilot evaluation's findings suggested that experiences at primary school were more positive than those at secondary.

Study design

The current research project was carried out over one year with two groups of first-year undergraduate students. The scope of the project included exploring student teachers' attitudes and subject knowledge in relation not only to their personal experiences of, and responses to, poetry, but also to the pedagogy of poetry teaching. The intention was to explore the impact of the taught modules and then track the experience of some students as they moved from the university classroom into their placement schools.

The study used a mixed methods approach with students being asked to complete two questionnaires: one at the beginning of the year and one at the end. The first questionnaire asked a range of questions about the students' attitudes to, and knowledge of, poetry, their poetry journey through to leaving secondary school and why poetry is taught. This was completed by 49 students. The second questionnaire, completed by 20 students, asked about their attitude and knowledge once again and also about their experience while on school placement. The findings reported on here are derived from the first questionnaire only. From the respondents of the first questionnaire, a number of students volunteered to be interviewed; four were selected, based on the age-phases they were working with (two in Key Stage One and two in Key Stage Two). All these self-selected students held positive attitudes towards poetry. The semi-structured interview developed key themes from the questionnaires. In addition, the class teachers of these four students were interviewed in school. Similar questions about early memories and attitudes were asked as well as some specific questions about their role as mentors in relation to poetry teaching.

Findings and analysis

One important theme that emerged from the data was the significant nature of the students' journeys from their early poetry experiences to primary school and then into secondary school. Of the 49 respondents, of whom four were English specialists or had taken A-level English Literature, only six recalled consistently positive poetry journeys. Here, Jane recalls:

> . . . having Zephaniah books at home. I was fond of Agard and Rosen poems which I would borrow from school and take home to read.
>
> We would study poems as part of English [at primary school]. Poetry books were always available to read and borrow. I remember 'A Poison Tree' which I immediately loved and it is still my favourite poem. Some teachers were enthusiastic about poetry and it was something we were encouraged to read and read aloud.
>
> We had to study lots of poems over the years [at secondary school] . . . make up our own poetry anthology . . . good way to explore poetry . . . heavily encouraged to read poetry. Favourite poets were Blake and Duffy.

Jane's journey includes two important strands: enjoyment and knowledge. From her home environment she was introduced to various poets and then, as she entered primary school, a synergy developed between the two as the primary school culture of lending poetry books encouraged her further poetry reading. The journey continued positively through secondary school as she encountered more poets and was encouraged to develop her own repertoire and responses through the creation of an anthology. As she matured, she continued to develop personal favourites, Blake and Duffy. From her comments there is a sense of a deepening repertoire as at each point she recalls specific poems and poets: Benjamin Zephaniah, 'A Poison Tree' and Carol Ann Duffy.

In common with many of the other responses, for Jane, the significance of her teachers is paramount. In the first questionnaire, 31 per cent were positive about their primary teachers with comments such as

My Year 1 teacher often read poetry
My teachers were enthusiastic about poetry
My Year 5 teacher was particularly encouraging.

However, Jane was not the norm and 69 per cent could not remember or gave lukewarm responses, such as 'My teacher would read a poem now and then . . . and that was it.' It should be noted though that there were no overtly negative responses about their primary teachers.

At the secondary level, there were some positive comments about the impact of individual teachers who inspired: 'My English teacher was a guiding light in my world,' said one student and another remembered her 'great teacher at GCSE who made it more like looking in on someone's mind and reading their thoughts'. But, set against these, were some emphatically negative responses: one student commented that 'My teacher deterred me from poetry' and another said that the 'teachers made it boring'. Deepa was moved by the poet in spite of her teacher: 'Wilfred Owen was very enjoyable but my teacher was horrendous'. Few students made any comment at all about Key Stage 3, presumably because little poetry had been taught or what had been taught was not remembered.

Despite the fact that a number of students could not remember much about their experiences of poetry at primary school, there was still a higher proportion of positive memories for this phase than there were for secondary schooling. This chimes with the pilot evaluation of *A Poem a Day* and Ray's research (1999). It would seem that, for some pupils, secondary school, particularly after the all-important transition from Key Stage 2 to Key Stage 3, is a site within which poetry is particularly vulnerable.

These findings deepened our interest in the student teachers' journeys and how these would play into the shifting loci of power within which they move as student teachers. This led us to focus more closely on the experiences of four of the students as they embarked on their first period of school experience. The two accounts that follow are drawn from interview data with the students and their class teachers.

Claire: Recycling experiences

Claire was an English subject specialist working with a Year 1 class in a primary school situated in a suburb just outside London. Her journey had been a positive one as she told us: 'I do love poetry but I don't read enough of it'. In the interview, she discussed her positive memories from primary school, including being read 'Please Mrs Butler' (Ahlberg), 'I can remember my teacher reading it'. This memory and the link the poems have with her childhood have stayed with her, and she described how she had recently read some of these poems to a childhood friend: 'For me it evokes so many memories of my childhood, growing up and the particular poems I was read by my teacher and my mum.' At secondary school, Claire remembers being introduced to the poems of Sylvia Plath and Carol Ann Duffy and the influence of her A-Level teacher. Even though she enjoyed studying poetry at this level, she was more cautious: 'My perception from A-Level is that you sit and read it [poetry] quietly in quite a monotone voice.' Significantly for one who has such acute recollections, she had no memories of the GCSE anthology.

Claire, thus, entered teacher education with a positive attitude to poetry, realizing that she needed to extend her knowledge of poetry and poetry teaching. She said that she bought a poetry book for the Year 1 English course and, as it offered a good range of poems, she recommended that this text should also be purchased for her niece. Her favourite children's poem was still 'Chocolate Cake' by Michael Rosen and she linked this to childhood memories of Rosen visiting her primary school and reading the poem. However, her experience on the course so far had brought her to the understanding that she needed to develop her subject knowledge further and move away from her comfort zone: 'I need to be braver and open myself up to a bit more discovery and other types of poetry.'

Once in school, Claire 'didn't observe any poetry being read to the children, even in story time at the end of the day . . . a missed opportunity. Even when the teacher read a story that had a poetic feel to it . . . it was not picked up on'.

When her class teacher was interviewed, she said that a poetry unit was to be taught in the next term, but she did not know what was to be covered in the unit. She also acknowledged hew own lack of confidence about poetry and poetry teaching. It was within this climate that Claire was required, as part of her course, to teach a poetry lesson and she managed to do this independently by finding poems to link with *RSPB Week*: 'I chose these [poems] because I wanted to keep the relevance.' Her teaching focused on the rhyming nature of the poems, and, just as she had experienced in her own primary schooling, she read them aloud and discussed the rhymes with the class. She said of the children's response, 'I was really surprised at how perceptive they were; I was really impressed . . . I was pleased how enthusiastic they were.' But she only taught poetry once.

In the absence of a strong role model of poetry teaching, students like Claire have to fall back on their personal poetry learning journey: what they remember from school, what they have learnt on taught courses as part of training and what they can take from commercially produced schemes. For any of these to come to life, they need to be embedded within what Lave and Wenger (1991) describe as a 'community of practice' where the teacher works in an empowering partnership with the student teacher.

Helen: Connecting worlds

Helen is a mature student with huge enthusiasm for poetry which she can remember writing as a child 'in order to express myself'. But she has no other memories of poetry at home and her recollections of primary school are 'vague with distant memories of reading and being taught to write poems'. At secondary school, her teacher was 'a guiding light'. She expressed caution about what she described as 'the more traditional, heavy type poetry' and this percolated through her practice. In the opening questionnaire, she could not name any children's poets.

Helen's first school experience as a student teacher with a Year 4 class offered an enabling 'community of practice' with a class teacher who 'loved' poetry. Her memories included early experience of nursery rhymes, reciting classics such as 'Tyger, Tyger' and loving the Ahlbergs and Rosen, both of whom are clear favourites in her classroom. Unsurprisingly, the class teacher was only too willing to give Helen free rein with her own ideas. As a result, Helen regularly shared poems with the children and these were ones that she chose with care: she frequently talked about the importance of 'connection', both for her and for the children. Believing that poetry is a 'medium through which children can express themselves', she was determined that the children would be able to connect with the poems she chose for them, for example, citing one that she felt they could link to *Toy Story*. She readily admitted that this arose from her own hesitations, saying that she 'actively avoided poems . . . that were a bit darker, a bit more involved'.

For Helen, an enabling interface between school and university offered both a comfort zone in which she could work with familiar, safe poems and also a secure place where she could reflect on herself as a learner: she was able to consider what she did well and what lay ahead:

> You've given me the doorway in which to pick a poem that you can relate to and hopefully that will give you the basis for delving into what I'd call the classics. . . to start off at the lighter end has built my confidence.

Conclusion

As illustrated by these two contrasting case studies, it is while on school practice that many student teachers encounter the tensions in their identities between being a learner and a teacher. They have to manage a multidimensional intersection of knowledge and attitudes towards poetry and its teaching. Their poetry journeys coincide with those of their class teachers; in addition, they have to balance the university's expectations with the school's curriculum requirements. Both the case-study students embarked on school experience with a positive attitude and were able, in different ways, to manage the settings in which they found themselves. However, given the power dynamics of the situation, for a less positive 'anxious' student, Claire's context would present a considerable challenge and one that would be hard to resist. These are not so much Dymoke's 'tentacles of assessment' as the hegemonic tentacles of each individual class teacher's underlying ideology about the teaching of poetry, often one that is infused with the same kind of cultural anxiety that Motion (2010) identified. Another teacher interviewed in the study talked about her fear of teaching poetry that had to be 'understood'; so great was her worry that she was reluctant to be interviewed and refused to have the discussion recorded. For student teachers, in the early stages of their training, it takes huge resilience and certainty to work against such powerfully felt affective concerns.

Teacher educators have a responsibility to acknowledge the significance of the students' poetry journeys and what these bring to bear on the interface between the requirements of the taught university modules and the teacher's culture in relation to poetry. This needs to involve rationalizing and characterizing poetry subject and pedagogical knowledge in ways that are empowering to students and acknowledge their personal and professional trajectories. Certo (2011) advocates consideration of a poetry pedagogy in teacher education that 'cultivates the widest possible definitions of poetry – and that sets teachers on a path of building their repertoire'. If such subject knowledge can be developed alongside a recognition of the significance of each student's poetry journey, then maybe student teachers will be better equipped to position themselves more powerfully in the classroom and to be better teachers of poetry.

4

Exploring Resistance to Poetry in Advanced English Studies

Gary Snapper

Introduction

'Introduction to Poetry', a poem by the American poet Billy Collins (*The Apple that Astonished Paris* 1988), has recently become popular among English teachers in Britain. Ironically – given its theme – it was relatively little known until one exam board set it as an unseen poem in a specimen GCSE English exam in 2010. The poem reflects on the transactions that take place in advanced literature classrooms when a poem is studied. Collins, a professor of English at Lehman College, City University of New York, is no doubt reflecting on personal experience when he writes that students prefer to 'tie [a} poem to a chair with rope' and persecute it to extract its meaning rather than to respond with sensitivity to its aesthetic effects.

The scenario Collins describes will be familiar to most teachers of English; as Collins himself says in an interview (PBS 2001), the poem suggests that the search for meaning in poetry study can be reductive and 'dulls us to the other pleasures that poetry offers'. The concluding metaphor of the poem seems to be one of resistance. The 'poem' is depicted as resisting the students' reductive reading strategies, while the students are clearly resistant to its wholeness and pleasures; they see it, like a prisoner under interrogation, as an object from which to extract data, rather than as a complex 'living' organism.

Such resistance to poetry – and often antipathy, too – is a common feature of 'main school' English classes. Perhaps surprisingly, however, it is also a noted feature of advanced classes, both senior high school (sixth form) classes and undergraduate classes. Collins is probably referring to undergraduate English classes in this poem, after all, and it is clear from other evidence that antipathy to poetry does not evaporate once students embark on the higher levels of literary study.

Drawing on my research into advanced literature teaching, as well as experiences with students, teachers and lecturers, this chapter seeks to explore the nature of this advanced-level resistance, examining some of its manifestations in high school and university English, and reflecting on the ways in which it might be related to broader issues in the constitution of literary study in schools and universities. While this discussion focuses specifically on experiences within the British education system – at GCSE, A Level and in higher education – it also asks more generally why those who choose to study English at advanced levels (some of whom even go on to become English teachers) often feel nervous, ambivalent, resentful or indifferent about poetry; how and to what extent these resistances are perpetuated even in advanced study; and how we might re-envision literature teaching at this level to try to overcome – or at least embrace – such resistance.

Advanced resistance

Many university lecturers complain that their English undergraduates do not like poetry. There is very little research into the attitudes of advanced literature students to the literature they study, but there is plenty of anecdotal evidence of the resistance of students to poetry at this level. Stephan Regan, a UK English lecturer, for instance, comments (2001) that 'some undergraduate students are likely to arrive at university with little or no interest in poetry, confessing that they don't know how to read it and therefore can't be expected to understand or appreciate it' and that 'while clearly there are students who excel in poetry classes ... there are others who painfully lack even the most basic critical skills in the analysis of poetry'. Elaine Showalter (2003) takes up the first two pages of her chapter on teaching poetry with accounts of lecturers' perceptions of the difficulty of approaching poetry with undergraduates who are often resistant to it.

I recently undertook a study of one class of first-year undergraduate students over the course of one year at one university in the United Kingdom (Snapper 2009a; 2011) and found strong evidence of this trend. In the introductory lecture at the start of the course, the head of the English department made it clear to students that poetry was at the heart of the first core module because the department had found that they found it most difficult to appreciate; indeed, he explicitly commented that he knew this would be unpopular with many students who did not like poetry. One (male) student asked, during the questions at the end, as if to prove the point: 'After you've done the poetry course in module one, can you do the rest of the course without doing any more poetry?'

Those few undergraduates who go on to become English teachers are not necessarily much more convinced – though, again, of course there are many poetry lovers and experts among them. It is relatively rare to come across a secondary English teacher who simply does not like poetry. On the other hand, it is very common to come across such teachers who read poetry rarely if at all, and who rely entirely on poetry they encountered while students themselves, or in their teacher training. There is plenty of evidence that many secondary English teachers lack confidence in the teaching of poetry and in the security of their subject knowledge about poetry. Andrew Motion's recent report, *Poetry and Young People* (Booktrust 2010), for instance, suggests that 'there is significant evidence to prove that many teachers, including the large number who feel affection and enthusiasm for poetry, need more support to develop their confidence and critical skills' (p. 6). Ofsted's 2007 report into the teaching of poetry similarly found that 'many teachers, especially in the primary schools visited, did not know enough about poetry and this was reflected in the limited range of poems studied' p. 4).

Clearly, there is the potential for a 'vicious cycle' here, whereby unconfident and ambivalent poetry teaching creates unconfident and ambivalent poetry students who go on to become unconfident and ambivalent poetry teachers, while nevertheless maintaining their overall commitment to English and English teaching. There are still many more questions to ask about *how and why* this happens, however. We might ask, for instance, to what extent the problem is *poetry*, or what is done *with* poetry in the curriculum? We might ask why is it that A Level English, which so many students enjoy so much between the ages of 16 and 18, and through which they are likely to be taught by relatively confident and knowledgeable literature teachers, does not 'convert' them to poetry? Similarly, we might ask why university does not always equip them with the secure foundations in subject knowledge they need.

The problem with poetry

In answering these questions, we need initially to go back to experiences in primary and secondary school, at home and in the culture more generally. Much of this ground is covered in Richard Andrews' text *The Problem with Poetry* (1991). In his introduction, Andrews identifies a number of issues about poetry in secondary schools that have conspired to make it seem problematic, summarized here in three groups. First, there is the perceived difficulty and difference of poetry in culture. Its language, form and structure mark it out as different from other literature, especially the plays and novels whose character-driven plots and long narrative arcs lend themselves so well to extended study in class, and with which children are so familiar from their own cultural lives through private reading, listening and viewing. Additionally, as Andrews writes (p. 2), 'it is seen as the most distant from 'everyday life', as the least 'useful' of the arts, as inhabiting an enclosed, self-referential world to which only an elite gain access.' He points out too that this situation is not in any sense new, citing, for instance, a 1930s' study which speaks of 'the unyielding resistance to the appeals of poetry' in schools.

Second, there is the way in which poetry is presented through the school curriculum and pedagogic practices. The dominant poetic in schools, Andrews writes, is characterized by a canon of 'lyrical poems to be read in reflective (often melancholy) mood . . . mediated to children through anthologies' (p. 3), in many respects exacerbating the problems identified earlier. In classrooms, the reading and interpretation of poems are too often 'appropriated by the teacher' – and 'there almost comes with poetry a moral obligation to enjoy it' (p. 4).

Third, there is the manner in which poetry is enshrined within national assessment systems. Poetry and examinations, Andrews argues, have a complex synergy: exams – for which poems are in some senses seen as the ideal focus (short and packed with 'language') – ensure that poetry retains a significant place in the curriculum, but often lead to pedagogies which do not result in a satisfactory classroom experience (p. 5).

In the rest of the book, Andrews argues in essence that, in order to overcome these problems, our notions and formulations of poetry in school need to embrace the multi-modality of poetry – its rhythmic, oral and visual dimensions; the diversity of poetry – its varied forms, modes of presentation and cultures; and the writing of poetry by children themselves, focusing as much on the forms and rhythms of verse as on the individual voice of the child.

Resistance from 14 to 16

Whatever fun students may have had with poetry in their primary and middle years, for many perhaps their most powerful experiences of it are in the charged years between the ages of 14 and 16, when, among other things, pressure to 'perform' in school is often steeply accelerated. In the United Kingdom, the national school-leavers' GCSE exams dominate this period, the results of which to a great extent determine both what kind of education or employment *students* will go on to and the way *schools* are placed in national 'league tables'. (Following their GCSEs, approximately 50 per cent of students will go on to do A Levels, which again will determine to a great extent what kind of education or employment they will go on to. All will have done English at GCSE; some will go on to choose English as one of their four A Level subjects.)

During the GCSE English course, examination pressure is intense; under high-stakes exam conditions, students study prescribed collections of poetry texts in specially published exam anthologies in order to write often highly formulaic answers to often highly formulaic questions on exam papers under intense time pressure. Dymoke (2003) comments:

> For teachers in my sample, the 'hard slog' to deliver the content-heavy KS4 [GCSE] curriculum dominated . . . They were concerned . . . that teaching poetry should not become a reductive process, solely geared towards preparing examination responses. During the course of the research, I sensed that they were constantly working to overcome the impositions of the poetry element of the GCSE specifications. (p. 11)

There are of course many students who enjoy the study of poetry at GCSE regardless; but there is also a great deal of resistance. Bluett's survey of attitudes to GCSE poetry among her A Level English Language students (2011) gives a snapshot of the range of their positions; their comments closely echo those of my own A Level English Literature students over the years. Some are positive:

- 'Yes, because I enjoyed finding the hidden meaning.'
- 'My teacher was amazing and made them exciting to learn. The format of poetry makes them fascinating.'
- 'Yes, it's very interesting to see how people express themselves and I really like poets who use clever words and play with deeper meanings.'
- 'They tend to be really sophisticated, makes them intriguing.'

Others are ambivalent, in telling ways:

- 'Yes, but not the poetry used at secondary school.'
- 'I enjoyed reading it but not analysing it.'
- 'Yes, but that's because I believe I have a wide imagination so I like to imagine what's going off, not being told by the teacher.'
- 'Colouring in the pictures in the poetry book, that's how boring it was. I'd read it when I got home to make it more enjoyable, or even at dinner.'

Others, wholly negative:

- 'In GCSE years I grew to dislike them.'
- 'Not really, because we were being told to analyse the poems without really being able to appreciate them as entertaining.'
- 'Got bored of the ones we did so much exam practice for. We should embrace it not have it pushed upon us.'
- 'We had to learn them religiously for exams so we got sick of them.'
- 'We were told interpretations and couldn't decide for ourselves.'

Here, in the latter two sets of comments, we can see at work at least two of Andrews' problem areas – the appropriation of the poetry by the teacher (e.g. 'we were told interpretations and couldn't decide for ourselves') and the negative effects of examination culture (e.g. 'we had to learn them religiously for exams'.) Arguably, these two issues are strongly interlinked, however, for it is the end-point of the teaching – the examination – as well as the intense time and performance pressures under which teachers and students work to prepare for that examination, which to a great extent determine the pedagogy.[1]

Is it inevitable that such pressure on poetry is problematic? It was following the introduction of the National Curriculum in 1990 that most students in the United Kingdom began to study large quantities of prescribed poetry for analysis in GCSE examinations. The specially constructed 'anthologies' of poems issued by the exam boards contained carefully selected and organized groups of poems, many of them well chosen, contemporary and multicultural. Many progressive practitioners and poetry enthusiasts saw this optimistically as a fine opportunity – in many respects, a step forward for poetry – placing it at the centre of the curriculum. Resources were ploughed into bringing the poetry alive for students through video and other types of performance. One of the most successful of these initiatives was *Poetry Live!*, the brainchild of Simon Powell, who wrote (2009):

> From November 2008 to March 2009 nearly 100,000 GCSE pupils will spend a day seeing and hearing six of the poets they are studying for their GCSEs. When I was 15, I hadn't seen or heard any poet, let alone 6. I wish I had. Then I might have seen poetry as something interesting and relevant to me, rather than a complex intellectual paper exercise, somewhere between a crossword puzzle and an IQ test.

Much as I admired Powell (who died the same year), I can't help feeling that his optimism was to some extent misplaced. *Poetry Live!* is a remarkable venture

– but the memory of four hours in a large hall with thousands of other GCSE students listening to poets read and talk is not, I think, enough to sustain most students' interest during the weeks of intense high-stakes exam preparation in which they have to learn to respond to a large number of poems in very particular, and often very reductive, ways. As Dymoke (2002) also points out:

> Within these syllabi there are no compulsory requirements to respond to poetry in written or oral coursework, to read poems other than those being studied for the final examinations or to write poetry. Therefore poetry has become solely, and one could argue deadeningly, linked with written response on terminal examination papers'. (p. 85)

Further, it seems to me that the 'nationalisation' of poetry which has taken place – which means that 50 per cent or more of GSCE students across the country are likely to be *studying the same group of poems* – has led to a proliferation of 'cramming' material – off-the-shelf responses – on the internet and in study guides. It is not surprising that many sixth form students' first impulse when presented with a poem to think about is to 'look it up on the internet'.

Resistance 16–18

It is clear from the above that few students are likely to start A Level Literature with wholly positive attitudes towards poetry, and some will harbour quite negative feelings, often particularly disliking the way that poems are 'requisitioned' for exam learning. Few of these students read or listen to (and even fewer write or perform) poetry, and most of them are looking forward to studying novels and plays, not poetry. At A Level, however, the regime is in some senses more humane, and students generally less resistant; there is more time to study more extended works of poetry in greater depth, often within a more sympathetic learning environment with other students who have *chosen* to study literature – even if the final target is once again to write under intense pressure in high-stakes examinations.

However, there is another problem: few of these students start A Level with much *knowledge* about poetry, despite the intensity of their work on it at GCSE. They will have studied many *poems* at GCSE, but are likely to know little about *poetry*. Perhaps this is as it should be. Previously, the emphasis has been mainly on response; when they start A Level, they are ripe for a higher-level exploration of the nature of poetry. They are ready to find out about the craft and motivations of poets, and to ask questions about the role of poetry in society and culture, and its historical origins. They are ready to understand the centrality of poetry in the oral culture of a pre-industrial age and the relationships between storytelling, singing, music and poetry. They are ready to learn about the importance of rhythm and sound in poetry and the connections between the 'lyrics' of pop and folk music and the traditions of literary verse. They are ready to learn about modernism and its transforming effect on poetry. They are ready to experiment with writing poetry in different forms and modes themselves.

Many – perhaps most – students, however, learn (or do) few, if any, of these things at A Level and know little of them by the time they start university, as lecturers' comments (above) and my own research testify. At the time of my case study, (and there has been little substantial change since), most students in my undergraduate focus group had studied two set poetry texts during the 2 years of their A Level course – and had read no other poetry. For many, these two texts were William Blake's *Songs of Innocence and Experience* and Carol Ann Duffy's *The World's Wife*; for others, selections of World War One poems dominated. There is nothing wrong with these texts of course, and many of the students had enjoyed them in some respects, but the exclusive and atomistic focus on these texts had not apparently significantly developed their knowledge of or confidence about *poetry*. (Dymoke (2002) comments: 'No matter how brilliant a poet she is, there may be more to poetry than torturing five poems by Carol Ann Duffy' (p. 92).) As at GCSE, the dominant modes of study of these texts were largely to do with understanding the meanings, thematic contexts and imagery of the set texts, rather than with placing these texts in the broader contexts of the production and consumption of poetry in culture – its forms, its conventions, its social functions, its history, etc. – or indeed in the broader context of other poetry.

Thus, few students at A Level have the chance to see what writing poetry feels like and what it might, therefore, feel like to be a poet. Few have the rudiments of poetic form explained to them in full. Few are given the opportunity to stand back and reflect on what poetry *is*, what it is *for*, what they *feel* about it and its role in their literary education, where it comes from, who reads it and who writes it and why. Few are given the opportunity to make connections between 'school poetry' and 'their own' poetry. Few are asked to select and explore poetry themselves. If they do any of these things, it is likely to be a fleeting experience, since the pressure to 'get the texts done for the exam' is always present.

The dominant focus on response to, and analysis of, the ideas and associated poetic devices within single poems is likely to continue for most, with little opportunity to develop a sense of the broader aesthetic of poetry – the life of poems as art works that exists outside the classroom and that are more than the sum of their surface meanings (see, for instance, Stibbs (2000) and Gordon (2004)). Under these circumstances, students find themselves in a sense trapped between personal response and critical semi-ignorance. As McCormick (1994) writes:

> While response pedagogy appears to give students a voice, it can also leave them unaware of the determinants of that voice, and therefore powerless either to develop or interrogate it. (p. 40)

Thus, when I tell A Level students that the first thing they need to know about poetry is that it was not intended to be studied in a classroom, they clearly think I am mad: but the discussion which ensues is almost always groundbreaking for them, as, for the first time, many of them can talk *as part of the formal curriculum* about what they think and feel about poetry as a form and as part of their cultural and educational lives, and can begin to acknowledge that, whatever they feel, poems have a social and aesthetic function: they are more than just obstacles produced by the educational authorities to test their literary sensitivity. In this way, they can perhaps begin to develop more informed, more *critical* personal responses. As Jackson (1979) writes:

> 'Intelligence and sensibility may be inhibited by too great a stress on conscious understanding: "explication" as a formal teaching method can turn the poem into an object almost as effectively as the museum-catalogue techniques of the past'. (p. 31)

Undergraduate resistance

In my study of first-year undergraduates, I was powerfully aware that there was a missing 'layer' of both cognitive knowledge and meta-cognitive awareness about poetry, the lack of which stood in the way of their full engagement with the course. The knowledge which students lacked, which might have opened up university study for them more readily, was precisely that which I have described above as being missing from much A Level study. Lecturers clearly expected students to have a narrow frame of reference, to have read little and to display ambivalence to a range of more difficult aspects of the course – poetry, Shakespeare and theory for instance. Yet, at the same time, lecturers often appeared to assume a foundational knowledge of and about literature which it was clear that most students did not have. In the course I observed, for instance, *The Waste Land* was the first text set for study in the literary theory module which formed the core of the first-year course. The students read the text themselves prior to the session and attended a 50-minute lecture on it, but discussion of the text in the seminar, and in my discussions with students, seemed to demonstrate that few of them had been able to grasp the nature or significance of the text – or indeed why anyone would want to read or write it: unsurprising, given their lack of foundational knowledge about poetry.

Whether A Level is to blame for not providing this foundation (above I have suggested that it might be) or whether higher education is to blame for not adequately catering for its absence, the end result is that many issues in relation to poetry remained unresolved for these students through their university experience, as they struggled to deal independently with modernist (and other types of difficult) texts, with little teaching time allocated. We can perhaps begin to see how this is translated into lack of confidence with poetry, and resistance to many of its powers. Many of these issues were also replicated more broadly in relation to the literary theory module as a whole, in which students were expected to deal with sometimes exceptionally difficult theoretical texts when many of them had never really even encountered 'standard' literary criticism before or understood what criticism is for.

Conclusion

As I suggested earlier, Billy Collins' poem depicts students who see a poem merely as 'an object from which to extract data, rather than as a complex living organism'. Their resistance to poetry, and the poem's resistance to them, is born perhaps of their ignorance about the true nature of the poem. In this chapter, I have hoped to suggest that many of the routines of our education system, and dominant modes of thinking about literature in schools and universities, might be at least partly responsible for such a situation. In the teaching of poetry, perhaps, we particularly see the ways in which reductive, de-aestheticized approaches can disable the text, cutting it off from its full expression.

Is it possible that we might re-envision the way in which we introduce poetry into schools in such a way that we can allow more students to retain a dynamic sense of its life as an enriching art form? If we stop 'beating it with a hose' under exam conditions, that might help. But we also need to make room for types of learning and reflection which are currently undervalued, especially in advanced study. We need to demystify poetry for our students, at the same time as helping them to become more understanding of its appeal. They need to learn that poetry is a part of culture about which different people feel differently; and they need to explore their own feelings and follow their own interests, rather than being instructed simply to 'appreciate'. They need to become aware of the sensual, aesthetic qualities of poetry, as well as to analyse its meanings. They need to hear and watch poetry, and read and perform it, in order to experience its sounds and textures. They need to be reconnected to the singing and storytelling origins of poetry. And they need to write it, and to learn about how[1] and why poets write it. Then, perhaps, they might actually *understand* it. Then, they might be able to respond critically to it. Then, perhaps they might become confident teachers of it.

5

Commentary: Confidence and Resilience in Poetry Teaching

David Whitley

The chapters in this section each contribute their own valuable and distinctive research perspective on the challenges currently facing poetry teaching. Reading the three chapters together, one realizes that they also tell a story that – between them – helps define the most significant issues in a larger territory. It is the story of a deepening malaise, of declining confidence among teachers of poetry and of increasing pressures to teach to the narrowly conceived objectives of examinations. But it is also a story of resilience – of continued faith in the power of poetry by those who come to understand it most fully; of poetry's enduring capacity to inspire and enable fresh connections, where teachers are supported adequately and the culture of classrooms made propitious. Most readers will recognize the negative portrayal of the current state of poetry teaching in England in these chapters as both realistic and perceptive. Just as important, though, is keeping alive a vision of other kinds of development and alternative practices. And a number of key questions for further research emerge with greater clarity from the dialectic.

These chapters offer a coherent, shared view (supported by a range of other research that is cited) of what characterizes the current malaise. The pedagogic principles in operation within primary schools – with their emphasis on creative response and performance – would seem potentially conducive to the development of a foundational culture within which poetry is enjoyed and experienced across a range of forms. However, as Teresa Cremin's studies – along with recent Ofsted reports and other UKLA surveys – have shown so clearly, primary school teachers generally do not read poetry for themselves, know of only a tiny number of poems/poets and lack confidence in working with poetry in the classroom. Within secondary schools, teachers tend to have more subject knowledge of poetry but, still, relatively few read independently for pleasure, and the examination system seriously distorts the kind of relationships with poetry that are developed in the majority of classrooms. Although the situation is theoretically improved at sixth form and university level, where students are self-selected literature enthusiasts, Gary Snapper shows that there are deep-rooted problems here too, associated with the kind of 'knowledge' about poetry that is valued within the education system. Although they will have studied a number of poems – at times quite intensively – most students entering sixth form, and later university, lack important elements in what Snapper calls 'foundational knowledge about poetry'. As a result, the intellectual and emotional pleasure they can derive from studying poetry at higher levels tends to be limited (with notable exceptions, of course), while higher education pedagogies continue to focus on analysis almost exclusively, rather than cultivating other ways of understanding or engaging with poems to any significant extent.

If one dimension or another of this bleak overall picture is a necessary starting point for each of the chapters in this section, then each uses this background both to raise crucial questions and to unearth other kinds of possibilities. For Teresa Cremin, these other possibilities are focused and activated through the closely observed case study of a primary school teacher, whose participation in a collaborative research project has enabled her both to expand her own repertoire of poetry reading and to develop confidence in communicating this enthusiasm with her pupils. The key to this teacher's professional development is the project's successfully creating a supportive community within the school, where her new, emergent identity as a poetry reader can be nurtured. Cremin's study is exemplary in evaluating the teacher's own development carefully in relation to its effect on attitudes and motivation of the pupils in her class. The crucial link between these two areas is often assumed in research studies, but teachers' enthusiasm for a fresh approach is not necessarily a guarantor of effectiveness, and the evidence this study marshals that sharing reading interests really can be a lightning rod, bringing new energies into the classroom, is scrupulous, as well as enlightening. This chapter is particularly interesting in terms of the way in which it resists instrumental remedies to the challenges posed in teaching poetry, addressing the issues, instead, at a fundamental level, though also very practically. If primary teachers' poetry teaching is stunted by extremely limited reading knowledge of poems, then the solution is not to introduce a raft of compensatory special techniques for 'delivering' the syllabus, but rather to create the social and professional conditions within which poetry can be rediscovered for personal pleasure and interest. This case study demonstrates how a personal interest that has been stimulated in this way can be translated into classroom practice and 'catch fire', as it were; many of the so-called 'problems of poetry' simply fade into insignificance in this context, as the domain of poetry becomes owned, in a shared way, by pupils and teachers alike. As so many of the problems that poetry appears to engender, especially at later stages of study, are caught up in the perception that it is an exclusive domain that requires special reading skills to master, studies that centre themselves on reader identity in the way this does would seem to have great potential in charting a positive way forward.

Taking up a slightly different angle with primary teacher trainees, Fiona Collins and Alison Kelly's chapter focuses down from a survey of initial teacher trainee's attitudes to more detailed case study comparisons. The case studies explore in detail how trainees' memories of their own experiences with poetry in school may influence their attitudes and motivation as they come into the profession. The authors here are particularly concerned about a cyclical process, in which those whose own experience of poetry has been characterized by anxiety and lack of confidence may pass this on to a new generation of pupils, when they themselves become teachers. The power of memory in relation to poetry more generally may well have been overlooked in contemporary research. In a recent study of my own, undertaken with Debbie Pullinger, we interviewed a range of poetry teachers from primary school through to university level, and found that a disproportionate number of teachers who feel themselves to be strongly committed to poetry also hold a large amount of verse in their own memories. We understand very little about how such memories function, but it is clear that poetry is particularly amenable to being embedded in long-term memory in this way and that those who carry verse in this form inside themselves nearly always experience it as an immensely valuable resource. Those we spoke to also felt that they 'owned' the poems they remembered in a way that was unique to them. This may well constitute an overlooked instance of the 'types of learning and reflection' that, as Gary Snapper points out, are undervalued in the current system. This is obviously a rather different function for memory than Collins and Kelly's study of the effects of remembered experiences of poetry in teaching situations, but both, arguably, help shape teachers' and pupils' identities and affect their attitudes in fundamental ways. Poetry has a special relationship to cultural memory generally, of course; even where it is most challenging and radical, it tends to draw strongly on elements of a deep past whose imaginative power is reactivated in the reader's mind. Contemporary pedagogy seems to have abandoned cultivating the connection between poetry and memory in any significant form, and it may well be timely for those working in the field to open up a debate as to the significance of this dimension. Collins and Kelly's chapter certainly suggests that bad poetry experiences may atrophy in the memory to create unexamined, negative attitudes. Becoming more conscious of the rich interconnections between poetry and memory in a constructive, shared context may be one way to break this cycle.

Finally, one of the things that is particularly valuable about the chapters in this section is that they range across the different phases of formal education, all the way up to university level. There is a tendency for all research to focus down, in order to gain depth and specificity. But sometimes it is important to keep energies in view that are part of a wider picture too. Gary Snapper concludes his chapter by asking whether the A-Level regime is to blame for not providing students with the kind of foundational knowledge in poetry that his research indicates they lack when embarking on university English courses, or if higher education is at fault for not addressing these gaps. But perhaps the broader picture opens up a third possibility? Many of the alternative types of learning and reflection he proposes – including learning through oral modes and performance – remain at the heart of primary school pedagogy. Perhaps the 'fault' lies in not keeping these modes sufficiently active through the long reach of further learning about poetry (which could be so much less exclusively analytical) beyond the primary years?

Part Two

Writing Poetry

6

Students' Metalinguistic Understanding of Poetry Writing

Debra Myhill

Introduction

Of all written genres, poetry is perhaps the most amenable to creative and playful exploitation of the potentialities of language. Poetry plays not just with words, images and ideas but also with line length, rhythm, punctuation and visual layout on the page. Poetry can release the creativity stimulated by constraint, for example, when writing a sonnet or a tanka with their respective tight forms, and it offers the unbounded freedom of almost complete absence from rules when writing free verse. In this chapter, I hope to illustrate how young people's thinking about poetry generally as a genre and what their responses to discussing specific poems reveal about their conceptualization of poetry and poetry writing. I have written elsewhere (Myhill 2011a) of the concept of writing as design: the idea that all writing, except perhaps the most transactional of texts, is an act of what Sharples (1999) called 'creative design'. We have to design our writing to match our rhetorical intentions, our sense of what we want to convey to our audience. While, perhaps most obviously, this demands design choices about the visual and multi-modal aspects of text, it is important not to underestimate the extent of potential decision-making that verbal text requires.

American poet, Adrienne Rich, evokes wonderfully the particular dynamism of putting words together to make a poem, likening the process to a force-field charged by the energy of word histories. She also draws attention to the design choices a poet has to consider:

> The theater of any poem is a collection of decisions about space and time – how are these words to lie on the page, with what pauses, what headlong motion, what

phrasing, how can they meet the breath of someone who comes along to read them? And in part the field is charged by the way images swim into the brain through written language: swan, kettle, icicle, ashes, scab, tamarack, tractor, veil, slime, teeth, freckle. (Rich 1993)

And if we conceive of writing as design, then the corollary for the classroom is that we must think of young writers as designers. Whether it is working with a particular poetic form or with free verse, we need to help students see beyond the words on the page to the full range of meanings, associations and connotations that those words evoke. We know that teaching poetry writing is not an area of confidence for many teachers (Dymoke 2001), and we know that all too often the teaching of poetic forms is reduced to obedience to the 'rules' of the form, rather than the creative possibilities they offer (Wilson 2005a). I am sure I am not the only one who has watched lessons where students diligently count syllables for a haiku, or beat out iambic pentameters, but never stop to look at the effect of the whole they have created. It is more important that we help young writers to think about the choices they make and empower them to be authoritative designers of their poem, rather than to teach mere obedience to the demands of form.

Composing processes and metacognition

All writing is a demanding process. Even writing a shopping list requires orchestration of motor skills to shape letters or type on a keyboard; orthographic skills to spell words correctly; syntactic understanding to construct phrases or sentences appropriately; and the retrieval of words and meanings from long-term memory. These cognitive skills are accompanied by the need to understand texts in context and the expectations of the intended audience and the goals of the text itself. When I write my shopping list, I try to order it so that the list matches the spatial organization of where items are stacked in my local Sainsbury's – which adds a whole new level of demand to the task! Writing texts with more subtle and complex possibilities than a shopping list, such as creative writing, academic argument or poetry, is significantly more challenging as the balancing of the need to attend to *what* you want to say with *how* you need to say it makes high-level demands. Because of this, writing is a process which requires high self-monitoring: the ability to become the reader of your writing and judge whether the words, phrases, layout and such things are fulfilling your goals as the writer. In the earliest and still most well-known cognitive model of the writing process, Hayes and Flower (1980) identify three core processes in writing – planning, the generation of text and revising. Critical to the focus of this chapter, they also highlight that these processes are not chronological, linear processes but recursive and our attention as writers switches between the processes through the executive action of a *monitor*. In very young writers, this switching between processes is very limited (Berninger et al. 1996), but as we mature as writers and low-level activities such as transcription, punctuation and spelling become more automatic, our ability to switch between processes increases. However, self-monitoring is only possible when we have strong metacognitive understanding of writing and the writing process. Research has consistently signalled the importance of metacognition in writing (e.g. Hayes and Flower 1980; Martlew 1983; Butterfield et al. 1996), underlining that to become effective writers is about far more than mastering how to convert ideas in the head to words on the page. Indeed, Kellogg argues that we need to '*teach the student how to think as well as write*' (1994: 213).

Metalinguistic understanding

Metalinguistic understanding is a subset of the concept of metacognition and refers to the ability to talk explicitly about language. This could involve the use of metalanguage, such as *alliteration* or *verb*, but it also includes understanding about writing which is expressed without the use of metalinguistic terminology, such as for example, the student who explains that 'I like the way that I described the fire by suggesting it was like a predatory animal'. If we adopt the idea of writing as design as a useful way to think about writing generally, and writing poetry specifically, then metalinguistic understanding is a crucial element of children's thinking about poetry. There is very limited research, however, which explores metacognition or metalinguistic knowledge in the context of poetry (indeed, poetry writing has been given very little serious attention in writing research!). From a metalinguistic perspective, poetry writing brings into focus both literary and linguistic language, although in general, teachers are much more confident with literary metalanguage (Wilson and Myhill 2012) and often struggle with linguistic metalanguage (Myhill et al. 2012).

Linked to the shortcomings of rather formulaic teaching of form, discussed earlier, is the rather perfunctory tendency to teach students to identify or to use literary metalanguage in their own poetry without any corresponding attention to literary effect or meaning-making. In our own research, we have witnessed teachers advising students to 'put in' similes and metaphors (Wilson and Myhill 2012), and Benton also noted the tendency to treat poetry as an opportunity for 'literary device spotting'. He argued that 'we are in danger of transforming pupils into trainspotting fanatics eagerly looking for assonance, sibilance etc. and ignoring the taste of it' (Benton 1999: 530). Some of this derives from subject knowledge issues: we know that teachers are less confident about teaching poetry than other aspects of the literature curriculum and this has a knock-on effect on the teaching of poetry writing. Although teachers' expertise in modelling writing has grown, Dymoke (2001) notes that teachers feel more confident about modelling the writing of prose rather than poetry. She argues that students 'need to be empowered to make their own decisions to write poetry' (2001: 39); we would add that students also need to be empowered to make decisions *in* poetry writing.

Poetic practice

Student empowerment in writing poetry is dependent upon an unambiguous understanding of the role of poetry in the curriculum. Successive studies (e.g. Dymoke 2001; Stables 2002; Wilson 2005a) have highlighted that poetry occupies an ambivalent status in teachers' minds. 'On one level, it is regarded as the ultimate creative endeavour, as high art, fundamentally associated with creativity, and free from the normative drivers of other writing in the curriculum. This is the Romantic view of poetry writing – the 'inspiration paradigm' which Hayes and Flower describe as 'pure bunk' (1980: 32). On the other hand, it is not formally tested so it is very easy for it to be relegated to a peripheral position, sidelined into the gutters of the curriculum. This ambiguity around poetry writing plays out in teachers' concerns about assessing poetry, with a common view being that it is inappropriate to assess it (Wilson 2005b). With my own student teachers, who would not hesitate to see it as a fundamental part of their professional role to provide both summative and formative feedback on literary critical essays, narrative, persuasive and other non-fiction texts, there is always a sense of real concern at the expectation that they should provide feedback on poetry writing. At the heart of this concern is the view that poetry is expressing deeply personal and intimate thoughts which cannot be exposed to the cold reality of critical comment, evaluation criteria and grades. Stables argues that, ironically, this view of poetry ultimately 'deprives poetry of its deserved status as a disciplined form of creative activity that is more than simply a vehicle for self-expression' (2002: 30). It is also in stark contrast with practice on undergraduate and Masters Creative Writing courses where not only is writing summatively assessed against benchmarked criteria, but also where peer critique of creative writing is a cornerstone of the learning process. Developing a pedagogical approach to poetry writing which articulates around a notion of writing as design would mean that teaching would actively encourage students' metacognitive understanding of their own composing processes, and metalinguistic understanding of the language choices they are making in order to foster learner autonomy in critical engagement with their own writing. Such a pedagogy would, in effect, be an 'induction into poetic practice' (Stables 2002: 34). However, in order to generate poetic practice, it is important to first understand current student thinking about writing poetry.

The study

This chapter draws on a strand of data gathered during a larger ESRC-funded study investigating whether embedding a focus on grammar and meaning-making within the teaching of writing would help students improve their writing. Overall, the study recorded highly significant positive effects of this approach (Myhill et al. 2012) and one element of this appears to have been the way that the pedagogic approach supported the development of metalinguistic understanding (Myhill 2011b). In a nutshell, the larger study involved designing three teaching units, one each addressing fictional narrative, argument and poetry writing, in which explicit attention to grammar was introduced at relevant points in the teaching sequence. The grammar points selected for attention were always meaningful and appropriate to the writing being taught and the focus on grammar was not on correcting error but on opening up understanding of design possibilities, what we have called 'a repertoire which generates infinite possibilities' (Myhill 2011a).

The poetry unit focused on a playful approach to language and included looking at, for example, how puns and riddles work, at concrete poetry, and encouraged experimenting with the possibilities of language. The findings reported here draws on 31 interviews conducted with 12–13-year-old students after the observation of one of the poetry lessons. The aim of the interviews was to elicit students' metalinguistic understanding and involved the use of their own writing generated earlier or in the lesson observed as a stimulus for discussion. A further part of the interview involved discussion of two prompt poems, ('Teacher' and 'Teacher's Red Pen') written by student teachers and available on the programme website (http://education.exeter.ac.uk/projects.php?id = 131) which students had had the opportunity to read earlier.

Students were guided in their thinking before the interview through a prompt rubric which invited them to 'be as specific as possible in explaining and justifying your answers' and which reassured them that the interview was not a test in which there were right or wrong answers, but that we were interested in knowing what they thought and they explained their judgements. They were also given the following prompt questions to consider:

- How well do you think each poem is written?
- What makes them successful or unsuccessful for you?
- How can you tell these are both poems?
- What about the sentences or lines? Can you comment on how effective the structure or shaping is?
- What about the word choices? Can you comment on the effectiveness of the vocabulary?
- How could the poems be improved?

Each interview was digitally recorded and transcribed and subsequently analysed, using NViVo, a software package for analysing qualitative data. The analysis provided an invaluable insight into students' thinking about poetry and led to the determination of four principal themes in their thinking: the distinctive nature of poetry, understanding rhyme and rhythm, poetic structure, and improving a poem.

The distinctive nature of poetry

The responses to the question 'How can you tell these are both poems?' provided an illumination of students' thinking about the distinction between poetry and prose. One cluster of responses signalled a strong perception that poetry was very different. Some of the answers linked this difference to the idea that in poetry there are 'no fixed rules', offering a freedom not found in prose. This has resonance with the teachers' views in Wilson's research (2005a): they also strongly associated with freedom and a sense of creative liberation from rules and constraints. Another response cluster was more concerned about the elusive nature of pinning down meaning in poetry. One student said that poetry was 'sneaky, like a puzzle', while another observed that 'it doesn't tell you exactly what it is'. Several students compared poetry with narrative, perceiving narrative to have much more overt meaning in contrast with the more covert way meaning can be expressed in poetry. In a similar vein, one student noted that poetry *'doesn't always make complete sense . . . it sometimes doesn't always flow like a story would'*, perhaps referring to the indeterminacy of meaning in some poetry compared with the neat plot resolution in some narratives. Almost certainly mirroring a teacher's advice, one student commented that poetry is 'not trying to tell you something, it's trying to show you about something', again pointing to poetry's perceived less transparent communication of meaning.

Another cluster of responses distinguished poetry from prose in more explicitly metalinguistic terms. The brevity of poetry compared with prose was a common observation, with one student insisting that the poem on the prompt sheet 'couldn't be a story because it's too short'. Several were prompted by the repetition in 'Teacher's Red Pen' to note that 'each sentence starts the same way': this patterning seemed to be part of poetry's distinctiveness because 'you wouldn't normally see that in a story or another piece of writing'. It does appear that this poem conformed more clearly to many students' thinking about what made a typical poem than the other prompt poem. The two comments below show students discriminating poetry from prose on the grounds of a range of metalinguistic features:

- That one's got verses, and the way it's set out it's like a song, like that's almost like a chorus and it's got verses and the ends of the sentences rhyme.
- You can tell that's a poem because the way it's set out it couldn't really be anything else, and it does rhyme and because it's like two short statements next to each other; that's the way quite a lot of poems are set out.

Understanding rhyme and rhythm

It is evident from the interviews that rhyme forms an integral element in students' thinking about poetry. Students suggested that the use of rhyme made poems 'fast and upbeat', with several referring to their perception that rhyme creates fluidity – 'it just like flows through the poem'. For some students, rhyme was linked with ease of understanding the poem, making it 'easier to read' or, as one student said, 'it kind of makes me get it more, I don't know why, just understand it more'. The majority knew that 'poetry doesn't have to rhyme', but many preferred poems that did. An association between an absence of rhyme and a more serious intent was made by several students, perhaps because so many comic poems rhyme: 'the less it rhymes it creates kind of atmosphere, like real, serious. Rhyming poems should only be with something not that serious'.

Although there was little difficulty understanding the concept of rhyme, including metalinguistic precision in talking about particular rhyming patterns such as rhyming couplets, students found it much harder to discuss or explain the possible effects of rhyme or the poet's reasons for different choices. In one of the lessons in the poetry unit, students read Auden's 'The Night Mail' and were asked to play with different ways of reading the poem aloud, and listened to the teacher reading it. This was intended to support students in seeing that sometimes there can be a connection between rhyme, rhythm and meaning. But students found this harder to grasp, as the following exchange illustrates:

Interviewer:	So how might the rhymes be linked to what you're basing the poem on?
Student:	It's like 'The Night Mail' one had line on line, like every single line rhymed to the one above it, but 'The Highwayman' had rhyming couplets in different places.
Interviewer:	Do you think there was a reason why 'The Night Mail' had pairs of lines that rhymed, whereas 'The Highwayman' had them spaced out?
Student:	No.

In general, students' understanding of rhythm was less secure than their understanding of rhyme. Rhythm was sometimes linked to 'different ways of saying a poem' and being able to 'say it at different pitches', in other words linking rhythm with sound. For others, rhythm was about movement, 'keeping the poem on the move all the time . . . flowing really well'. One student who played jazz piano made an interesting connection between poetry and music, commenting:

- They both have to have a very strong rhythm for it to work, and sort of each word is like a note and you've got to choose your words and notes carefully in both.

Another student revealed good understanding of how the rhythm can be used to reinforce meaning: she argued that if 'you need to emphasise certain words' you could use rhythm, but 'you've got to find the right place in the rhythm to put it', suggesting also an understanding of stress patterns in rhythm.

Poetic structure

One goal of the poetry unit was to draw attention to the possibilities of deliberate choice in line length in poetry, making links with work in the previous two units on variety in sentence length. Many viewed lines of poetry simply as a visual marker, without which the poem 'wouldn't really look like a poem'. One student, however, seemed to have an emerging understanding of the relationship between line length and layout, and how the poem might be read, and explicit understanding of concrete poetry:

- If it was like all one long line then it wouldn't look like a poem and you would just like read it all in one go but when it's set out you can make it shorter and stuff like that, or put it in like the shape of what you're talking about, like if you're talking about a hammer you can put it in the shape of a hammer, and it makes it more effective and more interesting to look at.

In general, however, there appeared to be very limited understanding that the lines in poetry can be significant structural features and can be used with effect to suggest nuances, emphases or meanings. There was a tendency to see lines as an accidental outcome of something else: the number of 'syllables in each sentence' or the requirements of the rhyme, or even purely arbitrary decision-making, as is evident in this student's reply to the question 'When you're writing poems how do you choose where to start a new line?'

- You just really think of a sentence, write it down and then think is that enough and if it is just put a comma or if it's the end put a full stop and then start a new line or paragraph.

In contrast to this general lack of understanding of line length and layout in poetry, students showed better understanding of the broader structural effects in the prompt poems. Several students commented on the single kenning at the end of *Teacher*, noting that 'all of the top leads to the bottom one, stress bin', and that this short line at the end 'gives you a little summary of what the whole thing's describing'. One student began to engage critically with the author's choices in terms of which kennings were attributed a line of their own:

- 'Blame absorber' isn't like really important, it's like the same as 'silence barker' so I don't see why that one's got its own line, it's not special enough, but I like the 'stress bin', on its last line. I think that's the good bit, like they've chosen where that would go quite well.

Similarly, students were aware of the structural contrasts in 'Teacher's Red Pen', identifying the oppositions in the tick and the cross and the No and the Yes, and the way the poem counterpoints 'the good side of the teacher' with the 'not as good sides'.

Improving a poem

Overwhelmingly, reflections on how to improve their own poetry and advice on how to improve the two prompt poems were framed around the idea of adding something to the poem. Sometimes the addition was in terms of making the poems longer, adding more words, or adding more punctuation. Often, however, it was adjectives to be added: students suggested additional adjectives they believed would enhance their poems and recommended more adjectives in the almost adjective-free 'Teacher's Red Pen'. Sometimes the adjectival addition was directly counter to the double meanings and language play in the poem:

- 'I force you to see red': I would have put a word in front of 'red', like a 'blazing red' or something because it sounds better, it's more descriptive.

This aspect of students' thinking appears to be common to both poetry and prose, as the same pattern was found in response to the narrative fiction and argument units of work. Adjectives, in particular, seem to be perceived as the panacea to all teacherly requests for improvement in writing! Very few of these responses related strongly to the design of that particular poem, appearing rather to be generic statements drawing on previous learning experiences. One student, however, began by suggesting that adding more kennings would improve the poem but then continued to begin to tease out some of her thinking about the structure of the poem:

- I'd maybe add a few more kennings and possibly an extra sentence so it isn't completely a list . . . if they had like one long sentence every three lines or something half way and then 'stress bin' on the end, on its own as the shortest line, it would be better.

Several students suggested adding an exclamation mark at some point in 'Teacher's Red Pen' 'because it makes you say it a bit differently, makes you say it like almost a bit louder, (with) more energy' or because it made a particular expression 'stand out a bit more'. Other recommendations for improvement related to making the poem's meaning more accessible, for example through making 'the vocabulary easier to understand', or by using 'nowadays vocabulary'. Some students found the personification in 'Teacher's Red Pen' difficult to grasp and with this in mind one student observed, 'it took me a while to understand that it was the red pen talking so if they made it maybe a bit clearer at the beginning'.

Conclusion: Weaving words

What, then, can these interviews tell us about children's thinking about poetry and their metalinguistic understanding? Although these students have some poetic metalanguage at their disposal – verse, rhyme, rhythm – they are more likely to identify their presence than to see them as meaning-making resources at the writer's disposition. They show limited understanding of the potentiality of decisions around line breaks for creating shades of emphasis, but there is a little more evidence of recognizing broader structural patterns in poems. Overall, because their metalinguistic knowledge of poetry is not robust, this leads to limited capacity for critical reflection and improvement of their own work. In the study as a whole, students in the intervention group who were taught the units of work intended to foster greater metalinguistic understanding did develop considerably in their ability to talk about their own writing and articulate design decisions. But this improvement was more marked in relation to metalinguistic thinking about narrative fiction and argument: in poetry, the growth in thinking was less evident. This is despite the fact that the poetry unit explicitly attempted to generate active discussion and understanding of how writerly choices in poetry can generate different nuances in meaning.

We know that many teachers fear or dislike teaching the reading of poetry and that, at the same time, they are more reluctant to intervene in the process of writing poetry or to give formative feedback (Dymoke 2001). Arguably, this means that students are not being inducted into the community of practice of writing poetry and not being given rich modelling experiences or scaffolds to shape their metalinguistic understanding. Stables argues for the importance of supporting growth in 'the understanding and practice of poetry' (2002: 30), but if teachers themselves lack 'familiarity with the poetry-writing process' (Dymoke 2001: 35), this induction is challenging. The students in our study showed high levels of engagement with the language play and the writing of their own poems: what is needed now is more opportunity to talk and think like poets, and to engage with poetic practice.

7

Teachers' Metaphors of Teaching Poetry Writing

Anthony Wilson

Introduction

As noted by Wilson (2009; 2010), the literature concerning poetry writing teaching and the place of poetry in the writing curriculum is largely non-empirical in nature, stemming from a synthesis of practical and rhetorical sources (Wilson 2010: 55). A significant influence on this literature, on teaching poetry writing and its discourse in England is the 'handbook' literature by poets and teacher-experts (Hughes 1967a; Rosen 1989; Brownjohn 1994; Pirrie 1994). In these texts, a repeated emphasis on the benefits of encouraging learners to write poetry can be found, namely 'discovery' (Pirrie 1994: 5), 'power' and 'release' (Brownjohn 1994: 4; Rosen 1989: 44) and 'grace' (Hughes 1967b: 12). As Wilson (2010) notes, these metaphors have their antecedents in Romanticism (Benton 1986; Andrews 1991) and are based on the tenet that children are 'natural poets' (Koch 1970: 25; Styles 1992: 74; Skelton 2006: 26).

It could be argued that the force of these metaphors have influenced generations of teachers and researchers, including those outside England, and still continue to do so. Recent examples of this can be found in recent work commenting on pupils' and teachers' use of poetry in classrooms. McClenaghan (2003) and Schwalb (2006) note the capacity of poetry to bridge or cross 'borders' (Schwalb 2006: 40) between different cultures within classrooms, including those of teachers and pupils. In a similar vein, Obied (2007) also speaks of breaking 'down barriers between classrooms and communities' (2007: 50). Drawing explicitly on the work of Hughes (1967a: 23), Yates (2007) uses this same metaphor to explicate free writing where writers 'produce works which they have not anticipated' (2007: 9). The goal of the activities described is the development of individual personal voices through poetry writing (Obied 2007: 51; Schwalb 2006: 43). The need for educators and learners to locate and liberate a 'voice' remains a powerful metaphor for researchers in this field from New Zealand (Fraser 2006), Australia (Mission and Sumara 2006; Morgan 2006), Canada (Sumara and Davis 2006; Hughes and Dymoke 2011) as well as England (Dymoke and Hughes 2009).

Two very different but nevertheless influential metaphors of the place of poetry writing in the curriculum have been used by Benton (1978) and Benton (1999; 2000). In a summary of poetry reading and writing pedagogy from a context which predates the National Curriculum in England and Wales (DES 1990) and the National Literacy Strategy (DfEE 1998), Benton (1978: 114) described poetry as a 'Cinderella' subject in schools. Revisiting and updating his research survey from the same era (Benton 1986), Benton (1999) described poetry as a 'rainbow' in the English curriculum. In contrast, he went on to describe the deleterious effects of the pressures within the English curriculum upon poetry pedagogy by using the metaphor of a 'conveyor belt' (2000).

The study

Theoretical framework

This study is framed by the sociocultural theories of Vygotsky (1962; 1978) and Bruner (1986), in particular, their assumption that learning is by nature a social activity and is a 'process by which children grow into the 'intellectual life' of those around them' (Vygotsky 1978: 88). The chapter also draws on the theory developed by Lakoff and Johnson (1980) in relation to metaphor playing a central role in defining everyday 'realities', including how we think and act.

This chapter examines the intellectual lives of teachers in regard to their teaching of poetry writing through analysis of their responses to a questionnaire survey. In doing so, this chapter presupposes that teachers themselves make abstractions, are in possession of a 'higher ground' of learning (Bruner 1986: 73) and construct 'formats or rituals' (Bruner 1986: 76) which give learners access to new concepts. Thus, language is not only useful for 'sorting out' how we think, but is also evidence of how we think. As Bruner says, language reflects back to us the tools available to us in the culture 'for use in carrying out action' (1986: 72).

Metaphor as a methodological tool

Metaphors describing poetry writing in the curriculum are various and always revealing of the context, time and culture in which they were written and spoken. They are powerful because, as Swanson says, our knowing they are not true causes us to take pleasure as we uncover their meaning: 'we hear a metaphor and become a cat after a mouse' (1978: 165). Armstrong et al. (2011) argue that it is possible to use metaphor as a valuable tool 'for uncovering participant conceptualizations' (Armstrong et al. 2011: 153). This corresponds with Miles and Huberman's (1994) description of metaphors as both potentially 'data-reducing' (1994: 250) and 'pattern-making' devices (1994: 252). Consequently, the view taken of metaphor in this chapter is of a tool (Zuzovsky 1994) which gives shape to a wide range of responses. Metaphor is, therefore, data-reducing in the sense of managing a range of responses to questions, not reductive in the sense of minimizing the potential of their meaning. Metaphors used by teachers to describe their poetry teaching are, therefore, a site of rich enquiry, both about the particulars of the subject itself and about its context in the wider English and writing curriculum.

It is, therefore, important to emphasize that the questionnaire survey used in the study described below was not disseminated with the purpose of investigating the metaphors used by teachers to describe their poetry writing pedagogy. However, on repeated close reading of the teachers' responses, it became clear that some teachers used metaphor when they described strong feelings about their teaching and the writing curriculum. I decided to focus on these as a potentially rich source of enquiry, for three reasons.

Attempting to codify and categorize teachers' metaphors is important because it allows researchers the opportunity to explore the beliefs and perceived realities of participants' settings and lives and of building hypotheses regarding their identity (Lakoff and Johnson 1980; Bruner 1990; Hunt 2006). Secondly, metaphors were deemed appropriate for analysis in order to explore the link between the subject matter of the study, poetry, and metaphor as a mode of expressing and discovering truth concerning it. Thirdly, no studies examining the metaphors of teachers' conceptualizations of poetry writing pedagogy exist.

Methodology

The study is a small-scale questionnaire survey of 33 primary and secondary teachers in England. The following questions lay behind the research survey:

- What can be learnt from the thoughts of the people who claim to be enthusiasts for poetry writing pedagogy?
- What are the models of learning which are modelled both consciously and unconsciously by these teachers?
- What do their responses tell us about the role of creativity in the writing curriculum of English?

Participants were invited to complete questionnaires at separate in-service training events, in different locations. Teachers at both events could be said to have an interest in the teaching of poetry writing, as this was the focus of the training. All questionnaires were anonymous and were analysed with the consent of each participant. Secondary and primary teachers were split on roughly equal lines. Participants ranged in length of service from 35 years to those in their first year of teaching.

The questionnaire (see Appendix 7.1) comprised two parts. Part 1 invited respondents to reflect on their conceptualizations of poetry, poetry writing and its place in the writing curriculum. Part 2 encouraged reflections on their pedagogical practices (including their views on poetry writing and assessment).

I coded the questionnaire responses iteratively to ensure the integrity of the coding themes that I decided upon (Strauss and Corbin 1990). The process was recursive and comprised four stages: open coding (Strauss and Corbin 1990: 61) 'over-inclusively' (Cropley 2001); grouping of clusters of metaphors thematically; labelling of themes where possible using phrases or words found in the responses themselves; and linking of codes to even broader themes or metaphors to describe and summarize the teachers' responses.

Findings

The most dominant metaphor of teaching poetry writing to be found in these responses was that of freedom:

- to explore personal creativity;
- to use integrated thinking;
- as a rejection of 'formulaic writing';
- from curricular 'directives'.

The different metaphors within these four themes are summarized in the table below:

Metaphors of poetry as a site of freedom to use personal creativity

The first group of metaphors are grouped around the theme of poetry writing as an opportunity to use personal creativity. Most common in this group were metaphors of experimentation (e.g. with language and with the drafting process), followed by metaphors of play. The latter were also characterized by references to playfulness with language, most notably in the example of '[reading, discipline and crafting leading to] the writer playing in a kind of ocean, a pool of freedom around a rock'. As found by Wilson (2010), there is evidence in these participants' descriptions of teaching poetry writing of their strong adherence to the personal growth model of English teaching (Cox 1991; Goodwyn 2001, 2004). With such a high frequency of metaphors relating to freedom, experiment, play and self-expression, in particular, it can argued that this is evidence of the enduring influence of the handbook literature (Hughes 1967b; Rosen 1989; Brownjohn 1994; Pirrie 1994) on teachers' thinking and attitude towards poetry, as well as their practice.

Table 7.1 Summary of codes: Metaphors of 'freedom' in teachers' responses about poetry writing instruction.

Metaphors of 'freedom' in teachers' responses about poetry writing instruction	
Poetry as a site of freedom to use personal creativity	Play
	Risk
	Experiment
	Exploration
	Voice
Poetry as a site of using integrated thinking	Connecting emotion with judgement
	A dialogue with the self
	Looking and seeing differently
	Thinking differently
Poetry as a rejection of 'formulaic writing'	Killing creativity
	The straitjacket of forms
	The restraints of prose
Poetry as freedom from curricular directives	A joyous lifeline

Evidence of the pervasiveness of the personal growth model can even be seen in the metaphors employed to describe difficulties with poetry teaching: 'finding a voice' and '[taking] a leap in the dark'. While this adherence to the personal growth model is strong, it would be wrong, however, to argue that these metaphors describe engagement with poetry as a 'soft' option for learners and teachers. This can be found in the metaphors of writing as travel 'not [out] of habit, but of experiment, if we ever want to go anywhere' and of 'playing in a kind of ocean, a pool of freedom around a rock', noted above. This metaphor seems to acknowledge the need to keep playfulness in tension with discipline, in order to make progress. I interpret these teachers holding playfulness in tension with discipline as an indication of a mature conceptualization of the personal growth model. This is a robust articulation; importantly it does not polarize these different aspects of poetic composition.

Metaphors of poetry as 'integrated thinking'

In the data I found metaphors which described thinking as, variously: a mechanism for 'getting the brain to operate in an integrated way'; a 'connector' (e.g. of emotion with judgement'); 'a dialogue with the self'; 'looking and seeing differently'; and as providing 'tools' (e.g. 'with which to edit' work). I infer from these metaphors that teachers are aware of the need for different kinds of thinking to come into play at different parts of the poetry writing process. That discipline is required for advancement of skills in poetry writing is borne out by Wilson (2010) in his analysis of 'deliberate processes' of thinking which unite unconscious and conscious procedures during composition. Also stemming from a personal growth model of English, these metaphors emphasize both self-development and the mental effort required by it.

In each of the categories of metaphors for integrated thinking, in Table 7.1, there is interplay between comments which prefigure the development of the individual ('emotion connected to the classroom') and corresponding cognitive demands of poetry writing, for example: 'One kind of thinking throwing light on another'. I would argue that the demands of the writing process are twinned to its rewards in terms of self-development. I infer that these are the kind of creative habits of mind that teachers see themselves as inculcating in their pupils as they instruct them in writing poems. Most complex of all these metaphors, perhaps, is of teaching poetry as a 'dialogue with the self'. As above, this is commensurate with the personal growth model of teaching English.

Metaphors rejecting 'formulaic' writing

The positive feelings in metaphors used to promote and defend poetry writing, above, contrast with those used by teachers when they respond to questions (see Appendix 7.1) about assessment of poetry. That these metaphors ('killing creativity', 'hostility to creativity', 'sapping of interest') express negative emotions towards the idea of formally assessing poetry according to National Curriculum statements of attainment (DfEE/QCA 1999) is perhaps not surprising. What is striking is the concentration and force of metaphors which use the tropes of death and constriction to respond to the notion of assessment ('suffocation', 'drilling the children', 'soul destroying').

The unenthusiastic associations held towards assessment of poetry can also be seen in metaphors which describe other aspects of teaching poetry writing (the 'straitjacket' of 'following forms'; 'conquering the impression' of difficulty) and of writing prose ('the restraints of prose'). These can be interpreted as metaphors of freedom in the sense that they express the opposite of an imagined ideal. I infer that teaching poetic forms is not what fuels the enthusiasm for poetry of these teachers. This is commensurate with metaphors which emphasize the importance of risk-taking and experiment in poetry writing and which foreground the needs of the writer ahead of the reader (Wilson 2010: 61). I would also draw attention to those metaphors delineating what appears to be a polarized attitude towards prose (poetry is 'freer than a story or article'). Prose is variously described as 'prescriptive', having 'demands', 'restraints', 'rules' and 'structures'. That poetry can also be said to contain much of these qualities is perhaps an indication of an overidealized notion of poetry.

Metaphors of freedom from curricular directives

A small but nevertheless important section of results continues in this vein of polarized images, particularly in relation to the status of poetry in the writing curriculum. It is described varyingly as 'marginalised' and 'isolated', culminating in the metaphor of the 'out-dated ornament'. These contrast with metaphors depicting poetry as 'the cornerstone' and the 'essence of literacy'. Furthermore, there is evidence of these teachers articulating a tension between the rewards of poetry teaching and the 'standards agenda' (Dyson, Gallannaugh and Millward 2003: 230) which forms the context in which they work. This is evident in phrases naming poetry as a 'guilty pleasure' and as a 'joyous lifeline in a target driven job'. There is a significant gap between teaching described as a 'pleasure', albeit a guilty one, and that which is a 'lifeline'. I interpret this as demonstrating an awareness of a context which is both pressurized and unyielding in its perceived lack of space for poetry. In these metaphors poetry itself becomes emblematic of a search for freedom from 'directives' and as an 'escape' from a 'suffocating' curriculum. The contrast between this and a 'joyous lifeline' speaks of personal investment and commitment to poetry which is not likely to receive high status. The rewards of teaching poetry in a context which is perceived as inimical to it appear slim. I argue that the 'pleasure' and 'lifeline' which poetry offers to these teachers must indeed be strong if they are to retain their commitment towards it.

Discussion

As Sainsbury (2009: 246) notes, these teachers are working in a 'high-stakes assessment context . . . driven by the notion of accountability'. Marshall (2000: 170) has summarized this as a cycle of 'sterile rhetoric . . . which has done much to debase the language in which we discuss education', and the central subject of English in particular (ibid). Ball (1990: 18) has called this the 'discourse of derision', which debunks and displaces terms such as progressivism and comprehensivism (ibid). It is important to note, therefore, that the responses of these teachers take place in a context where their professional autonomy is questioned; where external scrutiny on their work has never been greater; and, crucially, where the status of poetry in wider culture is mixed (Wilson 2009), or marginalized (Locke 2010) or variably taught (Ofsted 2007) in schools.

It is possible to see evidence of the influence of this discourse in responses describing poetry as a guilty pleasure, a lifeline and a pool of freedom around a rock. I interpret each of these metaphors as asserting personal autonomy while implying it is used within a context which is constraining. I would also argue that it is possible to interpret these metaphors as a reaction against metaphors of militarism to be found in the discourse of predisposing influences upon curricular recommendations in England (Beard 2000): 'targets' (DfEE 1998; Beard 2000), 'searchlights' for reading (DfEE 1998), the 'Literacy Task Force'(Beard 2000) and pupils performing in 'rank order' compared with other countries (ibid). It is ironic that this reaction can be seen most forcefully in metaphors of death and constriction, discussed above. These are, as it were, a reverse mirror image of the very set of affairs they oppose.

The data considered in this chapter suggests that these teachers display flexible characteristics in their thinking regarding the impact of poetry writing in their teaching, and thus the intellectual and emotional status they confer upon it in their lives. This can be seen in the apparently contradictory metaphors of poetry writing as both 'lifeline' and 'escape'. The former creates associations of something which is held on to while waiting to be rescued; the latter is an analogy of being set free.

Conclusion

We should ask, therefore, what rewards teachers find in teaching a part of the writing curriculum which they portray as simultaneously cherished and derided? On one level, perhaps, it is possible to argue that poetry retains and represents for them some kind of subversive appeal. Metaphors of experiment, play, risk, voice and exploration are common in these teachers' responses, and form a picture of an intellectual life which delights in the possibilities of teaching heightened use of language. Underpinning these metaphors, and also present in those of constraint, there is a tacit understanding that this writing is not subject to inspection.

On another level, poetry writing can also be seen to represent a humanizing event in that it promotes both self-determination and security ('a pool of freedom around a rock'), and an opportunity to test the limits of self-knowledge in a social context ('a dialogue with oneself which also expresses and speaks to something shared'). The metaphors describing this practice pay tribute to a space in the curriculum which cultivates growth of the self and of language use, therefore. This may account for the depth of feeling revealed by this survey, uncovering and uniting emotions which integrate these elements. In their definitions of 'risk' in particular, it is possible to see teachers relishing pupils' playfulness with and control over language. In this sense risk in itself becomes an overarching metaphor with which to describe these teachers' claims about their practice. They enjoy the prospect of entering creative spaces where they are by definition free of outside control while remaining aware that not to do so would be to risk losing ownership of the 'bedrock' of their subject.

Appendix 7.1 Questionnaire: small-scale survey of teachers' views of teaching poetry.

What age range do you teach?	How long have you been a teacher?	Are you male or female?

What do you think? – your opinions

- Can you give your working definition of what poetry is?
- How would you describe the importance of writing poetry within the writing curriculum?
- Do you think the process of writing is different or the same when writing poetry compared with other writing in the curriculum?
- What does 'getting better' at poetry writing mean to you?
- Do you think you could/should give NC levels to children's poetry writing? Please explain your answer.

What do you do? Your classroom practice

- Describe the typical teaching strategies you use to teach poetry writing.
- Describe one teaching strategy you have found effective.
- Describe on teaching strategy you have found less effective.
- Have you used any poems as models to teach poetry writing? If yes, please give examples, and explain why you chose these particular poems?
- What do you find most rewarding about teaching children to write poetry?
- What do you find most difficult about teaching children to write poetry?

Do you want to add any further thoughts about teaching poetry writing?

8

Ecocritical Approaches to Writing Nature Poetry

Sasha Matthewman

Introduction

My focus in this chapter is on the writing of nature poetry and the potential of ecocritical approaches for engaging children with poetry and environment. I will begin by illustrating the 'ecocritical' moves involved in reading a selection of nature poems. The implications of these ecocritical moves will be developed in relation to a summary of established methods for teaching children to write poetry and a case study of an English fieldtrip. I will argue that an ecocritical approach to the teaching of poetry can make sharp connections between learning to develop as a poet and learning about nature, environment and locality.

'Ecopoetry' and pedagogy

In *The Song of the Earth* (2000), Jonathan Bate develops a powerful 'ecocritical' argument for nature poetry as 'the song of the earth', deeply connected to the rhythm and pulse of nature. This groundbreaking ecocritical study of nature poetry has been recognized as offering implications for the teaching of poetry (Matthewman 2007; Matthewman 2011; Stables 2010). However, it is important to emphasize that Bate is not proposing a worked-out model of environmental pedagogy. Primarily, Bate's (2000) study of nature poetry is remarkable for his convincing and nuanced re-readings of romantic poetry locating authors and texts within their historical, geographical and environmental contexts. This suggests a subtle shift in teaching towards a more deliberate attention to the importance of environmental questions and shaping. This is part of a typical *ecocritical* move which makes the non-human central to interpretation rather than a focus on human culture and action. Thus, a traditional reading of Byron's poem 'Darkness' might respond to a representation of a universal apocalyptic nightmare, whereas Bate locates the suffering of the poem in a real ecological event – the eruption of the Tambora volcano in Indonesia in 1815. This explosion triggered a volcanic winter as dust filtered out the sun and lowered the earth's surface temperature, causing widespread famine, war and hardship in America and Northern Europe. Likewise, Bate re-reads Keats' 'To Autumn' as recalling a particular time and place when the air in 1819 really was clearer after the three cold damp summers following the Tambora eruption and traces Keats' precise evocation of a healthy 'imaginary ecosystem' (Bate 2000: 107). These readings show how environmental conditions have shaped the writing of these poets. Readers are equally influenced by their own environmental contexts. For instance, Bate's analysis becomes suddenly more compelling to me, writing from Auckland, a city that sits on an active volcanic field with suburbs distributed among approximately 53 volcanoes. Environment influences individual readers, but communities of readers or literary fans can have more tangible environmental impacts. In re-reading Wordsworth, Bate discusses how the tourist landscape of the Lake District has been moulded and marketed by Wordsworth's literary influence. The concepts of the picturesque and the sublime in art and literary writing have helped to define how we imagine and therefore shape and preserve landscapes in the United Kingdom. Likewise in New Zealand, the positive and symbolic qualities of 'the bush' are part of the white settlers' (Pakeha) identity, which is created as much through cultural work in media, literature and art as through tramping in the wild (Calder 2011). Bate's method involves researching the environmental context of the past and the ecological influences on the writer as well as acknowledging the way that texts shape and influence the way that we see the environment with indirect or direct impact on the way that the environment is valued and managed. For Bate, poetry is the genre that has the most purchase in creating a sensual evocation and memory of the natural world. Drawing on Heidegger, he defines 'ecopoetry' as poetry that can help us to access the meaning of dwelling in tune with the earth's rhythm and this is set against the alienation of politically didactic environmental poetry. Famously (at least within ecocritical circles) he concluded this scene-shifting study of nature poetry by writing that 'if poetry is the original admission of dwelling, then poetry is the place where we save the earth' (Bate 2000: 283).

So, what does Bate really mean by this bold claim? Is he serious or is this an ending written for rhetorical flourish? (After all, poetry is rather a minority interest – however we might wish it otherwise.) Of course, it is easy to attack this metaphorical language as overblown and overstated if responding in the language of rational educational planning. For instance, Andrew Stables (2010) who writes on environmental pedagogy and English has attacked the philosophical basis for his argument, while Greg Garrard (2010) has queried the lack of empirical evidence for such ecocritical claims to transformative pedagogy. However, this is to miss the point – Bate is a literary critic who has written a work of persuasive criticism that has poetic force rather than a policy document to be applied. Given that the effects of poetry are inevitably subtle and immeasurable, Bate's analysis of the way that poetry connects to the Earth is worth taking seriously in relation to poetry pedagogy without being too literal about measurable 'impact'. Bate writes that poetry has a unique and special power to make the natural world present to the reader and to prompt an emotional connection with nature. He argues that poetry is particularly attuned to the rhythm of the body and the sounds of the earth. It can embody experience to make us sensually experience the world – to make us feel the nestle of the tiny round of a bird's nest in John Clare's poem 'The Pettichap's Nest' (Bate 2000: 161) or the physical presence and smell of a wild moose in Elisabeth Bishop's poem 'The Moose' (Bate 2000: 200). So also in Heaney's poem 'Death of a Naturalist' (Heaney 1998: 5), the frogs act on all our physical senses in the evocation of the sudden wet movements, the smell, the noise, the tautness of the frog's skin. What poetry can do is to re-enact the sounds and rhythms of the Earth and make us re-experience it through all the senses. In this way, poetry captures what Bate calls the Earth's song.

If this is a persuasive line of thinking, then teaching children to write poetry about nature (and to read it) can (in a modest way) be as much about building connections between representations of nature and children's environmental awareness of locality and place as it is about teaching them to use and appreciate language in imaginative, concise and specific ways. In the following section, I will review established methods and approaches to teaching the writing of poetry in relation to how this might connect with ecocritical practice.

(Eco) approaches to teaching poetry writing

Close observation

This is strongly evident in the work of Ted Hughes in *Poetry in the Making* (1967). Young writers are encouraged to pay very close attention to the precise detail of what they experience through the evidence of all their senses. Hughes writes about 'capturing animals' and landscapes in this way, illustrating his method with his own poems and other literary examples and models. For instance, in relation to his poem 'The Thought-fox' (Hughes 1967a: 19), Hughes describes his impression of the fox emerging every time he reads it. Similarly, referring to Gerard Manley Hopkins' poem 'Inversnaid', Hughes puts forward a view of poetry as a way of experiencing nature more deeply:

> The value of such poems is that they are better in some ways than actual landscapes. The feelings that come over us confusedly and fleetingly when we are actually in these places, are concentrated and purified and intensified in these poems. (Hughes 1967b: 80)

This sense of poetry as distilling and re-invoking experience is also at the heart of Bate's thesis. Attentiveness to nature and environment is woven in as part of the process of reading and writing.

Shaping autobiographical experience

Jill Pirrie draws on the work of Hughes and is endorsed and praised by Hughes in his foreword to her book *On Common Ground* (1987). Pirrie emphasizes the importance of remembering 'with a special intensity' as well as the detachment of patterning and structure guided by and often inspired by literary models. Although rooted in common everyday experience, the pupils are encouraged to render the experience as exciting, fresh and unfamiliar rather than remaining humdrum and banal or drifting into their own idiosyncratic and 'unconvincing flights of fancy'. Ideas drawn from literary examples are used to prompt this – such as the poem 'Water Picture' by May Swenson which Pirrie uses to prompt pupils to see the strange juxtapositions created by really looking at the picture of a reflection in a window and the bizarre pictures it creates (Pirrie 1987: 80). In the Swenson poem, the reflection creates the image of a newsreader talking in the garden while the cats tread on his face. The children's poems show very precise and vivid accounts of real events and places. This is primarily an experiential approach which connects with an ecocritical emphasis on texts drawing on the value of real experiences in nature. Ecocriticism has challenged the poststructuralist idea that texts exist only in relation to other texts and language. While a naïve insistence on literature as a reflection of reality is open to ridicule, there is some purchase in remembering the referent of nature at the same time as being aware of how vision is constructed and distorted in the process of representation.

Language games

Language-based approaches such as Sandy Brownjohn's *Does it have to Rhyme* (1980) and *What rhymes with 'Secret'?* (1990) start by playing with words and using language games and move towards broader themes and models for writing. 'Success' in these poems is often guaranteed by the application of a formula. As the management of uncertainty in writing can be challenging in the classroom, then writing poems can often remain at the level of grammar and word games. This can devalue the writing as 'real' poetry with children having little investment and ownership in the content. This tendency to rely on form has been characteristic of the literacy strategy model of pedagogy (Matthewman 2007; Wilson 2007). Ecocriticism seeks to investigate the representation of nature and to engage with real environmental contexts and challenges. An ecocritical approach would, therefore, need to move beyond poetry as a language game to engage children in motivated writing about their environment.

Formulas for writing

This involves using structures such as repetition or forms as a starting point for writing as containers for experience. The work of influential American poet and teacher Kenneth Koch in the 1970s takes this approach in his books *Wishes Lies and Dreams* (1970) and *Rose where did you get that Red?* (1973). A formula approach can risk being applied in a literacy strategy style of 'add one noun, two adjectives and make sure you include two similes'. However, Koch's description of his way of working in the classroom suggests an intuitive and fluid reading of 'great poetry' alongside children's responses so that one feeds into the other, finding ways into the imaginative heart of each poem and making the connection with children's interests. Poetic models are chosen in response to the work of the children. For instance, Koch tempers children's self-conscious literariness and the anxiety to rhyme by introducing poets such as Walt Whitman and E. E. Cummings who work differently. The importance of having strong models is central to the teaching of writing, and the productive link between reading and writing poetry is taken for granted (Sedgewick 2003). However, Wilson (2007), in surveying the literature, cautions that the way that form is taught in the classroom can limit the development of children's own poetic voice. Equally, ecocritical approaches remind us that there is an important interplay between reading and writing texts *and* interacting with the environment directly.

Exploring speech in action

This approach emphasizes the language that children use and hear around them rather than taking literary language as the only model. It sees language as active, dynamic and dramatic and seeks to allow the expression of an authentic voice of the child writer. Michael Rosen is the key practitioner and poet here. The anthologized poems written by children in *I see a voice* (1982) and *Did I hear you write?* (1989) have a direct freshness and a dramatic quality which frequently involve snatches of found speech and dialogue. This connects with the emphasis during this period on the creativity of the child and on working class experience. The emphasis on the orality of poetry is often neglected in school approaches which concentrate on poetry as a visual and written form (Alexander 2010). This work can inform an ecocritical approach for urban contexts, which recognizes that the nature that children experience may be found in the garden or yard, the park, the building site and experienced in the seasons and the weather rather than in wilderness. Accordingly, nature is bound up with human talk and actions, and nature poetry should not be seen as a pristine and prettified genre set apart from everyday environmental contexts.

Workshop approach

Most practitioners employ a workshop approach emphasizing collaborating, drafting, feedback, sharing and presentation of poetry. Many also stress the importance of individual contemplation and silence as part of this process. Some emphasize the role of the teacher-poet (See Koch 1970 and Brownjohn 1994). Poets and teachers have also reported on the role of visiting poets in raising the profile of poetry (Coe 2006). Undoubtedly, an experience 'out of the ordinary' has an emotional impact on pupils which can be long lasting; this can be created in visits by writers, theatre companies, trips to the theatre or museum or fieldtrips. While cultural visits are very much a feature of English, fieldtrips are not a common part of the literary scenery. However, ecocritical pedagogy has established a strong investment in the value of place-based teaching which has the potential for interdisciplinary learning (See Crimmel 2003). Working outside the classroom in a particular natural or built environment creates a shared stimulus of experience and place which can facilitate collaborative writing.

In the next section, I will present a case study of a fieldtrip which was designed as an experiment in 'ecocritical pedagogy' focusing on the teaching of poetry.

Fieldwork in English: A case study

For this fieldtrip, 30 PGCE student teachers of English visited Tintern Abbey in South Wales and then took part in a 2-hour walk along the sculpture trail in the Forest of Dean which is just across the border in Gloucestershire, England. This trip was followed by a creative writing day. The methods and principles involved in teaching poetry through fieldwork are explained in the order of the process: 1. Reading Tintern Abbey, 2. Walking and Writing the Sculpture Trail and 3. Writing Workshop.

Reading Tintern Abbey

For the romantic tourist of the late eighteenth century, Tintern Abbey became the highpoint of the famous Wye Valley Tour publicized through a bestselling guidebook *Observations on the River Wye,* written in 1782 by the Reverent Gilpin (See Bate 2000). Tourists would consult Gilpin to check what they should look for, armed with a body of clichés about bold hills, rugged rocks, lofty heights and hazy hills. A ruined abbey was considered the crowning glory of a 'picturesque' scene – a scene which imitated art in the perfection of its beauty. Visiting the abbey today it is still possible to feel the grandeur of landscape and architecture which provoked Wordsworth's poetic response. Yet, it is a 'touristy' scene, and there is an effort of mind to blot out the crowds, signs, gifts and ice cream to get a sense of what inspired Wordsworth in his famous poem 'Lines Written a Few Miles above Tintern Abbey' (Wordsworth 1984: 131). This too is part of the experience of the visit – for as Hughes (1967) points out, to write about landscape is to re-imagine and recreate it rather than reproduce it – a concept which is essential to understanding 'the picturesque'. In pursuit of the picturesque, landscape views were sought which seemed artistic, but the artist also felt at liberty to cut or add his own finishing touches to improve the scene. For instance, Gilpin's illustration of the abbey cuts out the signs of human habitation and work to present the abbey in pristine nature. Wordsworth goes further to occlude any reference to the abbey in the poem. This suggests a challenge to the picturesque, with its notion of a ruined abbey as decoration, and a deliberate focus on the 'sublime' elements of the natural setting. In contrast, an ecocritical viewpoint would be likely to address the signs of human intervention and work in nature as part of the critique of the relationship between nature and culture. Students were asked to consider how Wordsworth's poem 'Lines Written a few Miles above Tintern Abbey' connected with their reading about the development of the picturesque and the sublime and to consider their own experience of the grandeur of the place among the bustle of tourist business. Some students chose to take pictures, some drew aspects of the scene and some worked on a draft of writing.

Responses to Tintern Abbey

Influences from the Wordsworth poem filtered into a number of contributions to the final creative writing anthology with some very deliberate, witty and modern takes on the problems of maintaining a picturesque viewpoint as in this opening from 'Tintern Abbey 2':

> Turner painted chickens picking through unmown grass
> I picture stained glass bright in lancet windows
> and black robed figures, ploughing early mist.
> Ravens caw across the mossy quiet;
> Coaches tear along the A466
> Try for a moment to visualise that fat American tourist
> In her vulgar yellow raincoat
> Composing lines
> She stoops to photograph the Northern transept
> Nobody writes anything

Another poet jokes in the middle of a long pastiche of Wordsworth's poem that he feels 'ecocidal' at the same distraction of the unfortunate tourist wearing a bright yellow coat:

> Fuck sake. Is she lost? Has she been thrown overboard?'

A third, more serious poem, 'The Window Frames of Tintern Abbey' integrates the context of picturesque rules for looking, with a glancing reference to the Reverend Gilpin's guidebook:

> We arrived at the Abbey around midday
> The approach was spectacular, showing the ruin nestled in the valley.

All clothed in ivy, the tumbled walls (as the Reverend writes)
Sit in contrast with Nature's elegant lines

These extracts from the students' poetry give a flavour of their experience of place during the fieldwork as well as their reading of poetry and context. It can be hard to engage students with a long, complex landscape poem like 'Lines Written a Few Miles above Tintern Abbey', but working with their own impressions and representations of place provoked sustained attentive readings of the poem. The questions of how and why Wordsworth had represented this location in the Wye valley in a particular way became more relevant in relation to actually experiencing the place first hand.

Walking and writing the sculpture trail

The second part of the day focused on creative nature writing inspired by the Forest of Dean sculpture trail. The structured guidance for the activities is described below:

a Sculpture response

There is a 'pedagogy of place' in the art works themselves which prompt questions which can lead to further exploration of the history and geography of the setting, as in the provenance of the rail tracks, the tin mines and the canal boats. Students discussed the sculptures in groups of two or three, focusing on the relationship of sculpture to place and considering narratives and histories of the setting as well as being attentive to comments made by visitors.

b How to capture a wild wildflower

Students carried simple field guides (Dickenson 2003) with them and were encouraged to use these to identify wildflowers that they came across. Students were asked to draw a wildflower using the analytical style of the field guide. They then wrote a description of the wildflower to try to capture its essence and to allow someone else to recognize and identify it. They were encouraged to include an emotional response to the wildflower. Next, students were asked to identify the wildflower in the field guide and to compare their response with the account given in the guide, noticing the field guide's use of specialist vocabulary and Latin names and noting down any words or phrases that they might want to use in a redraft of their piece.

Writing workshop

i   The writing workshop began with whole class exploration of students' impressions of the fieldtrip, sharing drawings and digital images from the day and hearing snippets of writing, anecdotes and ideas. Two tutors led this session, prompting with questions and drawing out and sharing information about the history and geography of the place and the names of wildflowers. A range of books were provided for reference: herbal dictionaries, wildflower guides and geographies of the area. Students also shared the published nature poems that they had selected to read in preparation for the fieldwork.

ii   Students were given time to research the name and habitat of their selected wildflower together with any myths, stories or herbal uses associated with it.

iii   Students were asked to discuss their ideas and drafts in groups. They wrote some more in silence, then they read each other's work in pairs, giving feedback on the working drafts. Students finished and typed their writing at home. This was a fairly typical creative writing workshop in terms of the drafting process. What made it special was the cohesion of the shared experience that they could draw upon. It was easier for students to respond to pieces of writing which were about the place that they too had visited.

A number of students combined the different elements of the tasks during the day into one piece of writing. Some students chose to develop poetry or descriptive pieces about the sculptures and others produced closely observed nature poems about their 'captured' wildflower. Most of the finished pieces showed a real specificity and confidence in relation to the natural subjects. One poem described a thistle, combining precise use of botanical terminology with religious imagery inspired by the abbey:

> *Canopied Seat*
> Spiny, rib-vaulted stems
> Vestments with green-purplish hems
> Florets, cloisters and liturgical bracts
> Branched transepts
> Hairy passages
> Egg shaped masses

Another poet also undercuts the reverence for place and nature with humour, but uses her new sense of authority on her chosen wildflower. She reflects on the moment of standing by the sculpture ('I do not like our site specific sculpture in its wonderful environment') and collecting and losing a sprig of St John's Wort:

> John ate my wildflower specimen:
> 'good for the gums' he informed me,
> wrongly.

Some students drew upon the nature poetry that they had brought in to share. Danny Dignan drew on Raymond Carver's poem '*Eagles*' (Carver 1986: 120) as he writes about a number of sightings of beetles along the Forest of Dean trail. This is a superb piece of writing which shows the power of a literary model and repays reading in full:

> *Beetles (with apologies to Raymond Carver)*
>
> It was a small, inch-wide black beetle
> Which appeared at our feet
> On the speckled brown carpet of the woods
> On the edge of the Forest of Dean.
> It stopped in its tracks and
> Stopped us in ours.
> A shining, black, unblinking carapace
> Stood there like the quietest, hardest,
> Meanest bastard in the pub.
> Defiant.
> Waiting for its moment to move on.
> So we moved on.
> We saw others along the way.
> Two of them loitering by the mangled chicken wire sculpture of the feral,
> Long eared goat.
>
> Like miniature museum attendants clad in Darth Vader costumes.
> Bored shitless with nothing much to do.
> There were others.
> One silent assassin scuttling by the bench as we ate sandwiches, salads and
> Stodgy sugary bread and butter pudding.
> Another in the upturned palm of the hand feigning helplessness.
> Playing dead, waiting for its moment to move on.
> So we moved on.

Talking about Tintern Abbey
but thinking about older, smaller, fiercer things

(Danny Dignan)

The most structured approach to teaching writing was in relation to the response to a wildflower. One of the students reflected on the teaching method in a prose poem titled, *How to Treat the Wildflowers of Britain and Ireland* (a play on the title of the wildflower guide (Blamey et al. 2003). The poem is in three 'stanzas' (1. Forgotten forget-me-not 2. Disowned forget-me-not 3. Remembered forget-me-not) and is accompanied by a sketch of the wildflower. The poet describes the process of finding the wildflower, discarding it and then finally choosing it as a subject, drawing it 'crudely' and in green 'the only pen I had with me'. The process of research is both a deepening of engagement and an expression of inexperience, uncertainty, and finally, humility:

> I learnt all about it, how it taught us about honey guided bees, how it was christened by a lover's dying breath, what it should have looked like. You were short for your kind, perhaps I misdiagnosed you.
>
> Calices x 2, Nutlets x 4
>
> I didn't understand what they were, but I remembered my forget-me-not. I remembered what it taught me.

Conclusion

These poems suggest that there is something very powerful to be learnt from the close observation and shared experience of environment. There are obvious connections here with established approaches to teaching poetry – such as the use of literary models, the emphasis on 'real voices', close observation and a workshop approach to shape autobiographical experience as well as valuing the notion of teachers as poets. The key developments are in the attentive ecocritical reading of nature poetry and the interdisciplinarity of the shared fieldwork experience. The work was interdisciplinary in that it connected with aspects of art and science involving a rich, multilayered 'reading' of sculptures and environmental sites drawing on field guides and geographical and botanical non-fiction texts. These influences can be traced in much of the writing that was created. The engagement was clearly with place and environment as well as with poetry as form. The process entailed developing knowledge and language to understand the environment as well as working from an engaged response to place and text. Obviously, the hope is that what student teachers experience in learning to teach their subject will be a positive influence on the children that they teach. Writing poetry, may in this sense, play a small, but significant part in the project of saving the earth as children learn to know and value nature more precisely and personally.

Grateful thanks to the PGCE students of 2007/8 and 2008/9 for permission to publish work in their creative writing anthologies.

9

Responding to Children's Poetry

Andrew Lambirth, Sarah Smith and Susanna Steele

Introduction

When one hears discussion of poetry among those who read and write it, it is clear that there are strong views about what 'good' poetry and 'bad' poetry is. It would seem that according to this discourse, there is no denying that bad poetry exists and that there is a lot of it about. On the internet and in books written to advise budding poets developing the processes and skills of writing poetry, it is clear that there is an interest and a basic belief in the concept of 'bad poetry'. Seamus Cooney, for example, has a website (2000) dedicated to the concept. He writes:

> To achieve memorable badness is not so easy. It has to be done innocently, by a poet unaware of his or her defects. The right combination of lofty ambition, humourless self-confidence, and crass incompetence is rare and precious.

Peter Sansom (1994), in his book about writing poetry, describes some poems as being 'tripe' and comments:

> There are literally thousands of bad poems sent to editors every week . . . most by people convinced their writing is not only original but almost literally crying out to be published. The bulk of it, frankly, is dreadful. (p. 20)

There is a strong fundamental belief by many that poetry can be very bad indeed. For some this is why the formative assessment of children's poetry by teachers is essential (Dymoke 2003, Wilson 2007) to improve the quality of written poetry. Sensitive and tailored interventions made by teachers of aspiring young poets may lead to the preservation of poetry as a unique crafted form of meaning making. Yet, what if a poet's motivation for writing poetry is for his or her own internal satisfaction and development and the reader is only of secondary importance. This view is echoed by Michael Rosen when he writes:

> As I see it, the value of poetry is that it should matter. It should matter first to the writer and then to the reader . . . to enable the writer through the act of writing, to discover something about herself'. (1997: 2–3)

With this perspective, Rosen argues, a teacher's direction of children on how to 'improve' their poems can contribute to the way in which society uses language as a means of instruction, correction, warning and control and sets up power relations in the classroom that may contribute to children's aversion to poetry. Here, the assessment of poetry by another party seems of much less importance to a child's poetic development.

Responding to children's poetry continues to be debated and is one of the reasons why we set out to ask a group of Primary School Subject Leaders to tell us how they thought teachers needed to respond and assess children's poetry. All Primary Schools in England appoint a teacher in the role of Literacy Subject Leader. We were interested to explore how debates about the nature of poetry, children's ability to write it and the overall necessity to direct children's poetic work have influenced the perspectives of those charged with the responsibility of promoting and guiding poetry's teaching in their schools.

In this chapter, we first provide an overview of the literature which presents some of the debates and tensions over the assessment of children's poetry and may provide the drive and motivations behind how poetry is being assessed in primary schools. We then describe and present an analysis of what a small group of subject leaders[1] said about responding to children's poetry in their schools.

Responding to poetry/assessing poetry

As has been already raised, those who read poetry often have strong views as to what is good and what is bad work. In addition to believing that writing poetry can in some way be good for the poet, one view of the reasons to try and develop the capacity of children to write poetry in schools is that it may be presented to the world and judged in various ways by an assortment of individuals. It may follow that teachers of the writing of poetry have a role to play in endeavouring to develop young people's capacity to produce poetry which may be considered by some to be good. Currently, there is much evidence and argument which suggests that the teaching of poetry by means of sensitive nurturing and development of students' work is impeded by a lack of availability of formative assessment measures coupled with ill-designed summative tools (Wilson 2005; Dymoke 2003). The problem is compounded by doubts over teachers' capacity and possibly will (Ofsted 2007; Lambirth et al. 2012) to intervene while young writers compose their work. This latter view emphasizes the sanctity of a young person's efforts to express themselves through the use of poetry; but we begin with the first tension over current assessment measures for Primary schools in England.

Since the report from the Task Group on Assessment and Testing (TGAT) (1987), from which the recommendations for national testing emerged, schools have been increasingly under pressure to provide a range of data on student attainment. The Kingman Report on the Teaching of English Language (1988) endorsed the recommendations of TGAT and supported the introduction of forms of assessment in the primary school that could most usefully enable teachers to 'look back over the child's language experience and identify the reasons for weakness in important areas, and which at the same time points to specific remedies' (1988: 58). Kingman, however, also raised concerns about the potential for the assessment in English to become a sowing of dragons' teeth, and the report expresses a concern that national testing may result in a *'backwash effect* where schools may narrow the experience of pupils, confining teaching only to what can be tested and the forms of the prevalent tests'. Kingman's concerns, we will argue, have materialized most markedly with how poetry has fared among a test-oriented curriculum.

It is more than 20 years since the introduction of Statutory Assessment Tests (SATs) in England and Wales. They were designed to assess student progress against national attainment targets, and in that time the use to which the resulting data is put has broadened. The prescient comments made in the Kingman Report are echoed in April 2010 from the Parliamentary Committee for Children, Schools and Families. This report also raised concerns about an overemphasis on the importance of national testing, the narrow focus on a limited range of skills and knowledge and the detrimental impact on teachers and pupils alike. As a consequence, the report states, teachers 'may feel less able to use the full range of their creative abilities' to explore the curriculum in interesting and motivational ways, while children 'may suffer a limited educational diet'(2010: 10).

The pressure of meeting national targets compels teachers to focus on those aspects of the curriculum that are likely to be tested and they have been supported in this by The Qualifications and Curriculum Authority's (2008) framework for Assessing Pupils' Progress (APP) assessment criteria for levelling writing. Although the general rubric states that the points for assessment are 'across a range of writing', the clusters of targets for each level are orientated towards prose forms. Dymoke (2003) draws attention to a similar emphasis on prose in both the National Curriculum (1995) level descriptors at Key Stage 3 and the Grammar for Writing (DfEE 2000) materials published as part of the National Literacy Strategy's (DfEE 1998) support for improving the standards of writing at Key Stage 2. There is a danger that as the assessment of the writing of poetry is rarely or never part of these high-stakes tests and assessment measures, teachers take arguably the sensible and pragmatic option of strategically providing more time for the children to practise the writing of prose. Poetry, therefore, becomes neglected and ultimately relegated to the peripheries of the offered curriculum. As the new Conservative-led government's education policy takes shape, there seems to be no real change in statutory assessment which might affect the place of poetry in primary schools. Promises made by the current Secretary of State for Education of more freedom for teachers in the future have yet to seriously materialize as high-stake testing is set to continue.

Teachers' capacity and will

According to Ofsted (2007), engaging and positive approaches to poetry are present in many primary classrooms where teachers have created 'the atmosphere of sympathetic sharing' which, Rosen suggests (1997: 5), poetry requires in order for it to flourish. However, the Ofsted Report also states that in many cases pupils were insufficiently challenged and too many promising drafts of poems were left 'undeveloped through lack of attention to re-drafting' (2007: 16). While this may reflect the prevailing emphasis on writing geared towards instrumental ends (Troman 2008), it also lends support to the view that developing teachers' subject knowledge and confidence as readers and writers of poetry is central to developing children's poetry writing (Dymoke 2003; Wilson 2005; Dunn et al. 1987).

Wilson's research (2010) into teachers' conceptualization of poetry and attendant pedagogy presents evidence that teachers' views of the poetry children write adheres to the twin strands of a creative writing movement and the ideals of the Romantic tradition. The personal growth conception of writing foregrounds writing as self-expression and arises out the creative writing movement of the 1950s and 60s (Dymoke 2003; Andrews 1991). Andrews (1991: 29) cites the work of Gilbert in this regard who states that if the poem is considered to be the vehicle of the emotions, a personal language form, this personal language is linked directly to the individual. To hold a perception of poetry that identifies the voice of the poem with the self of the writer and outside the constraints of form can leave teachers, according to Andrews, in a difficult position when it comes to responding to such writing (1991: 25). Benton (1999: 529) suggests that protecting what is considered to be the child's self-expression and viewing it 'as sacrosanct' leaves little room for intervention and consequently limits the writer's capacity to communicate.

There is, however, another perspective on the place of personal expression approach to poetry writing put forward by Wilson (2010: 67). He suggests that the approach may offer teachers some respite from current pressures on attainment and, aware that poetry is unlikely to be the focus of national testing, it can occupy 'a fertile space' outside the scrutiny to which other forms of writing are subject. Opportunities to write outside the constraints of the target-driven demands of the classroom can be a rare event for young writers.

Subject knowledge

The anxiety about primary school teachers' subject knowledge of poetry has been a consistent feature of debate in the United Kingdom. Many studies appear to show that some teachers do not know poets or poems and also display a lack of self-confidence to teach poetry (Benton 1984, 1999; Ofsted 2007; Cremin et al. 2008; Lambirth et al. 2012). Research into primary school teachers' subject knowledge in general has been the focus of many studies that have continued to highlight a significant deficit (Wragg et al. 1989; Aubrey 1997). Poulson (2001) writes that underpinning the work of those promoting primary teachers' knowledge of subject matter 'is the assumption that teachers who know more teach better' (p. 41). Yet, Askew (1997) showed that there can be serious methodological issues over how one identifies and quantifies teachers' levels of subject knowledge and that the subject knowledge required to teach primary school children may have a distinctive nature. There may be a need to conceptualize the often implicit beliefs, values and knowledge of effective primary school teachers. In this view, there needs to be a sound grasp of the content to be taught, along with the ability to represent this to pupils, and to make conceptual connections between different aspects of a topic or content – in short, what Shulman (1987) and others have referred to as pedagogical content knowledge. Shulman's contention was that teachers' subject knowledge was treated as being mutually exclusive to an understanding of pedagogy. He argued that pedagogical content knowledge includes knowing how to tailor the teaching approach to fit the content and making the learning experience stimulating and inspirational. For Shulman, this form of knowledge was distinct from the knowledge of a disciplinary expert and also from the general pedagogical knowledge shared by teachers across disciplines. The subject disciplinary knowledge can be embedded in the pedagogy and the two essentially coexist. Subject knowledge, in some cases, cannot be separated from the pedagogy. Medwell et al. (1998) and Poulson et al. (2001) have added to this argument by concluding from their work on literacy subject knowledge in general that there is no clear relationship between teachers' explicit academic knowledge and their effectiveness to teach literacy. They found the subject knowledge was pedagogically situated. We have found these perspectives useful in making our analysis of what subject leaders were telling us about the teaching of poetry in their schools.

Talking to primary school subject leaders

The *Leading Poetry* project examined the perceptions of ten Literacy Subject Leaders from primary schools in South East London. The purpose of the study was, through the means of semi-structured interviews, to explore the rewards, advantages, tensions and challenges that may be prevalent in being a Subject leader who is responsible for leading poetry. Ten Literacy Subject Leaders were asked to participate. All but one of these were part of a University's School of Education Initial Teacher Training Partnership group. The size of the sample for the *Leading Poetry* project was small and therefore, we make no claim for the perspectives being representative of Subject Leaders' views in general. However, in-depth interviews captured rich individual descriptions of the nature of the perceptions of Literacy Subject Leaders in their role of leading poetry, contributing to understanding within the field of poetry education scholarship. Each Leader was given one in-depth semi-structured interview that lasted between one and two hours. All the interviews were dyadic with one member of the research team and the participant present.

The interviews were audio-recorded and the data subsequently transcribed. The interview data were subjected to a coding process with the intention to 'dissect them meaningfully, while keeping the relations between the parts intact'

Table 9.1 Interviewee profile.

Interviewee	Gender	Number of Years in School	Number of Years as Subject Leader
Sally	F	22	10
Rowena	F	9	4
Mary	F	10	3
Rose	F	15	13
Helen	F	30	14
Gill	F	23	12
Debbie	F	15	2
Craig	M	15	2
Ruth	F	15	10
Anne	F	24	15

(Miles and Huberman 1994: 56). The object of the coding process was to make sense out of the text data, labelling segments which were picked out by the team with codes, examining them for overlap and redundancy, and then collapsing these codes into broad themes (Cresswell 2002).

Many of the subject leaders we interviewed voiced a concern over the assessment of children's poetry and their concerns in this area fell broadly into three sub-themes – struggling with assessment tools, teachers' knowledge for assessment, the untouchable and the individual. The majority found matching children's poetry to official assessment framework criteria difficult and this contributed to an uncertainty about the nature of progression in poetry. In some cases teachers recognized that their own subject knowledge in poetry was not strong enough to know how to move the children's learning forward. There was also evidence to suggest that some teachers considered the poetry children wrote to be 'untouchable' in a way that other genres were not. These factors contributed to a reluctance to teach poetry because of an overemphasis on assessment and inconsistencies in approach.

Using official assessment tools

A number of subject coordinators indicated that their staff believed that assessing children's poetry was challenging because it did not easily fit within the assessment frameworks provided. Most of the subject leaders subscribed to the Assessing Pupil Progress (APP) framework for assessing writing. While this framework may support teachers in developing genres other than poetry, they are, in common with the National Curriculum level descriptors, orientated towards prose (Dymoke 2003). Poetry was not used by any of the subject leaders in our study to level children's writing because, as Rowena observed, 'It is not the easiest medium in which to measure progress'. With increasing pressure on teachers, at the time of the interviews, to level children's writing against APP criteria, genres that fitted more easily into the APP framework were taught more regularly than poetry as teachers focused more on forms of writing that they could use to level and report on. As Helen said 'it is much easier to assess writing from other genres you have done. (Poetry) will get pushed aside to make way for other things.'

The pressure on schools to meet national standards in writing has meant that teachers focus on areas that are more likely to be tested (Troman 2008). The views of subject leaders in the sample bear out both Kingman's concerns about the 'backwash effect' of national testing and those of the more recent parliamentary report which raised concerns about the distorting impact of high-stakes assessment culture and the consequent tendency to offer children 'a limited educational diet'. This type of assessment may lead to teachers, as Craig describes, 'teaching towards a tick list rather than what the child wants to say'.

However, while none of the subject leaders' schools focused on poetry for formal assessment procedures, it had a presence in the curriculum of all the schools represented in the study and, in keeping with OFSTED, (2007) attitudes towards children's poetry writing were both 'engaging and positive'. Evidence from all the schools in the study suggests that while poetry writing may not have a place within formal assessment, it was still part of the classroom pedagogy.

Knowledge for assessment and response

None of the schools in this study had procedures in place for guiding the assessment of poetry. In some cases, however, subject leaders who felt unsure about how they could assess poetry considered the need for a set of specific criteria. In one school, it was thought by the Subject Leader that some of the teachers would appreciate criteria to assist them with deciding if the children had met their poetry lessons' objectives. Criteria, however, were considered by others to be 'dangerous' as they could lead to 'a tick list' for summative rather than formative assessment, a view which suggests that poetry is placed outside the scrutiny to which other genres are subject (Wilson 2010).

The view that assessment of poetry is a subjective process that made any objective decision on its quality 'impossible' was held by most of the teachers. According to Helen it is 'hard to quantify the quality of poetry as it is such a subjective thing to mark', and any formal assessment of poetry would need to be based upon the way the children had understood specific structures which reflects the National Literacy Strategy's emphasis on form-driven approach.

When Helen assessed children's poetry she looked for whether their poetry 'spoke to the reader', and judged the way the poems engaged and interested readers. To do this, she used children's self and peer evaluation. In her classroom, the children were asked to assist each other in refining their poems and they 'did a lot of sharing poems, talking to talk partners about what they thought could improve the writing and what they liked about it'. In Rowena's school, individual year groups – the children – 'marked to their own criteria - whatever it is they've decided they're looking for because (poetry) is so individual'.

While encouraging young writers to respond to each other's work may be viewed as positive, setting criteria for development without the informed support of the teacher is unlikely to occur in relation to any other form of writing and perhaps reveals teachers' lack of confidence in their subject knowledge. This echoes the findings of Wilson (2005) who suggests that 'the problem for educators of young writers ... is that there is no agreed vocabulary for discussing poetry by children in this country' (2005: 228). However, if subject leaders were to support teachers in developing criteria for assessing poetry, they could, as suggested by Dunn et al. (1987) and Wilson (2005), develop a set of formative guidance for developing writing that includes ways of responding to the writer, the poem and the form of the work.

The 'untouchable' and the individual

As has been already mentioned, the majority of Subject Leaders in the study made reference to assessment of poetry being in some way made more difficult because of the perceived relationship between the individual and the writing. Gill commented that 'children's poetry is from the heart'; Craig believed that 'the child's voice is the most important thing'. Rowena contended 'it's so individual'. Helen's view was that 'I don't think that you can level a piece of poetry because it is up to whatever the child was thinking as they were writing it, which is why we never use it for our summative assessments'. Poetry is conceptualized as a unique and, consequently untouchable, expression of self, a view that resonates with Andrews' (1991) contention that teachers find difficulty in separating the poem from the individual. The resulting 'sacrosanct' approach may in some part be responsible for a lack of development in the children's capacity to redraft their poetry that was noted by Ofsted (2007).

The idea that children's poetry writing has a special status is also reflected in views held by the majority of subject leaders that more care had to be taken when responding to poetry than to other genres. Craig, for example, considered that 'the child's voice is the most important thing':

> You need to be careful how you respond to it . . . when a child is struggling with a word then the teacher can discuss it with the child. You need to respond with thought and feeling.

Rose took a different approach to her teaching of poetry. She drew a distinction between poetry written independently and poetry written as part of the curriculum. In her view, poetry written independently and unprompted by others should not be assessed. 'Anything they write out of school,' she said, 'is absolutely untouchable or in school but on their own . . . because that's their expression' and she reads those poems 'as a reflection of them and I probably don't read it thinking is this a poem?' She describes how children take their journals to swimming and will:

> sit together on the coach . . . and write really funny little poems – something to do with the swimming instructor and they are cheeky . . . those lads will be the ones to read back their poems and those are untouchable . . . .

Yet, she saw her role as a teacher of poetry as being appropriate within the classroom domain and in moments of what may be called 'pedagogic action'. Rose described how, working in small writing groups, she guides the children with their use of language as developing poets, using the same levels of intervention she would with other types of writing. There would be a form of negotiation between teacher and child on how to go forward with the poem. A shared delight and enthusiasm is generated within the context of the teaching of poetry in the making. Rose described her own delight in watching the children become engaged in what they do:

> Children's enthusiasm is reflected in the teachers . . . I don't think I'm a good teacher of poetry. It is my children. They are the inspiring ones. You know how kids talk to each other and ideas grow. My children definitely do that for me.

Although Rose does not see herself as being what she would describe as a 'good teacher' of poetry (she is sceptical about her own levels of subject knowledge), when she is working alongside the children her enthusiasm and confidence grows with the children's and among all this joy the nurturing of poetry proceeds. Rose explained in the interview that, although poetry does not play a significant part in her own personal life, she recognized its importance and the impact it has on her children in her class in terms of their engagement. As a professional, this motivated her to explore poetry further with her children. She told us that she would spend time researching poets on the internet after school and finding their poems to read to the children in subsequent sessions. This preparation fed into her literacy sessions and assisted her in providing feedback to children's own work, creating satisfying experiences for her and the children. We felt very strongly that Rose's description of how she taught poetry came close to Shulman's view of pedagogical subject knowledge. The experience of teaching children poetry encouraged her to find out more about poets and poetry and this nourished the quality of her interventions when formatively assessing their work. Poetry with pedagogy brought compelling results.

Conclusion

Primary School teachers and their Subject Leaders in school have a different role to a critic and as such require different skills, experience and knowledge to assist their students to develop as poets. It is the nature of this knowledge which has proved elusive and difficult to capture and to pass on to others. As we have shown, it has proved difficult to find a clear relationship between teachers' explicit academic knowledge and their effectiveness to teach. Primary school teachers seem to require something close to Shulman's (1986) concept of a pedagogical content knowledge, synthesizing knowledge of a subject with the ability to represent it sensitively to children through teaching. Successful poetry pedagogy may also require the formation of a special relationship between teachers and children but also between the knowledge of poems and the teaching itself.

It would be wrong for the poetry children produced in schools to be judged harshly as adult poetry can be within the literary world. Yet, developing children as poets may require critical guidance from the teacher. Rose's approach to teaching poetry in the classroom combined a determination to make interventions into the development of children as writers of poetry in school alongside the recognition of the sanctity and uniqueness of the children's private individual work. With poetry, how to balance sensitivity for the unique poetic representations produced by children with the application of a form of pedagogical content knowledge to assist development is what the Subject Leaders felt that their teachers in this study needed but still struggled with. In an increasingly instrumental philosophy and approach to education policy in England, poetry will remain marginalized as a school activity. The teachers with whom we spoke looked for guidance, time and direction to help develop children's poetry and until this is provided teachers will continue to do what they can in finding the time for poetry in the school day.

10

Commentary: Writing Poetry, Teaching Poetry

Jane Spiro

The four papers offer us a powerful insight into teacher and learner experiences of poetry writing. A number of shared themes emerge across them and lead us towards critical questions about why we teach the writing of poetry, how it sits within the curriculum and assessment framework, and what are its underlying values and content knowledge.

Creative dualities

Through the voices of teachers, subject leaders, year 8 children and PGCE student teachers, a central paradox emerges in the teaching of poetry writing. On the one hand, teachers note the 'untouchable' 'sacrosanct' qualities of poetry writing. At best, learner poets write for 'fun', for themselves, not for the teacher or assessor (Rosen 1997). Both Andrew Lambirth and Anthony Wilson give us examples of teachers experiencing this free and unrestrained writing among learners; for Wilson's teachers, this is described in powerful metaphors of freedom, joy and escape. On the other hand, teachers in Wilson and in Lambirth's sample comment on the constraints and 'straitjacket' of assessment, judgement and curriculum standards. Formulaic, assessed writing is described by the teachers in Wilson's study, with metaphors of stifling, suffocation and killing. They are unsure about what 'progression' in poetry writing would look like, and are ambiguous about how far a monitoring of this is helpful or appropriate. They are concerned that rigour might stifle creativity and that poetry is best left free of judgement or critique.

Debra Myhill's study, however, suggests that this ambiguity about 'rigour' in poetry teaching has left children with an inadequate understanding of why and how poets write. The year 8 learners in her study lacked confidence and precision in talking about poetry meaningfully. Her examples include one student for whom the poet's choice of line length had no particular meaning or purpose; and another who edited out pun and double entendre by adding an adjective into the centre of an idiom. This is part of an overall picture in which the children seemed to manipulate poetic metalanguage without any reference to the actual effect, message or purpose of the poems they were describing.

It is interesting to note that teachers communicate a sense of unease about linguistic detail and precision, fearing it will lead readers away from the poetic heart rather than towards it; yet data from learners suggests that it is this very precision which gives them the means to appreciate poetry holistically and deeply. It will be useful to explore later in this section how poetic and linguistic crafting can be reconciled with affective and holistic appreciation of poetry, and why it is that teachers experience a divide between these two dimensions.

Poetry teaching and authentic poetry practice

Interestingly, poets such as Heaney (1981) frequently describe the intertwining of rigour with inspiration as a critical part of their own practice. Myhill suggests that poetry teaching should involve a mirroring of how poets really think and act, allowing children to join a poetic community of practice with a sense of 'design' rather than compliance. Sasha Matthewman's paper offers us a model of what this might look like in practice. In her example of an eco approach to poetry writing, poetry is a vehicle for exploring and describing the real world. The PGCE students in her study visited Tintern Abbey, engaging with their environment through Wordsworth's poem. The poems that emerge use precise and technical language to describe the wild flowers and wild life encountered on the path and demonstrate humour, originality and emotional engagement. Matthewman offers us a completely different paradigm of poetry-making which emanates from a researched observation of the outside world, and which recognizes the link between learning the language of nature and the language of poetry. But what is also happening here is that the PGCE students are engaging with poetry in the way that poets do: not as a 'technical event' but to convey precise messages using language and form with purpose, passion and meaning.

We might see this example as an opportunity to define a poetry pedagogy based on the actual practice of poets. Here we might ask: what is it that poets actually do to combine personal and public messages, personal and public knowledge? What resources, experiences and processes are needed to make this take place for learner writers too?

Intervening in the poetry process: Judging and assessing poetry

While all our authors acknowledge that there is little shared language or agreement regarding criteria for poetry progression, Lambirth reminds us that readers, writers and teachers have strong feelings about the distinction between 'good' and 'bad' poetry. We have cause to note that these ideas of 'good' and 'bad' are also subjective and differ from context to context. The children in Myhill's study make suggestions for 'improving' poems which actually make them less effective to an adult reader's sensibility; for example, they suggest adding adjectives which detract from 'double meanings and language play'. However, Lambirth asks the question: if children are writing for themselves, for the sheer 'fun' of doing so, how far is it helpful for the teacher to intervene and how far would children's poetry 'play' really develop as a result of top-down judgements? Lambirth's teachers believe that teacher intervention and judgement is neither desirable nor necessary for the 'poetry play' enjoyed by learner writers. For them, the fact that poetry writing lies outside National Curriculum assessment practice offers opportunity for poetry writing without teacher judgements or interventions, and without a controlling audience. Helen, a teacher in Lambirth's study, describes the transfer of power from teacher to learner when children work together to develop their own and their peer's poetry writing. In this process, they are simulating the way poets actually work together in poetry workshop settings, developing their own judgements collectively, and writing for and with one another rather than for the teacher.

Both Lambirth and Wilson lead us to the view that notions of 'good' and 'bad' poetry are unhelpful not only within a paradigm of poetry as personal growth, but also within a paradigm of poetry as technical knowhow. It is perhaps more valuable to guide learner writers to fulfil their writing intent and purpose, to develop with peers their own skills of evaluation and refinement, and thereby give them the opportunity that Myhill describes to 'think and feel' for themselves like a poet.

Poetry, audience and teacher intervention

Emerging from this discussion is the notion of two kinds of poetry written by children, with two kinds of audiences, and two kinds of teacher response. 'In-school' poetry generated within a learning and teaching context could be instrumental and artificial as in the examples described by the teachers in Lambirth's and Wilson's studies. Conversely, an instructional context could be inspirational as in Matthewman's example, where the teacher/trainer has provided an experience of deep engagement. Yet, the two are similar in that the writing generated in these settings is outward-facing, written with a sense of 'publication' or audience. Matthewman acknowledges that one of the poems written after the Tintern Abbey fieldtrip is of publishable standard and could reach an audience well beyond the normal expectation of a school activity. Rose, one of the subject leaders in Lambirth's study, separates poems written for the teacher, which have an instrumental purpose and are devoid of personal intent or engagement, with those they might write for fun or pleasure outside class and for one another.

The primary subject leaders in Lambirth's sample describe 'out-of-school' poetry writing which the children do 'for fun', often collectively, such as jingles about the swimming instructor written on the school bus. These the teachers consider entirely inappropriate to assess: they describe these as written by the children for themselves and their peer groups. It might be useful to differentiate between these two outcomes: self-initiated, or initiated as a result of a learning activity? Initiated for self or peer group, or initiated explicitly for an audience? Transferring to children the skills of evaluation and refinement for their chosen audience, as in Helen's example (Lambirth), is an exciting example of empowerment; here, the children not only 'become' teachers of one another, but they become peers working with one another as poets do for maximum impact on their chosen audience.

Establishing a poetry pedagogy and language

What emerges strongly from these voices 'in the round' is that a clearly articulated poetry pedagogy which enshrines best practice is lacking, leaving teachers and their learners unprepared both for poetry writing and reading. As a community of poets, teachers, writers and researchers, it is this question and deficit which it is most pressing to address. Each of the papers suggests that prose pedagogy is much clearer and more thoroughly articulated within the curriculum than poetry pedagogy is. The studies have also shown us that this lack of clear pedagogy has made teachers less confident in making (or choosing not to make) poetic judgements. It has made teachers step back from rigour, and made learners separate out the poetry-making they enjoy from the sterile formulaic poetry they write for teachers. To take account of these voices, we might move towards a poetry pedagogy that brings together the communities of writers, researchers and teachers and takes account of best practice. Such a jointly informed pedagogy might ideally provide teachers and learners with the clarity and inspiration they need to make poetry a lived and living art form. Three questions might inform such a pedagogy, concerned in turn with the poet, the learner and the reader.

What do poets actually do and how can this inform poetry pedagogy?

Sharples (1999) and Stables (2002) at the turn of the century asked 'how do we write' and where does 'poetic experience' come from: is it 'found or made'? These questions remain urgent a decade later. The teachers in Lambirth's study show us activities involving peer development of writing which simulate real writer practice; Matthewman's eco-poetry mirrors the combination of cause and rigour in poetic practice. Spiro (2007, 2009) unpacked a number of poetic strategies she uses in her own writing, and showed how these could be translated into classroom activities, and with what effect. In a further study (2013), she explores how writers of learner literature find and craft artistic ideas, and how these insights can inform the teaching of creative writing (Spiro 2013). Insights from writers reveal the detail and rigour poets impose on their own processes; the way they join 'technical knowhow' with deeper message. It would also be interesting to ask how poets learn from one another and arrive together at collective judgements. Thus, a poetry pedagogy authentically informed by poets may address the teacher's sense of divide between 'craft' and 'heart', as poets reveal how they themselves reconcile these dimensions of poetry practice.

How does the poetry writing children do 'for themselves' differ from the kind generated through classroom design? What can children tell us about the two kinds of writing, and the ways they wish to be judged or supported in each?

The papers in this section suggest that we can locate children's passion and delight in poetry writing outside the classroom rather than inside it. The question of how we might dissolve the boundaries between writing 'for fun' and writing for teachers is a fruitful one both for research and for pedagogy. Benton (1999) suggested that the outcomes of poetry play should be open to refinement and study, just as the more formulaic classroom activities are. The studies here suggest that it is urgent that we rise to this challenge and look at its implications for the classroom. We might learn more precisely from learners themselves how the conditions of freedom and play found outside the classroom could be mirrored inside. The characteristics of the 'creative classroom' might include notions of 'flow' (Csiksentmihalyi 2002), creative delight (Robinson 2009), language play (Cook 2000; Crystal 1998) and 'creative space' (Spiro 2009). We might also look at how children learn from one another as they refine and edit their work for themselves and take control of the poetry writing process.

What language and metalanguage are needed to talk precisely and purposefully about poetry?

The papers in this section suggest that we have not yet arrived at a shared and adequate language for describing poetry and its associated pedagogy. This lack is experienced by teachers and communicated to their learners. It would serve the poetry teaching community to identify, classify and systematize the language used by poetry readers and writers when they articulate poetry knowledge. The studies by Wilson, Myhill and Lambirth in this section, and Spiro (2011) include teacher and reader articulation of their poetry assumptions and judgements. Spiro (2011) set up a small-scale project in which eight readers, teachers and poets talked about their response to poems and explained how they arrived at literary judgements. These studies offer some insight into the concepts and terminology used by practised readers when they talk about poetry. It is from this 'living' poetry language that we might evolve a shared language for talking about poetry which could inform the new poetry pedagogy.

As we reach towards a more clearly articulated poetry pedagogy, we are also reaching towards a clearer join between the authentic practice of the poet, the experienced reader, the play and delight of the child, and the creative opportunity of the classroom. An ideal poetry pedagogy would take account of all of these and bring them together in a virtuous cycle that joins up poetry worlds inside and outside the classroom.

Part Three

Speaking Poetry and Listening to Poetry

11

Preadolescents Writing and Performing Poetry

Janine L. Certo

Introduction

Poetry is underrepresented in the US curriculum in elementary schools, in spite of its potential to develop children's perceptions, draw their attention to language and help them respond to and make meaning of the world (Elster and Hanauer 2002). This chapter draws from a larger study of classroom- and school-based poetry writing and performance among US children. This chapter describes the project, as well as two trends in the research findings, from one of the participating classrooms. I and several visiting poets facilitated poetry writing and performance sessions three times per week across one month with 24 fifth grade children (ages 10–11, often a stage referred to as preadolescence). Students selected one poem to read at a school-based reading, and their performances were videotaped. Afterwards, they were interviewed with their poetry portfolios (containing all poem drafts) to explain/describe: why their texts are considered poems, why they revised their poetry, and their experience of performing poetry. The research question addressed in this chapter is: What do fifth graders' poems, their discourse about their poems and their discourse about their performances reveal about their poetry writing and performance practices? Through use of ethnographic, textual analysis and interpretative methods, findings revealed that fifth graders, writing about a subject that was meaningful to them, appropriated and remixed topics and linguistic features from the multiplicity of voices that surrounded them. Preadolescents' reports suggest that their poetry reading performances brought forth feelings of pride, exhilaration, a literate identity, and, for some, an understanding of genre. Results suggest that a genre approach to teaching poetry paired with acknowledgement of children's topics and interests may support their poetry writing and performances.

Context and rationale

Poetry is an underrepresented or narrowly taught genre in US elementary schools (Certo et al. 2010; Duke 2000; Elster and Hanauer 2002). The American Common Core Standards (2010) privilege the reading of poetry over the writing of poetry. In fact, according to the Standards, a student can progress through 12 years of schooling and never be asked to write a single poem. This genre void seems problematic from a literary, educational and humanistic perspective. Genre theorists have argued that successive, multiple experiences with a range of genres are key to becoming a reader and writer across contexts (Fowler 1982; Rosmarin 1985). If this is indeed the case, then certainly schooling should be a primary space where young people are provided such exposure. I and my colleagues have argued elsewhere that poetry is not a luxury, but is rather necessary and inspiring, for it potentially contains universal themes that may comfort, move and please readers (Certo et al. 2011). With poetry, children are (perhaps more than other school genres) given the rhetorical power to use words in new ways, to study the often-condensed language of poetry and to discover what language can do.

Children writing and performing poetry: Theoretical and conceptual considerations

Theories of genre (Bakhtin 1986; Miller 1984), including poetic language theory (Jakobson 1987; Friedrich 1979), performance theory (Boal 1995; Hymes 1996; Schechner 2003) and Vygotskian learning theory (in Lantolf and Appel 1994) are all highly relevant to this study. Genre is a term used in literacy pedagogy to connect the different forms text take with variations in social purpose. I approached this study with the dual interests of how texts work (their formalities and linguistic features) and also with the living social reality of texts-in-use. Bakhtin (1986) argued that the words people use belong partially to others, as they appropriate words from others and adapt them to their own purposes. Put another way, he established that our words are built on the words of those that have come before, and of those that currently surround, us.

This study is framed, too, by Hymes (1996), who explained that any written and performed texts must be understood in the context and through the communication norms of the community that produced it. Supported by

Vygotsky's notion of the zone of proximal development (in Lantolf and Appel 1994), I intended for children to try out poetry writing and performance with 'scaffolding' from expert others: teachers and visiting poets. However, I also assumed that children would try out (and adjust their) writing and performing as they were moved by, and responsive to, their peers' writing and performances.

For the purposes of this study, I define a poetry performance as an aesthetically heightened and more formalized mode of communication (Boal 1995; Schechner 2003) that has some form of 'stage' or 'space'. I argue that when the poem meets the body, children have a new literary experience. The poem becomes felt, seen and heard through their body for a completely fresh interpretative event. For children who may not have had access to this before, it can be exhilarating. Depending on the child, however, I understood that this event may come with complications and challenges. Children are faced with *writing* a poem, then writing a poem they are pleased with (and perhaps one that they feel would please an audience). Then, the *body* is involved as it is the vehicle for taking the poem off the page. Studies have found that (Fisher 2003; Jocson 2005; Weinstein 2009; 2010) youth spoken word performances can increase participant confidence, self-efficacy and understanding of genre and process.

The study

Twenty-four fifth grade students in one US school composed poems across one month before performing one of them. Afterwards, they were interviewed to explain: (1) why their text is a poem, (2) if/why they revised their poetry and (3) why individuals may be moved to write poems. A semi-structured interview protocol was adapted and piloted, which allowed children's responses to dictate subsequent probes. I and a group of doctoral students conducted the individual interviews. I engaged in descriptive/interpretative textual analysis by doing multiple readings of children's original poems to get a sense of poems. The interview data was transcribed and entered into Hyperresearch© software where transcripts were coded along interview protocol questions for a thematic content analysis (Miles and Huberman 2002). I then analysed each poem and interview transcript in relation to other data sources (e.g. children's drafts of poems, audiotapes of classroom instruction, videotapes of poetry performances, field notes and demographic data).

The setting and the students

King Elementary is a public elementary school in a mid-sized metropolitan area in the mid-north-eastern part of the United States. At the time of the study, the school enrolment was 235 K-5 elementary and 32 preschool students. African-Americans made up a substantial population of students, at 70 per cent. Approximately 90 per cent of the student population qualified for free or reduced-price lunch. The teacher, Ms Jorgenson, had been teaching fifth grade for several years. I had previous experience working with her (in a project on conducting peer writing conferences) who, in my assessment and by school reputation, had a commitment to writing pedagogy. She also had a literacy-rich classroom where experimentation and student-to-student talk were encouraged. Unlike some of the elementary classrooms I have visited to observe writing, this was a classroom with a healthy hum of talk around writing – not just when students were peer-reviewing or sharing, but also when students were composing.

Twenty-four students aged 10–11 participated in the study (13 girls; 11 boys). (See Table 11.1).

A genre approach to poetry

I facilitated poetry lessons three times per week across four weeks with students. On five of these occasions, I brought another visiting poet from the community to work with the students. The pedagogical views that primarily informed this poetry unit study included a genre approach to writing instruction (Cope and Kalantzis 1993) and process writing (Graves 1983). It was my hope to cultivate genre knowledge according to Chapman's recommendations (1999), considering 'engagement, inquiry, exploration, personal connections and meaning-making, participation

Table 11.1 Demographic Summary of Student Participants.

	African American	White	Chicano/ Latino	Hmong American	Gifted/ Talented Programme	Speech and Language Services
M	4	2	3	2	1	1
F	7	2	3	1	3	

N=24.

in a discourse community, apprenticeship and mentoring, collaboration, and talk about text' (p. 473). Poet Mary Oliver has written, 'to write well, it is entirely necessary to read widely and deeply. Good poems are the best teachers' (1994: 10). It was important, therefore, to distribute and read many poems. The poems were diverse in terms of author, historical context, subject, form, theme and mood. Students received a poetry pocket folder (for handouts of poems), a poetry notebook and an 'at-home' poetry journal should they be so inspired. Students also had the opportunity to select a poem from the project for inclusion in a class anthology.

I wanted children to witness not just me as poet, but also a variety of poets (by gender, age, cultural background and performance style) reading or performing their work. This opportunity not only increases the likelihood of them connecting with or relating to one or more poets, it helps to give them a broader exposure to a range of poets who, in turn, can help them see expanded possibilities for their poems. Visiting poets included Laura Apol, David Blair ('Blair'), Joseph Harris ('Logic'), William Langford III ('Will the Poet') and Rina Risper. When any poetry session was held, it simply began with a reading or a performance. If a poet was visiting, there would be some sharing of that poet's writing practices, followed by a question- and- answer period. Students had opportunities to engage with poets in ways that satisfied their curiosities and addressed their authentic questions. For example, one child asked: 'Why do you poets always wear those things around your necks [scarves]?' Another asked a visiting poet: 'What got you started writing poetry?' Following the Q&A, we moved into poetry writing. Peer-to-peer talk and poet-to-peer talk were encouraged. The session always ended with students doing some sort of sharing of their work that day.

During the poetry unit, the students, with the support of adults, planned a culminating event, which they titled, *The Super Spring Poetry Jam* – a school-based reading held in the media centre where each child could invite 'anyone who cared about them'. Naturally, the audience included intimate or extended family members, as well as teachers, the school principal, university interns, staff members and a few local professors. Many of the visiting poets were also able to return to see the project come full circle.

Children writing and performing poetry

In this next section, I elaborate on two primary claims. First, all children, in particular and sometimes complex ways, appropriated and remixed poetry topics, lines and other poetic language features from the multiplicity of voices that surrounded them. These included slogans from advertising, phrases from other poems and lines from songs. Secondly, students' reports overwhelmingly suggested that their performances brought forth feelings of pride, exhilaration and a literate identity. Owing to space limitations, I will draw on specific students' poems and their discourse about those poems (pseudonyms used throughout) to represent exemplars of descriptive findings.

Rejeanne, through visiting poet, Laura Apol, was asked to write a poem about a family member. Laura, before moving students into writing their own poems, shared several 'family' poems with differing forms and moods, including Joseph Bruchac's 'Birdfoot's Grampa' and Margaret Walker's 'Lineage'. In Rejeanne's poem, she appropriated the advertising slogan 'Just Do It', making it clear in one of her drafts that 'it's [the poem] a reply to her mother'.

Notice the distinct child-to-parent voice – an in-poem dialogue. She reported in her interview that she drew on the use of a thesaurus to 'impress the audience' with 'insignificant' as opposed to 'small' things that her mother tells her to correct. The poem contains a clear structural poetic turn – there is a set up to a punch line in the last sentence – a metaphorical retort to her mother, much like the literal retort of 'Just Do It'. The appropriation of 'Just Do It' is an intertextual practice that functions as a scaffold for her writing. Indeed, Nike's familiar slogan carried a meaning that was very likely shared with her peers and many other audience members, but Rejeanne is using the slogan in a new way in her poem to achieve a specific rhetorical goal.

Another student, Aiesha appropriated lines from a popular song, 'Worry', from the R&B recording artist Jazmine Sullivan. Aiesha reported that she mostly gets ideas 'from things that happen or are happening, or by listening or watching something'. She explained in her interview, '"I'm not scared of lions and tigers and bears" – that's the only line I used from the song . . . I wrote it the day before the Poetry Jam when I went home, and I had my radio on and I was watching the Discovery Channel, and they were talking about how people die from different diseases, and so I wrote a poem.' This exemplifies one of two students who composed an entirely new poem the evening before the event. An interpretation of this is that with repeated performances (in the classroom and in the performance space for the rehearsal the day before) Aiesha was realizing the kinds of performance and written texts that could be taken up to achieve her purposes.

Booker's poem demonstrates a common theme in children's writing at this school: incarceration. When talking with Booker about his poem, he explained that his family 'kept telling this story over and over'.

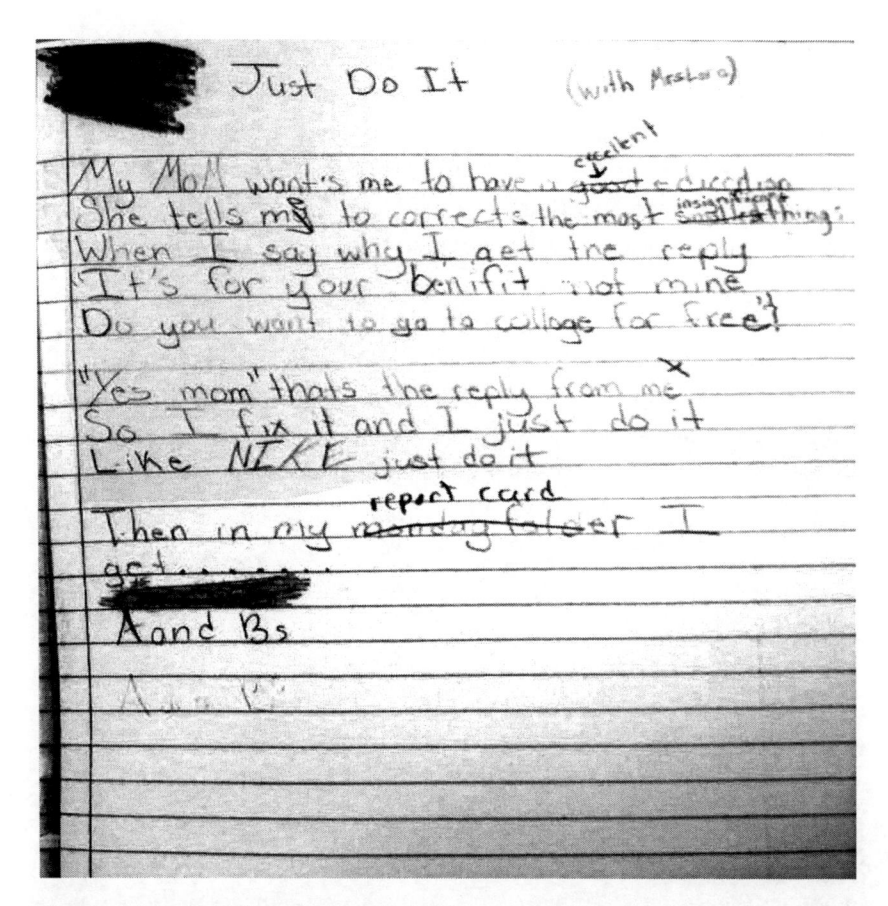

Figure 11.1 Rejeanne's poem 'Just Do It'.

My Uncle Matt
MY UNCLE MATT HAS BEEN
ARRESTED TWICE BECAUSE HE
WAS ALMOST BLIND OF HOW DARK
IT IS IN JAIL IT IS AS DARK AS THE
FUR ON A BLACK BEARS BACK.

BY BOOKER

Booker described how, in sharing an earlier draft of his poem with one of the guest poets, Logic, Logic suggested to compare the darkness to something. Booker explained, 'You know, how like Dr. Certo, she compared her husband to a Komodo Dragon, so I wanted to compare the darkness in the jail to an animal.'

'My Uncle Matt' was an anthologized poem. Though Booker did not comment on this practice, the reader can wonder if he is using the all Caps graphics to enhance his rhetorical goal. When asked in his interview what made 'My Uncle Matt' a poem, he responded, 'Um . . . in stories, it's like in a paragraph form. And in stories they have to be with the lines longer. I wrote it about my Uncle Matt, because he's my favorite uncle. He does everything with me.' Interestingly, in his interview with his poetry portfolio, the interviewer asked him why he crossed out the bottom line in an earlier draft that read, 'I hope you get well/and I cannot wait to see you.' Booker replied, 'Um . . . I took it out because I thought it didn't go with the poetry. And um . . . I didn't like how it sounded.' Thus, at first, Booker appropriated a turn of phrase that he knew in another context (perhaps a letter or card), then he self-monitored and adjusted this inter-contextual practice, realizing that letter- or card-like phrases were not working in this particular poem.

As mentioned previously, reading or performing an original poem for an audience can carry with it some challenges, not the least of which is trepidation. When students in this study were asked what it was like to read their poem for a live audience at the Poetry Jam, 23 students reported a sense of nervousness followed by or coupled with exhilaration and feelings of pride. Some comments also suggested that their performances brought forth a literate identity. For particular students who elaborated in their interviews on their reading or performance style, their reports suggest that performances are shaped by a want to honour their subject in their poems, to please the audience and/or to please themselves.

To begin, Long explained in his interview, 'I was kind of nervous. I was twitching my hand. And when I was done reading, I felt like so happy to myself.' Owen shared that 'it was pretty fun to get up there, and, like read, in front of lots and lots of people. I was a bit nervous. But it ended up being really cool. I thought about it all day.' And Carter explained, 'I didn't sleep the night before I was so excited. When Angelique [the MC] called my name, my heart was pounding. But I was so proud I did it.' Fifty per cent of the class reported that they felt a sense of a literary identity – that they could not only write, but also read or perform a poem. Six of these students' reports suggested that there was a sense of solidarity with the rest of the class. Jon explained, 'We got a chance to show adults and students that we could write poetry even though we were young.' Tia replied, 'I didn't know I could be a poet, but all the people saw us doing it, and all the poems were so good!'

Children's poetry performances (and the way they talk about them) do not tell us everything about their practices, but they do shed light on what might influence their decisions. Interviews with students demonstrated that students' performance practices were informed by honouring the subject of their poem, pleasing the audience and/or pleasing themselves. As Long noted, 'What helped me is believing that I could do it. It doesn't really matter as long as you like your poem. That's all that really matters.' Students overwhelmingly seemed motivated to read their poems, and they reported that 'confidence' and 'preparation' were most important when reading for an audience. When Rajeanne, the author of 'Just Do It' was asked about her experiences, she explained,

> I wanted to do a really good job. I wrote it [the poem] over as neat as I could, and I put certain things on the paper that said "pause" or "read kinda sassy" cause the poem is kinda sassy, or something like that. And then, so when I read a line, I could look on the side to read what it said on the side, and I just read off the piece of paper. Some of the adults, they were laughing, like Mr. Blair and Logic and Laura Apol, they were laughing when I said "She tells me to correct the most insignificant things."

At the *Poetry Jam*, 7 of the 23 students who read a poem (one elected not to read, as will be discussed later) chose to memorize their poems (3 boys, 4 girls). It is likely that these students were influenced by the performance styles of spoken word poets (Logic, Blair and Will the Poet) who visited the classroom and frequently memorized their poems (and/or perhaps children wanted to please these poets, who would be returning for the end performance). When asked why they chose to memorize their poem, responses were along the lines of 'I wanted to do something different.' Though, six students also thought it honoured the subject more. As DeMarcus explained (who had free hands to make a mock basketball shot at the end of his poem), 'Well, my poem was about basketball. I practiced in my room in front of my mirror. Cause I just didn't want to stand there stiff, and it is about basketball afterall.' The notion of the poem's subject suggesting its form was also evidenced by Booker's exchange, which additionally suggests he saw his peers as influential audience members in his decision to dramatize the last line of his poem.

> I: You said you memorized the poem. Why did you choose to do that?
> B: Because um . . . how I said that my Uncle Matt is my favourite one, so I wanted to memorize it.
> Then when I said that he was arrested, I put my hands behind my back.
> I: Oh, why did you decide to do that?

B: Because when they arrest people they put their hands behind their back. Also one of my friends told me that it would be good to put my hands behind my back so that people will get the feeling about it.

Conclusion

The fifth graders' poems and their talk about their poems revealed much about their writing practices which are interwoven with their performance practices. All but one student chose to read their poem at the Poetry Jam, and most certainly, Ms Jorgenson, the visiting poets, and I respected and honoured his wishes. As critical pedagogue Lensmire (1994) found, some children feel there are serious risks involved in writing for and speaking in front of their peers – risks to self, to their values and what they care about, and to their social positioning with audience members. Overwhelmingly, however, students in this study wanted to control their poetry writing, but they also craved the experience of reading or performing it. In the week after the performance, when my team was conducting interviews, two groups of students told me they started their own poetry readings in basements of each others' homes. My own interpretation is that students were given access to a way of working they had not had before, so some novelty was at play here. I also sensed that they found the performative aspect of inviting guest poets as highly motivating.

Anne Haas Dyson (2003) found that children can craft particular voices in multiple genres of their writing and essential resources for this can be found all around them in their daily lives. Findings in this study of preadolescents are commensurate with her work. It seemed that in addition to the resources available in their communities, homes and lives, a social community with diverse poems and poets in a school culture can socialize preadolescents into poetry writing and performance. Although the poetry pedagogy had some framing (e.g. distribution of poems, topical ideas such as writing about a family member), it was important to let students take their poems in any direction they wanted. The appropriations of media and popular culture that peppered students' poems functioned as scaffolds for trying on poetic voices, but they also positioned students favourably with peers. Preadolescents' reports suggest that their poetry reading performances brought forth feelings of pride, exhilaration and a literate identity. This was perhaps possible with the scaffolding of oral reading and performance throughout the project, as it was a resource for developing students' performative voices, topical play, linguistic play and even composing or revision activity. It was also powerful to acknowledge literacy as a social practice (Street 1993), providing social spaces (in the classroom, school and in the community) for focusing on the practices surrounding the reading and writing of poetry. Students' poems, performances and the way they talk about them suggest that poetry matters. Poetry matters, for it is one form of writing that touches students deeply and keenly by engaging their interests and emotions. Poetry matters, for it is a form of performance that can potentially exhilarate children and develop their confidence, all the while having their literal and metaphorical voices being heard.

1 2

Hearing the Voice of Poetry

Joy Alexander

Introduction

In this chapter, I relate reading a poem to hearing a voice and then reflect on an appropriate research-informed pedagogy for hearing the voice of poetry. Three principles are proposed as helpful for sharing with pre-service teachers and the consequent challenges and rewards are discussed and exemplified in the practice of one student teacher, Megan.

Hearings

The tale which the Ancient Mariner is fated to keep telling has two hearers, in Coleridge's final version of his poem. They are, according to J. T. Netland:

> the Wedding-Guest who is compelled to listen to the Mariner . . . . and who emerges from the encounter deeply moved; and the gloss-writing editor who, in the written record of his reading, demonstrates a sympathetic, scholarly interest as he seeks to explain and interpret the tale, but who never shares the Wedding-Guest's affective response. (Netland 1993: 39)

The glossing marginalia were later additions to the poem by Coleridge himself, but they give the appearance of being the work of an academic student of ballads, whose marginal prose narrative reveals him (presumably?) to be a precise, analytical reader. He 'domesticates the sublime and reifies conventional platitude' (ibid: 53), reducing the Mariner's experience to a succinct moral, namely 'to teach, by his own example, love and reverence to all things that God made and loveth'.

On the other hand, there is the Wedding-Guest who, despite the 'merry din' and 'the loud bassoon' in the background, has his ear held captive, though initially it is the eye of the Mariner that holds his attention:

> He holds him with his glittering eye -
> The Wedding-Guest stood still,
> And listens like a three years' child:
> The Mariner hath his will.
>
> The Wedding-Guest sat on a stone:
> He cannot choose but hear;
> And thus spake on that ancient man,
> The bright-eyed Mariner.

By the time he has listened to the Mariner's tale to its end, he is deeply affected, turning away from more immediate concerns, and enriched by what he has heard:

> .... and now the Wedding-Guest
> Turned from the bridegroom's door.
>
> He went like one that hath been stunned,
> And is of sense forlorn:
> A sadder and a wiser man,
> He rose the morrow morn.

His response is both cognitive and affective and his imagination has been receptive as well as active.

Which of the two has been the better listener to the Ancient Mariner's tale, the one who can prosaically recount what he heard or the one who absorbed what he heard with full attentiveness? In a lengthy consideration of the teaching of *The Rime of the Ancient Mariner*, David Holbrook similarly implies that there are two types of readers:

> But one often finds students who will run away into a discussion of such a poem before they have assured themselves that they have *read it*, by taking in fully the meaning and flavour of each word (Holbrook 1967: 146, author's italics).

The ballad editor and Holbrook's students miss the poem; the Wedding-Guest imaginatively engages with it. I am uncomfortably familiar with the ballad editor and his limitations and consequently am always gratified to find a Wedding-Guest in the poetry classroom. The latter enters into the poem; the former is an onlooker. Every English teacher who has had an examination class knows of the syndrome where young people dissect and annotate poems so that they will be able to write about them in the exam, but in the process lose interest in poetry. The stance of the Wedding-Guest proffers an alternative strategy: quite literally, to give the poem a hearing. *The Rime* provides reference points for teachers in relation to reading poetry: reading with the eye/knowing about/analysing a poem or reading with the ear/listening to/experiencing it. The tension for the teacher lies in finding the equilibrium between ensuring that a poem has been truly heard and developing skills in reading the printed poem on the page.

Reading a poem as hearing a voice

Before discussing practical considerations germane to the teacher's important role in developing young people as readers of poetry, the theoretical context should be outlined. The focus is on readers who can hear the voice of poetry, who read poems aloud and for whom reading a poem is in part an aural experience. Relevant to this would be background studies of oral culture and of the history of reading habits (Alexander 2000). There once was a time when it would have seemed odd to see a ballad written down; it was a story designed to be spoken in a way that could be remembered. The fact that most poems are written to be heard connects to the English curriculum by means of the positioning of listening within constructions of English as a subject; historically, listening and reading were commonly paired as the receptive functions of the subject, complemented by its expressive functions – talking and writing (Alexander 2008).

Denis Donoghue has helpfully distinguished between graphi-readers:

> The graphireader deals with writing as such and does not think of it as transcribing an event properly construed as vocal and audible. (Donoghue 1981: 151)

and epi-readers, whose inclination, by contrast, is to read with the ear and who 'say to poems: I want to hear you' (ibid: 152). The epi-reader participates in the dialogic nature of the text:

> The only requirement in epireading is that reading be construed as a personal encounter, the reader enters into a virtual relation with the speaker. (ibid: 99–100)

The words on the page are experienced as voice; the text – and this is especially true of poems – demands to be vocalized and heard. Donoghue regards style as compensation, making up for the defect in the condition of writing that it is writing and not speech. Style is a strategy to restore the poet's voice. From this perspective, the imagination both sees and hears and a poem is a multi-modal text.

In her essay 'The How of Literature', Ruth Finnegan explores what this means and coins the word 'en-performancing' to describe its consequences for literary experience:

> Literature is experienced in terms of its immediacy, in the temporal moment. This can come in a variety of forms: through embodied enactment, for example, or public theatrical display, or, more subtly, through the en-performancing of a written text, the 'now' when the reader personally encounters and re-creates it – 'performs' it. (Finnegan 2005: 176)

En-performancing is involved, even in a silent reading of a poem, where that reading is sensitized and attentive.

Wordsworth's Solitary Reaper is a poetic icon of vocal art. The en-performancing Reaper has the equivalent of the listening Wedding-Guest in Wordsworth himself, recording an incident from a visit to Scotland in 1803. When I asked 31 experienced teachers how they would teach 'The Solitary Reaper', more than half of them developed their lesson from a reading aloud of the poem. A few suggested that the class would listen to the poem before they had a copy of it in front of them to read. For most, a core activity was exploring 'rhythm, rhyme, tone and pace'. One teacher confessed to the chagrined realization that 'I wouldn't usually put much emphasis on listening to the poem.' Another said that 'the proper reading of this poem gives an insight clearer than explanation.'

An example of this might be the two occasions in the poem where the word 'listen' is used: 'O listen!' in the first stanza and 'I listened, . . .' in the last. The brief but marked pause that follows in each case enacts the attentiveness elicited by the reaper's song which instigates contemplation, so that the poem allows 'an analysis of the listening process itself'. One teacher proposed asking the class:

> The poet invited us to stop. What exactly have we stopped for?

In terms of the poem, the reply is that we stop to have our visual and auditory imagination engaged. Figuratively speaking, these are also always good reasons to 'stop' in the English classroom. 'The Solitary Reaper' is quite strongly visual, beginning with sight:

> Behold her, single in the field,
> Yon solitary Highland Lass!

and ending with hearing:

> I listened, motionless and still;
> And, as I mounted up the hill,
> The music in my heart I bore,
> Long after it was heard no more.

Although the speaker addresses his companion – 'Stop here'; 'O listen!'; 'Will no one tell me what she sings?' – he also enters into dialogue with himself. The fact that the girl is singing in her native Gaelic means that he has to listen carefully to catch the tone and hence surmise the meaning. The poem progresses from an appreciation of the sound in itself to reflection on the emotion the sound expresses, vicariously contemplating the lived experience that is transmuted into melody; and then to the lasting trace of the song left upon the imagination and memory. The music is a medium to define the identity of the Solitary Reaper; the act of listening exercises and increases the speaker's emotional intelligence and activates human sympathy. The poem challenges teachers to honour the process it enacts.

Poetry pedagogy

The emphases by Donoghue and Finnegan on epi-reading and en-performancing are helpful in formulating a methodology for teaching poetry. The student teachers with whom I work in post-primary pre-service education are looking for such a methodology, though it cannot be handed over as a neat package. Contemporary students are arguably at an advantage in that their culture is characterized by what Walter J. Ong has described as 'secondary orality' (Ong 1982: 11). In contrast to a print-dominated society, communication technologies have engendered a marked predominance of the oral and the aural. There are, however, also obstacles which can confound young teachers as they begin to teach poetry. One is the prevalent idea that English should have content:

> Operating within an educational marketplace, English teachers have been increasingly seen to deal in knowledge rather than in meaning-making, being expected to 'deliver' the goods rather than to teach young people to engage in deep learning. (Dymoke 2011: 145)

This has led to the commodification of poetry teaching, where there can be more teaching about poetry than actual reading of poems. Poems are encountered as examples of a range of genres – limerick, haiku, sonnet – or as assemblages of techniques – simile, metaphor, rhythm, onomatopoeia and so on. This 'naming of parts' approach is exacerbated in the current target-driven and outcomes-obsessed curriculum. Instead of simply being read and enjoyed for themselves alone, poems are, in the manner lamented by Billy Collins in his poem 'Introduction to Poetry', tied to a chair with rope and beaten with a hose. The advice with regard to classroom practice – 'just read a poem' or 'read the poem and see where it takes you' – seems lame to English graduates in whom the habit of analysing poems is engrained. I find it fairly common that student teachers, arriving in a school on their first placement and given the responsibility of teaching some poems to an exam class, fall back on the security of teaching methodologies which they experienced when they were pupils or even undergraduates, and the torturing of the poem into a confession, to again use Collins' description, becomes a perpetuating cycle.

In making these remarks I am not wishing to be critical of young teachers who are endeavouring to find their way in the English classroom. On the contrary, as someone seeking to help them to share poems with young people, I am all too aware that the present context is not conducive to an affirming confidence in simply reading poetry. I recall watching a student teacher take a lesson on ballads in line with the English department's scheme of work. The first thing that happened was that the pupils copied down a definition of a ballad; the one thing that never happened in the lesson was that a ballad was read right through. In conversation afterwards, I suggested to the student that 'Sir Patrick Spens' or 'The Wife of Usher's Well' would be good poems to read with the class but she demurred, on the basis that they were hard to understand. I think she meant for herself as well as for the pupils. I wanted to tell her that if she tried reading it aloud she might find that the problem would recede. I should stress again that I am not criticizing her; I know that she was anxious to do as she had been asked. However, she was hampered by the desire to have a demonstrable outcome to the poetry lesson, by a lack of confidence in a poem's ability to speak for itself, and by insufficient experience of understanding poems by reading them aloud or hearing them read.

Three principles

Against this backdrop, my advice to my student teachers comes down to three basic principles. They are spare and stark and may seem like stating the obvious, but I want the trainee teachers to have clear guidelines that are easily remembered and that have the blunt force to confront the monolithic pressures to conform to other curricular agenda for poetry.

You learn to read poetry by reading poetry

Young people need to get into the habit of reading poems so that they can gradually build up their poetry-reading stamina. Teachers have to find natural ways in which numbers of poems are read for their own sake in the classroom. English teachers wanting to infiltrate poetry in a seemingly casual manner into their class routines need to be purposeful and to believe that it is worthwhile. It should not be the case that the only poems read by GCSE or A-level pupils are the poems they are studying for their exams. I encourage student teachers to spend lessons, especially in the junior school, just reading poems with their classes, for example, poems with a common theme such as humour, mystery, animals, and allowing whatever conversation may arise. Several students have done enjoyable and productive anthology-based work, where, for example, groups of pupils have a range of anthologies from which they have to find and present or record their own selection of favourite or themed poems.

Poets write poems so as to direct us to read poems in the way they intend

Roger Shattuck records that the composer Claude Debussy informed the poet André Mallarmé that he was making a musical arrangement of his poem 'L' Après-midi d'un faune', to which Mallarmé replied, 'I thought I had already set it to music' (Shattuck 1999: 189). Poets deploy their skills so that the reader is artfully nudged into en-performancing a poem's particular emphasis, pace, tone, pauses, cadence, which in turn unfold its meaning. An example of the impact on reading development of having an attuned mind and ear is found in Seamus Heaney's account of how using the auditory imagination helped him to understand and appreciate Eliot's poetry. For Heaney in his late teens, Eliot was the writer of whom it was true that 'until one had found him one had not entered the kingdom of poetry' (Heaney 1989). However, Heaney found Eliot obscure and bewildering, until two things came to his aid. One was Eliot's definition of the auditory imagination which 'confirmed a natural inclination to make myself an echo chamber for the poem's sounds. I was encouraged to seek for the contour of a meaning within the pattern of a rhythm' (ibid). The other was the experience of hearing the actor Robert Speaight reading aloud T. S. Eliot's *Four Quartets*. In addition to sight-reading, Heaney listened to the soundscape, and suddenly discovered that 'what I *heard* made sense' (his italics). In practical terms, Heaney found that Eliot orchestrates language so that the voice realizes meaning.

To illustrate this, I sometimes ask my students to recreate a poem from a prose version of 'To a Poor Old Woman' by William Carlos Williams (to read this poem go to http://www.poetryfoundation.org/learning/guide/236558). Their instructions are that the resulting poem should have four four-line verses (counting the title as a line), and the only punctuation is one full stop, which is not at the end. This task can best be done on a computer, since the only permitted change is to delete punctuation, and the line lengths can be determined by trial and error through clicking the mouse. Williams orchestrates the reading he desires by running the syntactical unit against the rhythmical unit so that the light pattern of stress builds variance into repetitions of the line 'They taste good to her' and by carefully placing words such as 'Comforted', which forms a one-word line. This exercise demonstrates that 'the poem in print is a notation designed to make what one hears as clearly apprehensible as possible' (Pinsky 1998: 43) and that craft can render punctuation superfluous. The line 'a solace of ripe plums' has to be said aloud to appreciate its juicy, lip-smacking effect – which leads to the third principle:

Find as many ways as possible to get young people reading poems aloud for themselves

Attaining understanding of a poem by Williams or Eliot in this way is, as Heaney admits, 'available through a silent reading . . . . . since . . . . . it operates below the level of sense; but it operates much more potently when the poem is spoken aloud' (Heaney 1989). It can be both salutary and instructive for any English teacher to carry out an audit after a series of poetry lessons of how often poems were read aloud and by whom. My feeling is that too often the privilege lies with the teacher and many pupils rarely have the experience of voicing a poem.

In an essay titled 'Reading Out Poetry', F. R. Leavis claimed that 'the mere reader of poetry who doesn't do a great deal of full reading out won't be able to read out in imagination' (Leavis 1986: 254). Obviously, it is not choral reading and recitation that are to be placed on the curriculum:

> Faithfully reading out a poem . . . one should think of oneself as both the violinist and the violin, and not as an impressively personal elocutionary voice blessed with an opportunity. (ibid: 260)

Leavis explains what he means by violinist/violin:

> ... the ideal executant musician, the one who, knowing it rests with him (*sic*) to re-create in obedience to what lies in black print on the white sheet in front of him, devotes all his trained intelligence, sensitiveness, intuition and skill to re-creating, reproducing faithfully what he divines his composer essentially conceived. (ibid: 260)

The aim is for the pupil to combine apprehension of authorial intention and reader-response, and reading and hearing poetry aloud is a way towards accomplishing that. Leavis's image is used by Hirsch in a detailed justification of the 'sounding' process:

> Poetry is a voicing. . . . When I recite a poem . . . I become its speaker and let its verbal music move through me as if the poem is a score and I am its instrumentalist, its performer. (Hirsch 1999: 5)

Before leaving the image of the violinist, we find it used to strike a cautionary note by the Australian poet, Les Murray:

> Would David Oistrakh take his violin to parliament? And expect ears coarsened by dissension, rhetoric and the noise of competing egos to hear his more delicate nuances? (Murray 1997: 8)

Murray's words are admonitory to teachers with their warning that ears can be coarsened as well as sensitized. There are uses of language of which the cumulative effect may be to give young people cloth ears. Overemphasis on talk, too brisk a pace, too little exposure to imaginative language: these are some of the practices that might result in deficient, deadened listening.

As part of some classroom research, I asked groups of pupils to prepare a reading of a poem about which they were told nothing, the objective being to discover afterwards how much they had understood purely on the basis of reading the poem (Alexander 2008). Like a one-trick pony, this is the single strategy that I recommend to student teachers, advising them to find as many variations on it as they can, without deviating from its central thrust. Usually, I demonstrate by 'teaching' one or two poems to them, telling them nothing about the poem myself and giving them activities requiring them to read the poem aloud numbers of times (group preparation of a reading for presentation; recording a reading as voice-over to PowerPoint pictures) and then investigating its meaning through reflecting on their reading. This maximizes the reading aloud and hearing of the poem; it is a process of pupil discovery rather than teacher talk; and it is inclusive of, and accessible to, all pupils.

Megan's practice

Following the three basic pedagogical guidelines enumerated above will genuinely help pupils to get the poetry reading habit, but it requires confidence in poets and poems to move away from safer, more didactic and controlled approaches. In an account of her first teaching placement in an all-boys' school which she has given me permission to reproduce, Megan, a student teacher, discusses her early poetry classes:

> One of the issues I quickly identified with my first lesson is that I had only really provided the pupils with time to read the poem once, or in this case listen to a reading of the poem once at the beginning of the class. Noticing quickly that imploring students to 'read through the poem again, possibly twice, before you start on the questions' results only in a cursory glance through, if at all, I set out to design classroom activities that would require the boys to read, re-read and think explicitly about the process of reading.

Megan reflects on the shortcomings she observed in what is common practice and thinks through a range of alternative procedures:

> The easiest way I could think of to get boys reading and re-reading a poem was to have the boys 'perform' it. This was appropriate to this group as they were all keen to read or perform in front of their peers. In a less enthusiastic or 'secure' environment I would have still included reading aloud/performance but would have limited it to within small groups or pairs.

Further reflection leads her to develop her methodology and to add to her repertoire of poetry teaching strategies. Her capability in handling poems in the classroom is increasing and so too is the pupils' enjoyment:

> I noticed initially that the boys were not at all proficient in reading poetry aloud, though this improved drastically with a little practice either individually or in pairs. I also remembered the importance of *modelling* reading for pupils and discovered a useful means of delivering this through audio or video files, and which had the added advantage of increasing the boys' engagement with the poem further. Witnessing the class spontaneously erupt into applause following a performance of 'Jabberwocky' by Richard Griffiths was definitely one of the highlights of my teaching practice.

The pleasures of the text are evident here. Megan comes to realize that her strategy brings about a highly significant outcome, for as their reading got better 'I noticed that their understanding also improved. It was immensely rewarding to see pupils improve their grasp of a poem in this way.'

Conclusion

Megan's practice of developing in her pupils the ability to read orally and aurally is endorsed by C S Lewis. In a memorable image, he describes the process of reading:

> To see things as the poet sees them I must share his consciousness and not attend to it; I must look where he looks and not turn round to face him; I must make of him not a spectacle but a pair of spectacles. (Lewis and Tillyard 1939: 12)

Although the reader may subsequently turn to face the writer and engage in dialogue, his or her first activity is unself-conscious participation, which can then be followed by analysis and self-aware understanding. The tension I drew attention to at the start can be resolved by being the Wedding-Guest first and only then the editor. Appreciation of any art form yields to a simple but demanding formula:

> The first demand any work of art makes upon us is surrender. Look. Listen. Receive. Get yourself out of the way. (Lewis 1992: 19)

Megan managed to get out of the way of her pupils and devised ways to get them out of the way of the poem. She illustrates how both teachers and learners are empowered when young people are put in direct contact with a poem so that by reading with eye, ear and mouth they are able to tap into the poet's own 'orchestration'.

Sometime ago, I watched a student teacher handling a poem quite effectively with a class. In a discussion afterwards, she said that she felt a conflict between what she perceived as the department's wish to approach poetry through techniques and her wish to keep the focus on reading and understanding. The problem was that she thought the latter was risky – would the pupils know the things they needed to know? My answer was and remains: try it and see, get out of the way, and above all, trust the poet and trust the poem.

13

Heard Poetry and Oral Response

John Gordon

Introduction

This chapter is about teaching and learning where poems are treated as literary items, not just enjoyed for their own sake but used to prompt responses concerned with either their content or design.

When students of any age write about poems, plays or prose, it is common that they make use of quotations in their commentary. Each of us probably feels we understand what a quotation in writing is: the direct transcription of a word or phrase drawn from another existing text. We are likely to signal that it is borrowed with quotation marks, and perhaps go a step or two further in providing reference details. A similar thing happens in classroom talk about literary texts. A teacher can ask 'Can you give me a quotation from the poem that links with what you have suggested?', and a pupil can supply a word or verbatim phrase that is taken from the source text.

There are some important differences of context to consider with respect to these two examples, though. When someone uses quotations in writing, they do so in a private realm, shaping a line of discussion on the page with only a notional reader in mind. In a classroom, things are different. There may be an exchange between two people just like the one mentioned, or there could be more people involved. If words from a text are repeated, they are shared publically for all present, even if in response to one person's question. In a written assignment, quotations are used within a cohesive piece crafted in reaction to a specific title or brief – and as such contribute to a piece that aims at completion. The classroom exchange by contrast is more fluid, exploratory and provisional. Repeating details in a classroom is, therefore, social and tentative, less of a binding commitment. They are also shared aloud, and can't be marked as quotations in the same way as they might be on the page, where spaces, inset margins and punctuation all guide the reader to recognize the borrowed items. Further, these devices in writing do more: they serve to isolate the extracts from the author's own commentary, the sentences and paragraphs which offer explanation and analysis of the selected details. In writing, the function of the components is marked in the sequence of the assignment and in their layout.

You may have assumed so far that in remarking on the act of quoting I have meant quotations selected while studying poems in print, and it would be quite reasonable to do so. For the rest of this chapter, discussion will be about different texts. I want to think about how pupils respond to poems they *hear* in classrooms, and specifically what happens when they select words or phrases from what they have heard and then repeat them. Is this quotation as we usually understand it? I don't think so. That they are working in sound, and in the process of conversation, makes the process rather different.

I propose that we distinguish this differing phenomenon by calling it *echo*. It performs actions distinct from quotation in writing. While on the page the actions of presenting and analysing textual detail occur in separate sections of writing, in echo they can happen simultaneously.

Why is it necessary to make such a distinction? Poetry itself is often understood to make meaning through resources beyond semantics alone, and this contributes to its status as poetry. On the page these include features of layout that signal to us we are looking at a poem even before we are manipulated by line breaks or guided by stanzas. Where we experience poems through listening, these additional resources include volume, intonation, pace and silences. The pedagogy of poetry needs to allow for the possibility that pupils respond to these resources in a manner distinct from how they react to semantic meaning and that they may articulate their responses in a unique way too. Pupils do repeat details of poems in classroom discussion, but as they do so they have at their disposal resources of sound not available to them when they write about poetry.

In the endeavour of supporting pupil learning around poetry, it is important to consider what their responses to texts tell us about their engagement and understanding, and this includes gauging their sensitivity to the play of sound in poems. Conventionally, this is done through recourse to an analytic metalanguage describing features such as alliteration, rhyme and metre. When pupils talk about poetry they have heard, however, pupils may convey response in sound itself, with the possibility that some aspect of their understanding of texts could be revealed if we were in the habit of attending to it.

The research method

Drawing on transcripts of recorded classroom discussion, I will illustrate the use of *echo* in pupils' responses to heard poetry and explain its function. The conversation used as illustration here happened in a primary classroom setting. The female teacher worked with a group of 10 male pupils (aged 9 and 10) and was involved in the discussion herself. First, the group heard a performance of a poem from a CD audio recording read by the authoring poet. Next, they responded to what they heard, with the teacher prompting talk little by little. The learning focus for the session was on pupils offering and elaborating response, exploring what the poem is 'about'. The poem for attention was Liz Lochhead's 'Men Talk',[1] which pays attention to relationships between gender and communication.

My research method treated the recorded poem as the first turn in the conversation, the performing voice effectively a participant. In the structure of conversation, the poem was also the common point of reference for all that followed. For a teacher guiding learning, pupils' contributions shared in group or class discussion provide key information by which to gauge their understanding and progress in learning. To see how these responses develop orally and through interaction is thus useful to refine assessment practice in literary pedagogy. It concerns recognizing that the text for study is oral in character and that responses are shared in the same mode. It is about making sure that the details we are alert to in formative assessment are matched to the nature of the study text. In this example, the voice of the heard poem manipulates intonation, volume and pace to prompt varying emotional responses. Often, these reactions merge with intellectual judgements about relative value – in this poem around qualities associated with each gender.

This short extract will give you a flavour of the poem as it is encountered in print:

> Women
> Rabbit rabbit rabbit women
> Tattle and titter
> Women prattle
> Women waffle and witter
> Men talk. Men Talk.
> Women into Girl Talk
> About Women's Trouble

Trivia'n'Small talk
They yap and they babble
Men talk. Men Talk.

And here is the same extract rendered for the research through the transcription conventions of Conversation Analysis[2]:

Wo:men
(0.5)
> rabbit rabbit rabbit < women ta:ttle and titter
(.)
.h women pr*attle women waffle and witter
(0.7)
.hh↑me::n talk:
(0.5)
.hh°↑me::n talk:°
(0.7)
> wo↑men < into girl talk! about women's trouble
(.)
.hhtri:::via:ansmall talk they yap and they babble
(.)
.hhh ↓me::n talk::

Of course, it cannot really be regarded as the same, because the transcript represents a different text. It represents a recorded version of the poem performed by the poet, and therefore is a new text in a different mode: sound rather than print.

The Conversation Analysis transcription method supported attention to aspects of delivery both in the recorded poem heard by pupils and in their own conversation. When a pupil's repetition of a phrase is set aside as an extract from the source text, we can see how patterns of delivery echo the original. This pupil turn illustrates the point,

Luke = women > rabbit rabbit rabbit < (.) whatever =

corresponding with and echoing the swift repetition of the word by the poet:

Lochhead > rabbit rabbit rabbit < women ta:ttle and titter

Just as we would expect of written quotation, the pupil replicates the word used by the poet and repetition of it three times in succession. Additionally, and of course in a way not possible in writing, he also mimics intonation and the increase in the pace (signalled in the transcription convention by bookending the faster word or phrase with arrows). In other instances of *echo*, though, the parallel is less true, for example, they may not replicate intonation exactly. The *echo* lies in mimicking the patterning of poetry, for example, where words or phrases become marked as important relative to their context. This marking occurs through variation in aspects of delivery, which listeners have a tendency to notice. In their own *echoes* they recall this marking, though specific aspects of delivery may differ. Like naturally occurring echoes, there is gradual loss and faithfulness to the source diminishes. The way in which the poem directs attention through patterning in sound is retained.

The research method does more than help us examine the response of individuals. Conversation Analysis also permits attention to how pupils involved in a conversation interpret one another's contributions, evident if we look at any contribution next to those made by others or how contributions build and accumulate across an exchange. What they say, how they say it and when they say it are part of the analysis and can suggest what participants in the conversation understand the turns of others to achieve. This need not be complicated – for instance, if one pupil provides an echo of the source poem and another pupil makes a new comment about the poem, it indicates that the second pupil considers the echo as allowable, normal and relevant.

What normally happens with quotations?

This next example illustrates a pupil using quotations to support discussion of a poem for study, encountered in print. It is the response made by a young adult of 16, writing in an examination setting[3]. Its structure will be very familiar to teachers of secondary-phase English. The pupil is commenting on the poem 'Two Scavengers in a Truck' by Lawrence Ferlinghetti:

> In 'Two Scavengers' the poor garbagemen are described as wearing 'red plastic blazers' and in a 'yellow garbage truck' whereas the rich are in a 'hip three-piece linen suit' in 'an open mercedes'. At a first glance the rich have lavish vehicles and more sophisticated clothing, but a second look suggests otherwise. The colours 'red' and 'yellow' are bright primary colours whereas the linen suit is usually white and a mercedes is often associated with silver. In comparison the colours used to describe the rich are more subdued than the colours used to describe the poor. Perhaps Lawrence Ferlinghetti is subtly suggesting the poor lead more vibrant lives, hence giving them the upper-hand. . .

The example demonstrates a three-part structure, often summarized in formulae like 'point-evidence-explain' (acronym PEE) or 'point-evidence-analyse' (PEA). Clearly, quotations (here, the details extracted from the Ferlinghetti poem) constitute content – what the given paragraph is 'about' – and in other instances this might be even more obvious where marked spatially by use of inset and/or empty lines either side of the quotation. Sometimes teachers present the PEA formula through the analogy of a sandwich or as 'the burger method'. In the analogy, the quotation is clearly the bit we add in, inserted between an introductory 'point' and then explanatory or analytical comment. The example here shows a genre in which initiating statements and observations about the text, as well as elaborating discussion, are distinct from the repeated textual details as a consequence of the modality of writing to the conventions of a literary essay. Quotation in writing can be no more than an exact semantic and syntactic copy of a detail in source text, a clone if you like. It can't do any more. Other words, other sentences have to provide the analysis.

The poem used in the research example

As we might expect of poems presented orally, Lochhead's performance has fluctuating emphasis, volume and speed. When she says 'men talk' in the recorded version, her intonation clearly rises on 'men' and then falls on 'talk'. On its own, the fall would not draw attention, but becomes very apparent after the rise. Sometimes brief pauses mark items even more obviously. For me, the rising tone builds suspense, as if to say 'Look what we men can do!'. The elongated 'e' suggests a further attention-seeking flourish to typify male self-regard.

Other play around sound suggests male claims to composure, steadiness and pragmatism, but because Lochhead is speaking in a female voice, this seems gently mocking and ironic. Most conspicuously of all, the clear rise and fall of the tone usually happens after a quite prominent pause, which sets the phrase 'men talk' aside as a distinct unit. It parallels isolation on the printed page through line breaks and spacing, though the combined resources of sound and silence arguably bind the words together more completely and with more resonance.

At other points, volume seems to convey a male persona who is convinced of being right. This typifies shifts of intonation that guide listeners to work out whether a male or female perspective is most dominant at any given point. Sometimes Lochhead is representing a male utterance (often with irony), sometimes a male voice rendering a female utterance and sometimes a female utterance. In combination, these examples make obvious the significance of resources other than words themselves in the performance. My research looked closely at how pupils repeated parts of what they heard, and if they drew on these resources too.

An example of *echo* doing something different from quotation

In the extract of conversation in Figure 13.1, a pupil named Mark echoes the heard poem at turns 8 and 10. To understand how the *echo* works, we need to look at the broader conversation:

Look at Mark's exclamation in turn 2. It may express disagreement, annoyance or disapproval, perhaps to reject Joe's point. Yet, it could also be construed as agreement with Joe's proposition, as if to say 'yes it does say that, what rubbish'. That Joe carries on suggests that he doesn't interpret Mark's interjection as a challenge, implicitly accepting it as reasonable. The teacher's reaction may be

1 Joe	= we:ll (0.2) theyyerr basically saying men are borrri:ng=
2 Mark	=PFFYEAHH! =
3 Joe	=Men just talk =
4 Ben	=.men DO: ju:st ta:lk…
5 Joe	They're li:ke men just ta:lk about no:thing in particular.
6 Graham	[hhcchiccuhnff! and ???
7 ???	and then =
8 Mark	= Mme:n ta:lk =
9 Teacher	= George?
10 Mark	Mme:n ta:lk
11 George	Oh well in a wayyy (0:2) whoe:ver it is wrote the um (.) poem is being er-kind of ne<u>ga</u>tive about men (.) cos they're saying (.) wo:men a:re >talkative< and men are <u>bor</u>ing.
12 Teacher	That's ri:<u>gh</u>t, does that-this is a compl↑etely diff<u>erent</u> pers<u>pec</u>tive <u>then</u> i:sn't it, you've kind of moved on =
13 Ben	= That's going into a woman's ((role)), they're saying good things (.) they're say:ing women're really (.) like (.) <u>GOOD</u> and interesting and men are jus- (.)↑<u>bor</u>ing, they don't talk =

Figure 13.1 Extract of conversation about 'Men Talk'.

different, and the actions her speech performs imply that Mark's turn may not be viewed as constructive. After Mark's echo of 'men talk' (8), she invites another pupil to speak. In between, Ben (4) takes the opportunity to confirm Joe's remark.

There may be more to this exchange, and to Mark's contribution. Joe was paraphrasing the poem, but Ben seems to be making instead a statement about how men conduct themselves in the world at large. His is not a comment about the poem. Joe goes on to sum up the perspective of the poem with an overt reference to the poem's voice ('they're like . . . '). The next couple of turns appear to appreciate that he is reflecting an assertion *in* the poem rather than offering his own opinion.

After all this, Mark offers the echo '= Mme:n ta:lk'. In the jargon of Conversation Analysis, it is latched (shown by the 'equals' sign), indicating that it follows on immediately from the prior turn. That it follows fleetly shows us that Mark sees this as a perfectly valid place to comment both in terms of the etiquette of a conversation and with respect to the logic of ideas. It can be considered sequitur to Joe's recognition of the poem's assertion that men 'talk about nothing in particular'. There is no other turn which elicits Mark's echo of the poem, but because he captures the differentiated emphasis of the original, we know this is not just a general observation about men. Instead, this deliberate echo acts as a *demonstration* of Joe's point. It serves to say 'here is evidence in support of Joe's point found in the poem', and in that respect it acts rather differently from quotation in writing. The aspects of intonation and choice of timing in the architecture of the full conversation convey the purpose of the interjection.

At turn 9, the teacher directs a question to another pupil. In the sequence of the conversation, this action does not treat Mark's turn as a useful contribution. Yet, Mark does not accept that he should give up the conversational floor, and he continues to echo the poem. Here is an interesting problem: Mark seems to have an understanding of a part of the poem and its relevance that does not coincide with that of the teacher. His interjection could just be a quip, a distracted repetition with no purpose. An alternative function, though, is to demonstrate again Joe and Ben's earlier comments that gloss and comment on the heard poem without citing it directly. This implies he has been listening throughout, and with care. His comment is in fact part of an 'adjacency pair' with Joe's turn at 5, Mark's turns (8 and 10) combining to echo the 'men talk men talk' of the original and then to confirm the proposition that male talk is mundane and about 'nothing in particular'. Perhaps, then, it is laden with purposeful intent.

Additionally, Mark's *echo* is accurate in words, and shows he notices that sound marks emphasis in the original, even though he does not recall the pattern perfectly. He mimics Lochhead's falling intonation in his 'mme:n ta:lk', but also the pause. Significantly, he mimics the unit – the two words used in the same formula, with approximate sound patterning – which suggests that they are perceived as having meaning *only* in this entirety. It is this item with this completeness that is worthy of note, not just the semantic meaning of the two words.

In summary, this example points to Mark's specific contribution being far from random. It has a function in the conversation that is more than just the presentation of details replicated from the source text. In acting to demonstrate the points of others, his verbal action is multitasking in a manner that is not possible through quotation in writing.

So what is an *echo*?

Based on this example, we can identify characteristics of *echoes* that make them distinctive from quotations on the page. First, an *echo* is an utterance by a pupil or teacher that in some manner repeats a part of a study text that has been presented through sound. Second, an *echo* is not necessarily an exact or pure repetition of every element of the selected detail drawn from the source text. Syntactic details may vary slightly, or aspects of delivery may be altered in some way, though it will be possible to trace the *echo* to a parallel item in the original.

The key trait is that the repetition reflects the distinctive character of details in the source text derived from *how* they are uttered. They could, for example, differ in pace and volume from surrounding details. When a listener echoes a text, it indicates that they recognize a detail is significant in some way as a marker, though the resources for marking may not be replicated entirely.

At the level of interaction across the conversation, *echo* can function beyond the mere mimicking of the source text. It is methodic and serves two or more functions. By this I mean that as well as existing as a repetition, ostensibly a recollection for its own sake, it has other functions too. These can be considered analytic: because the deployment of *echo* is methodic, it acts to express a pupil's position relative to the source text and is thus more than a simple recollection of the poem shared for its own sake.

Conclusion

The transcripts for the research showed what teachers know from experience – that pupils repeat words and phrases in their own discussion in the manner I have termed *echo*. On occasion they preface such repetition with a phrase confirming the act of repetition (for instance, 'he said'), though their repetition of a phrase may be inexact.

When *echoes* are made, other participants accept them as relevant to the flow of conversation, even though further explanation as to their relevance is not provided. For the contributor, they can be a source of pleasure, one of display and performance, assuming an audience that may be entertained. Use of *echo* is not trivial, however, and appears to function in support of the progress of an exploratory conversation. It can convey a speaker's position about an idea or item relative to the preceding turns, depending on where in the conversation it is offered.

Sometimes pupils provide *echoes* that may not seem to follow from immediately preceding contributions, but which are relevant to the general pedagogic focus, for instance, relating to a teacher's question further back in the exchange. The example presented above shows a use of the echo that on the face of it does not seem immediately relevant, though attention to interaction and intonation suggests that it is constructive and could indicate something of the pupil's own interpretation of the poem.

The use of *echo* here by Mark to demonstrate the observations of another participant also reveals what he perceives to be relevant and salient. He treats the echoed parts as a complete and coherent single unit, hinting at the possibility that listening to poetry evokes responses not oriented to semantic meaning alone but to units of patterned sound. Mark assumes that his reasons for doing this action now – making echo without elaborating comment – will be understood by others.

The significance of this for teaching is that though in some respects akin to quotation in writing, repeating details of heard poems in subsequent classroom discussion is not exactly the same. Crucially, some of the analytic work that might be articulated overtly in writing is not necessary in interaction. The resources of intonation, emphasis and volume, together with the timing of contributions within a sequence, are distinctive resources by which a contributor's interpretation of an item can be conveyed. Listeners apparently understand the meanings conveyed in such ways.

In terms of teaching, this should not mean that we refrain from asking pupils to express their analysis explicitly, but it does mean that if we are trying to gauge how pupils have understood a poem, we need to be alert to these subtle aspects too. Pupils may understand more than we believe they do. It helps at least to appreciate the distinction between a pupil who is not able to respond in a way that signals comprehension and one who appears to comprehend but may not communicate that understanding in the discourse of a recognizable commentary. If we are not attentive, we overlook the sensitivity pupils may have to poetry they hear, which would be ironic if we hold the specialness of poetry to reside in part in its play and craft in sound.

A version of this paper, entitled 'Echo, not quotation: what Conversation Analysis reveals about classroom responses to heard poetry', was first published in Classroom Discourse, 3:1 (May 2012), 83–103.

14

Commentary: Poetry as a Matter of Spokenness

Julie Blake

In their different ways, the authors of the three papers in this section ask us to think about poems not as words on a printed page, to be wrangled like a semantic Rubik's cube until *the* solution is found, but as multimodal texts inviting interaction with the *voice* of the poem, and through that interaction to other interactions beyond it, with teachers and classmates, with public audiences and with the wider world of the literate community. This is poetry as a matter of spokenness, part of a deep cultural heritage of literary meaning-making, in which orality is encoded in the form even as it moves into the mono-modality of standard print production.

This dimension of spokenness is foregrounded most strongly in the work of poets who would describe themselves as 'stage' poets rather than as 'page' poets, or 'performance poets', or 'spoken word artists'. This naming directs our attention to the idea of poetry as a social experience of voices and to the resonance that comes from hearing the poet perform the poem exactly as they intend it to be heard. In Janine Certo's account of running a poetry writing programme with children in school, this foregrounding of the spokenness of poetry is evident in her involvement of other poets as readers of their own poems, and in her support for the students' public performance of their poems. This is not just a poetic position but also an ethical one in its educational context, one which the growing popularity of school 'slams' attests to and which often informs the rationales for such events: it is about valuing what young people have to say about their lifeworlds and experiences, and giving them a valued opportunity through which to invite interaction about those. Poetry is a voiced, social experience for talking about, for discovering personal and shared meanings that may not be immediately reducible to Point Example Explanation.

This voiced dimension is not absent in poetry and poets not labelled as 'performance', though some poetry might attend closely to its visual representation on the printed page and some poets might be more active than others in giving readings of their work. Neither is it absent in popular understandings of what poetry is and does: the Poetry Archive website,[1] the premier online collection of recordings of poets reading their own work, has millions of page views per month; poetry festivals, and poetry tents at music festivals, thrive; as do the UK's *Poetry Live!* curriculum-related poetry events. The demand for poetry as voice has further encouraged the Poetry Archive to make recordings of contemporary poets reading 'classic' poems by poets who lived before recording technologies were invented. The interaction generated by attending to the voice of poetry happens across time and space too, connecting us with past voices and other lifeworlds that help us to understand where we have come from and make sense of where we are now.

This belief in poetry as voiced interaction underpins the work Joy Alexander describes in encouraging beginning teachers to think about the form of a poem as designed by the poet to show how it was intended to be read, in an act of 'enperformancing'[2], silent or aloud. This is about how teachers support young people in encountering poetry first hand, as a lived, embodied experience, co-constructed in the here-and-now by the poet and the reader. This is a position that entails young people learning to read poetry by reading poetry, and being guided to pay close attention to the way in which the poetic voice is realized in the deployment of its language. This too is deeply ethical in its educational context: it is about learning to listen to another's voice, a listening that is deeply attentive, empathetic and present. It is about so much more than whether there is or isn't a metaphor in line three.

Poetry as voice has another dimension: the opportunity it affords young people to 'try out' different voices, to respond imaginatively to them and to appropriate them for meaning-making. Janine Certo describes the way that the young people in her poetry workshops appropriated the voices of popular and commercial cultures in their own writing. The specific example is of a young woman appropriating the Nike slogan 'Just do it' in a poem about her relationship with her mother, the potentials for meaning layered into its intertextuality and ambiguity. This is a wholly different encounter with the 'stuff' of poetry to the lists of terminology more commonly encountered in the curriculum materials supporting secondary school English, at least at the time of writing in the United Kingdom.

There is an interesting connection to be made here between this kind of work with young people and the revival of interest in children memorizing and performing the poems of published poets. In the USA, *Poetry Out Loud* is well established, *Poetry In Voice* is developing in Canada, there is *Poetry Aloud* in Ireland and *Poetry By Heart* is in the process of being launched in English schools. Teachers sometimes regard these activities as oppositional, sometimes pejoratively, with student 'slams' constructed as the liberation of young people's voices and student recitals of poetry as its repression. The papers in this chapter point to an alternative framing: that a pedagogical multiplicity of encounters with poetry as voice, through inhabiting and appropriating the voices of others, across historical time and cultural location, gives young people a far greater richness of resources through which to find their own.

John Gordon's work takes a different approach, methodologically, but there are interesting connections in his thinking about the appropriation of voice. His use of the linguistic methods of Conversation Analysis to analyse classroom interaction about poetry allows him to focus intensively on the way in which young people respond to poetry they have heard by appropriating the poet's voice. He calls these appropriations 'echoes', in which selected words and features of the poet's stress, timing and intonation are replicated by students for purposes akin to written quotation, but with more significant social functions within the emerging classroom discussion of the poem. In class, such 'echoes', without any offer of more conventional analytical response, can irritate teachers (I speak with the conviction of my own impatience), but Gordon argues, as all of the writers do in their different ways, for a pedagogy that is better able to listen to the tentative meanings young people are making in the modes and manners they have access to. This too is a deeply ethical pedagogical position, as well as an interesting line of enquiry for future research which might usefully contribute to debate about the validity of the ways in which our education systems seek to assess student responses to poetry.

Joy Alexander's paper starts with a very important reminder about Coleridge's *Rime of the Ancient Mariner*: that it is not just the narrative of the wedding guest whose situated, attentive listening leaves him changed forever, in almost unspeakable ways, but also the narrative of the marginal glosser, offering us his picky little analytical comments and moral judgements that are painfully recognizable to the best of teachers as standard pedagogical method. In the three papers here, we are invited to do better, and in the ideas that their different interests and approaches suggest, we have the starting point for a pedagogy of poetry that is about voice, interaction and deeply attentive listening. We may, however, first have to learn how to do those things ourselves.

Part Four

Transformative Poetry Cultures

15

Developing Poetry Pedagogy for EAL Learners within Inclusive Intercultural Practices

Vicky Obied

Introduction

Our class

Bring lots and lots of humour to the boil with
Some Iranians and Arabs,
A healthy part of China,
A bit of India,
A chunk of France,
A slab of Sri Lanka and a tablespoon of Tanzania.

Add a blend of Harrow, London, England,
Nepal, South Africa and a pinch of Ireland
Before stirring vigorously.

Fill up the pan with Ecuador,
Pop in a couple of sachets of sparkles and
Mix with some art,
Before sifting in some drama and fun –
Not to mention a good sense of justice –
And stirring in some purple.

Sprinkle some pinches of Japan,
Video games and a touch of fun sports.
Drizzle with smiles
And serve with Dalek Bread.
Note: Serve with joy and happiness.
By a Year 7 class (London Secondary School)

The poem *Our Class* was written by a group of 11–12-year olds in a London classroom. In constructing the poem, a single line was taken from different students' writing and amalgamated into the poem. The lines illustrate the diverse nature of a typical secondary school in central London and the range of cultures within one classroom. There were many English as an Additional Language (EAL) learners in this group, and the writing of the poem engaged and empowered them to explore their identity and perceptions about living in London. The teacher wrote and shared her own poem about identity which started:

> Take a hearty slab of Yorkshire
> A morsel of Poland,
> A pinch of London and
> A good dose of humour.

This openness and collaborative approach towards the writing of poetry supported more inclusive practices, and this perspective recognizes the importance of viewing classroom interaction as multidirectional as 'students accommodate to school routine and repertoires, but teachers accommodate to students' repertoires as well' (Rymes 2010: 538).

In this chapter, I explore the development of poetry pedagogy for EAL learners and examine how trainee teachers of English approach poetry in diverse multilingual school settings. I contest existing relationships between language, power and pedagogies and look at pressing questions that arise when teaching poetry in inner-city London schools. I put forward the premise that poetry uses language in aesthetic, imaginative and engaging ways that have considerable potential to extend the learning of EAL pupils. Here, I draw on earlier research that recognizes the importance of the imagination in learning a language and sees the interface between language and literature as 'the richest vein of learning potential for learners at all levels of language' (McRae 1996: 23). Poetry opens up spaces for EAL students to learn the musicality of the new language and develop a deeper understanding of intercultural practices.

Developing an intercultural perspective

Pertinent to this debate about viewing poetry from an intercultural perspective is an innovative research project 'Bombing of Poems' (Bianchi 2010) which investigates the transformative power of poetry in reframing past experiences and creating an alternative image for the future. The ability of both researchers and teachers to move across boundaries and take poetry back into the community, or to bring pupils' sense of poetry and identity into the classroom, has helped to create alternative pedagogies and new ways of teaching. However, this is not without challenge as although creative teachers are able to introduce an intercultural perspective into the curriculum, 'it must also be recognized that the current compartmentalised curriculum and high-stake testing regime constitute a powerful barrier to the kind of transformative pedagogy implied' (Anderson and Obied 2011: 24). Research and practice indicates that there are certain areas that trainee teachers find difficult: teaching poetry, teaching EAL learners and developing intercultural practices.

In a report into 'Who's prepared to teach school English?', Blake and Shortis (2010) highlighted concerns regarding the teaching of poetry: 'confidence, capability and familiarity with the genre was said to have been impeded by limited prior exposure to poetry in the trainees' own earlier schooling and at degree level' (Blake and Shortis 2010: 26). In a report into EAL provision in England and Wales, researchers found that 'any sense of an EAL Pedagogy is strikingly absent' (IoE 2009: 11), while *The Newly Qualified Teacher (NQT) survey* (TDA 2008) found that only 37 per cent of NQTs felt their preparation to work with EAL learners was good or very good. In developing an intercultural perspective, distinctions between different domains of learning become more fluid and links are developed between home and school, study and leisure, and local and global. However, 'there is a danger that underdeveloped pedagogy for EAL learners may lead to teachers having low expectations, simplifying tasks, and providing a limited, reductionist form of the curriculum' (Anderson and Obied 2011: 20).

Recent studies investigating EAL children's encounters with textual worlds recognize the potential of stories and poetry to help these learners experience the whole shape and rhythm of the new language (Datta 2007; Obied 2007). EAL learners can bring a wealth of experience into the classroom. Erickson (2003) argues that rhymes and songs are seen as a way that children pick up the musicality of speech and learn the regular patterns and timing of talk across different educational and cultural settings. Stories, images, rhymes and melodies are at the core of our cultural identity and children form a deep connection with texts 'revelling in a tale's drama and music and patterning' (Crossley-Holland 2000: 24). The language of poetry provides students with the opportunity to question rules, play with language and start to understand the complexity and nuance of deeper word knowledge.

Developments in the field of intercultural communication and ideology raise important educational questions about how knowledge is conceived and how this is reflected in curriculum content, design and assessment. While education systems tend still to base achievement on a narrow, fragmented view of learning, it has become increasingly clear that such an approach fails to prepare young people for the realities of the modern world, a world in which an ability to move comfortably across linguistic and cultural boundaries has become vital. Cummins (2006) argues that 'a multiliteracies approach that attempts to incorporate students' language and culture into the curriculum is much more capable of including all students productively within the learning community' (ibid: 57).

Context of the research study

The part of the study presented here developed from a larger year-long research project carried out in a London-based university and across London secondary schools from 2009 to 2010. The original research question looked at how teachers support EAL pupils' academic language development with a focus on the language of literature and how teachers can design pedagogies that effectively support language learning for EAL pupils. The main part of the study focused on situated practices in four mainstream secondary schools and examined how teachers of English support EAL learners access a diverse range of literary texts. The part of the study examined in this chapter investigates how trainee teachers grapple with the tensions between theory and practice and look at how to develop poetry pedagogy for EAL learners within inclusive, intercultural practices. An ethnomethodological approach (Cameron 2001) was employed to analyse data collected from focus group interviews with trainee teachers, video recordings of English lessons inclusive of EAL learners and samples of research projects carried out by trainee teachers.

The challenge for educators is to open up 'ideological and implementational space for multilingualism and social justice' (Hornberger 2010: 563) and challenge existing relationships between language, power and pedagogies. There is an urgent need for research-informed practice as 'despite growing numbers of students with diverse language histories attending school across Europe, systematic and structured professional education to prepare teachers and educational managers for work in multilingual schools is still relatively rare' (McPake et al. 2010: 5). In this chapter, I frame perspectives towards intercultural communication and ideology within a dynamic paradigm that teachers and students are continually negotiating. 'It is at the level of discourse that individuals are able to negotiate, make sense of and practise culture; and it is within this process that imaginations about culture are generated and ideology is both experienced and manufactured' (Holliday 2011: 1).

Developing poetry pedagogy

Bakhtin's concept of the living heteroglossia of language (Bakhtin 1981) places EAL learners in an ideal position to understand this notion of multi-languagedness and to engage in intercultural discourses around literary texts. However, the reality of poetry teaching in London classroom has often moved far away from this dialogic, exploratory approach. A trainee teacher in this study, frustrated by her experience of poetry pedagogy in schools, explains this dilemma thus:

> Poetry teaching in English secondary schools today is locked in a vicious circle. Poetry, arguably the purest form of emotional expression in literature, is often taught by methods that leave no room for pupil exploration and thus inhibit understanding. It is often the case that poetry teachers take on an authoritative role as instructors of meaning and pupils are shuttled through what becomes a series of inaccessible poems, a ubiquitous set of class annotations their only guide to the words on the page of their poetry anthologies. (Melinda)

In developing more inclusive practices in poetry pedagogy, trainee teachers enter a landscape which is both political and contested. A trainee English teacher exploring the poetry anthology as an artefact of English education explains the shock of his grandfather's English teacher when his grandfather, on his first day of primary school, recited 'The Red Flag' in a south London classroom, the anthem of British leftism.

> At the time, the shocked reaction of the teacher left him thinking he'd done something wrong. Of course, he had. The poems and songs which are taught in school, which we interpret, perform and commit to memory have always been part of a contested educational landscape, one in which ideological viewpoints are put forward and reinforced. (Nigel)

The trainee English teachers in this research study were interested in exploring the concept of relevance regarding the selection of poems to teach in the classroom. This raises questions about the teaching of particular poems and whether a poem is relevant when students can see their own lives reflected in the text. There is concern about the disconnection of teaching practice from contemporary culture and lack of opportunities for pupils to bring more of their own knowledge and experience of contemporary poetry into the classroom. This particular trainee views rap as the contemporary world's most popular poetic form and its history as providing a cohesion for socially and economically marginalized groups. He argues for giving rap an appropriate place in the English curriculum and understanding its social and historical context.

> By using the classroom as a space in which poetry is brought from the outside world to be re-examined and reinterpreted amongst the pupils as well as with the guidance of the teacher, the range of material and cultural understanding may be expanded and deepened. (Robert)

The trainee teachers recognize the potential of poetry to be experimental and to draw on the experiences, languages and cultures of the pupils. This development of an intercultural perspective towards teaching poetry takes up the view that there are many correct ways of using language depending on the social and cultural context, and that dialects and languages are understood as fluid and interrelated systems. 'It is essential for teachers to respect the whole of their students' linguistic repertoires if they want to provide them with the best possible chance of educational success' (Weber and Horner 2012: 2000). This particular trainee teacher articulates the need to see the links between poetry writing and individual voice.

> Poetry writing allows us the freedom of expression often denied us by formulaic prose writing and, in today's multi-lingual and multi-dialectic society, it also qualifies and affirms individual's voice – regardless of it being 'correct' or Standard English. (Luke)

In this chapter, I argue that poetry opens up new worlds for EAL learners and that 'pedagogical language practices that are ritualized and allow for little meaning-making on the part of students may limit the learner's language learning and access to more powerful identities' (Norton 2010: 361). There is a danger in relation to poetry pedagogy that existing school structures in England marginalize children, particularly EAL learners new to English, who are placed in low-ability sets and become even more likely to receive 'monomodal literacies and transmissive forms of pedagogy' (Mills 2009: 109).

Developing poetry pedagogy for EAL learners

The next part of this chapter focuses on the research and practice of two trainee English teachers in London secondary classrooms. Luke, the first trainee teacher in the study, was working in an inner-city school in South-East London. The school is an all girls' 11–19 comprehensive school with 1860 pupils and around 40 per cent of these pupils are EAL learners speaking 51 languages. The school was praised in its 2011 Ofsted report for employing many successful strategies that ensure students work extremely well together and celebrate the cultural and ethnic diversity within the school. Influenced by Gibbons's work in Australia (Gibbons 2009: 166), Luke was interested in investigating the role of poetry from different cultures in empowering students to use home languages and promote their own cultural identity within the English classroom.

In developing poetry pedagogy for EAL learners within inclusive intercultural practices, it was important for the trainee teachers to reflect on their approaches to learning, as well as views on language, literacy and culture. An intercultural perspective towards learning can be viewed as having an integrated interdisciplinary orientation and be 'interactive, dialogic and collaborative' (Anderson and Obied 2011: 21). Luke in his work on poetry from different cultures with 11–12-year olds adopted a collaborative approach with extended group activities. There were 27 students in this mixed-ability class and the majority were EAL learners from ethnic minority groups.

As part of Luke's research project, the students completed a questionnaire about their cultural background, languages/dialects spoken with the family and attitudes towards studying poetry from different cultures. Some of the advantages students voiced about poetry from different cultures were the use of different languages in the classroom, learning about new cultures and learning more about their beliefs and lifestyles. Some of the concerns raised included the use of different languages, the idea that 'we don't need to know about them, we need to know about us' and the fear that they might change religion. He was interested in exploring these different attitudes within the English classroom with particular reference to the use of home languages to promote cultural identity.

After discussion about his research project and reading of related theory with particular reference to Cummins' work in Canada on identity texts, Luke was keen to experiment with the use of bilingual poetry in the classroom. Cummins argues that 'if we focus only on one of the bilingual's two languages, or keep them rigidly separate, then we miss a very significant opportunity to enhance bilingual students' linguistic and academic development' (Cummins 2000: 198). Luke printed a poem in each of the five languages listed in the Language development data for his Year 7 class and arranged the students into groups of six, with one of the students listed as speaking the language at home, taking the role of reader. He explains the difficulties he encountered in putting theory into practice and opening up the English classroom to the range of languages his students spoke in the home.

> After I had distributed the poems and was expecting to hear a chorus of other languages, the class was struck with a sudden silence. Approaching one of the bilingual students, I asked what was wrong and was told that she couldn't read the Punjabi script as she could only speak it. Another student raised her hand and said the same for Vietnamese, Nepalese, and so on. Before long I was left with just one student who could confidently read in Albanian and she had already explained how she found speaking it "embarrassing", so I decided to stop the activity and instead annotated the translations of the poems instead. (Luke)

Luke's experience in this diverse London classroom demonstrates how quickly language attrition may occur for many EAL learners. This links with Barton's ecological approach towards diversity: 'Literacy has a role in maintaining diversity; it can either be seen as the main force of standardization of languages, or it can have an important role in maintaining the range of variation in language' (Barton 2007: 32). This implies that educators need further training to support the specialist needs of EAL learners and increased knowledge of bilingualism (Obied 2010).

However, the EAL learners in this class are beginning to forge their own intercultural identities and these pupils explored both language and culture in the writing of their own poems 'for these pupils cultural barriers are more permeable and experiences, aspirations, dreams and desires are negotiated and redefined within the dynamic of everyday life as an integral part of survival' (Rassool 2004: 212). The EAL students in this class now have the courage to experiment with language.

Who am I?

> Who am I?
> I am Asian
> Ma Nepali ho
> I am proud.

Luke commented that the EAL students' writing of poetry was transformative:

> 'Poetry from different cultures', in particular writing a poem about their own culture, had proven its value as a form of transformative pedagogy. (Luke)

Lucy, the second trainee teacher in this study, was also working in an inner-city school in South-East London. The school is a mixed 11–16 comprehensive with

822 pupils and around 40 per cent of these pupils are EAL learners speaking 30 languages. The school was praised in the latest Ofsted report (2012) for the progress students make in languages, but the report highlighted the overall need in the school to improve students' oracy skills. Lucy was particularly interested in oracy. In her research project, she decided to explore the contribution that EAL learners make to classroom discussion of idiom and metaphorical language in poetry written in English. Her study of 13–14-year olds in a bottom set Year 9 class focused on the 6 EAL learners in a class of 22 students. Lucy investigated the premise that bilingual pupils are better at concept formation and divergent or creative thinking. 'Bilingual children tend to give more responses, and replies that are more varied, original and elaborate' (Garcia 2009: 96).

This research project shows how bilingual learners' vocabulary can be extended in the English classroom when they are given the space to rehearse new words and phrases and develop real knowledge of a particular literary genre, such as war poetry. McRae advocates an interrelated pedagogy at all levels of language learning and argues that this is integral to developing a deeper word knowledge. 'The acquisition of vocabulary which goes beyond the merely synonymic is frequently the turning point in this process' (McRae 1996: 18). Lucy decided to explore creative and divergent thinking of EAL learners in their oral responses to poetry.

> My research study was sparked by the idea that EAL pupils are able to think more conceptually . . . there's all this kind of evidence around divergent thinking and creative thinking and I was really interested in that, in looking at it within the English classroom to do with things that you would imagine would typically be exceptionally difficult for EAL pupils which is looking at idioms, and figurative language and metaphorical language in texts that we study. So I set up a study which was around classroom talk and looking at some of the metaphorical language in war poetry. (Lucy)

In focusing on the EAL learners' response to war poetry in this bottom set English class, Lucy found that the EAL learners dominated class discussion in most instances except during more formal debate. The EAL learners were more likely to seek clarification of context, play with words and infer meaning from the poetry (including words and phrases). In responding to Wilfred Owen's poem 'Anthem for Doomed Youth', the EAL learners used language in a more creative and flexible manner.

> And so I had English kids looking at the grid going 'stuttering guns sssss stuttering guns' and making the obvious connections. And the EAL kids making

'innocent candles shine wailing goodbyes' and 'silent tenderness who call now for death', making really incredibly unusual creative connections. (Lucy)

Lucy recognizes the importance of developing poetry pedagogy for EAL learners within inclusive intercultural practices of moving away from basic comprehension-type questions to allow these learners to draw on their own prior experiences and interpret the poems in new and distinctive ways. The EAL learners were being given space by this trainee English teacher to audibly process thought and be imaginative in their interaction with poetry.

> The EAL kids were the ones that said 'but maybe it means this, maybe in 'War Photographer' he's not just carrying this baggage on his back because he's been there, but he's carrying the world and he's got the world on his back'. One of the things that it's really hard to teach in English is the deeper layers of meaning, and it was the EAL kids that were essentially teaching the rest of the class, not only how to have those thought processes but how to express them. (Lucy)

EAL learners in this bottom-level set slowly became attuned to the musicality of the new language and explored the emotive power of words. They were able to play with the language of the poems to create meaning and explore the power of metaphor to describe experience.

> But with the war poetry we had three of the people in my study group: one recently arrived from Iran; and two, brother and sister, recently arrived from Afghanistan. And for them . . . when they kind of playfully used the language of the poets to create their own ideas, there was a much greater sense of noise in what they were creating, there was a much greater sense of action. And there was always the grittiness with those kids that you could tell had heard it, seen it, known someone that had talked to them about it. (Lucy)

This mirrors with earlier research on writing poetry and the bilingual child where EAL learners were able to discuss their own experiences as refugees and 'draw on these experiences to interpret the images in their heads and create their own poetry using a highly personalised voice' (Obied 2007: 44).

Conclusion

The research presented here points to the role that a culturally inclusive curriculum plays in the successful learning of EAL pupils and the importance of creating creative spaces of learning. Poetry can encourage EAL learners to understand the richness and variety of a language and gain agency in the process, as they actively make meaning and enter dialogues around texts. The trainee English teachers in this study critiqued existing approaches to the teaching of poetry in London secondary classrooms and explored alternative poetry pedagogies. Poetry teaching in this context is linked with cultural identity and seen as both situational and dynamic.

Poetry can help EAL learners to draw on past experiences and memories and 'reappropriate their history, culture, and language practices' (Freire and Macedo 1987: 157). In an inclusive intercultural classroom, these EAL learners can create powerful images of their lives. This poem opening is by a Year 7 student in the study.

> When I think about my family in Vietnam,
> I imagine my grandma is picking apples in the trees,
> And singing in the sun.

There are complex situational practices to negotiate in opening up the classroom to the many identities and languages of EAL learners, but the poetry pedagogy described in this chapter shows how writing and talking about poetry can empower these learners.

Teaching Poetry in New Zealand Secondary Schools at a Time of Curriculum Change

Sue Dymoke

Introduction

This chapter focuses on one element of comparative research about the impact of new assessment regimes on how poetry is taught in senior English classes in the diverse cultural contexts of New Zealand and England. It reports on emerging issues from data collected in New Zealand at a time when the newly aligned National Certificate for Educational Achievement (NCEA) standards were being assessed for the first time and becoming embedded within classroom practices. These issues are explored with an eye to the opportunities in New Zealand classrooms for reading and composing poetry that represents a range of cultural perspectives and embraces the specific contexts in which students live and learn. The chapter also identifies points of comparison with poetry teaching for the General Certificate of Secondary Education (GCSE) in English schools that were to be investigated subsequently.

Conceptual canvas

The conceptual canvas of this research is underpinned by critical perspectives on examination-level preparation and assessment of English (Kress et al. 2004; Locke 2008; Myhill 2005; Yandell 2008) and the specific challenges of teaching poetry within high-stakes testing regimes in international contexts (Thompson 1996; Benton 1999/2000; Dymoke 2001, 2002; Ofsted 2007; Faust and Dressman 2009; O'Neill 2006; Hennessy 2011). The pressure to deliver results is juxtaposed by a desire expressed by educators to plan for teaching that is both culturally responsive (Sleeter and Cornbleth 2011) and acknowledges the social literacies of students beyond the classroom (Street 1995). These cultural and social factors are significant in the way in which English is framed within the New Zealand curriculum.

Research questions

The project was driven by three key research questions which ask how poetry is

a   prescribed by national curriculum and assessment criteria;
b   flexibly interpreted by examination boards[1]; and
c   locally interpreted by an English department or an individual class teacher.

I sought to discover to what extent can teachers respond to contextual factors and what choices they (and their students) can make about the poems they read, write and perform.

Methodology

The methodology combines desk study (examining specifications, exemplar questions, marked work, published and in-house teaching resources) with semi-structured interviews and classroom observations. Additional data were collected through scrutiny of resources and displays, discussions with students and teachers at specially organized events. All data were collected using ethical principles and with the informed consent of participants. An iterative, grounded theory approach (Charmaz 2006) was used, thus affording more flexible opportunities for discussion points to emerge.

The NZ data were collected in educational contexts that were unfamiliar to me. It was surprising to enter a New Zealand school for the first time and observe English being taught with different emphases (and different accents) from those I had experienced as a teacher educator in the United Kingdom. A list of broad topics for discussion, closely linked to the research questions above, was given to participants prior to my arrival. Specific questions and observation foci were generated and refined throughout the data collection period. The material was analysed through repeated readings and re-codings.

Data sources

Data collection took place during 2 3-month periods in New Zealand (2011) and in the United Kingdom (2012) in English departments in six contrasting secondary schools in two cities. The NZ schools are located in differently decile-rated[2] (3–10) multiculturally diverse communities. They include single sex and coeducational institutions from both state and private sectors. Approximate school populations are

- A: Pakeha (of European descent) (70%): Maori, Pacific Islander and Asian students (30%).
- B: Pakeha (60%); Maori, Pacific Islander and Asian students (form largest groups within the remaining 40%).
- C: Pacific Islander, Maori or Asian (90%); Pakeha (7%).

This was a convenience sample chosen with guidance from an experienced teacher educator. The NZ sample consisted of 13 experienced English teachers; 3 small groups of Year 10–13[3] students; 10 English classes; work samples, departmental activities, resources and displays in each school and a wider sample of 18 English teachers from the region who participated in an in-service event; 2 teacher educators and 10 pre-service English/Media teachers.

National Curriculum for English

The 2007 New Zealand National Curriculum for English aims to develop students' appreciation and enjoyment of texts *in all their forms*. Its underpinning key concepts are Identity, Communication, Story and Meaning. English can be studied both as a heritage language and as an additional language. The curriculum document states that 'the study of New Zealand and world literature contributes to students' developing sense of identity, their awareness of New Zealand's bicultural heritage, and their understanding of the world' (Ministry of Education 2007: 18). The curriculum consists of two interconnected strands (each encompassing oral, written and visual forms of the language):

1 Making meaning of ideas or information they receive (Listening, Reading and Viewing)
2 Creating meaning for themselves or others (Speaking, Writing and Presenting).

It is suggested that this reframed curriculum has allowed 'for a more holistic and integrated notion of texts' than in previous versions (Ministry of Education 2012). Poems are but one textual form amidst the range exemplified in support materials. Those cited include 'play scripts, news media editorials and reports, games, game scripts, poems, speeches, letters, essays, reviews, documentaries, Computer Generated animations, graphic novels, mime, blogs, mockumentaries, video diaries, electronic journals, lyrics, novels, oral narratives, oral histories, short stories, films, and re-use and mash-up texts across a variety of platforms' (ibid). The two interconnected strands of the NZ English curriculum appear to facilitate an integrated and flexible approach to teaching and learning in English that is reflected in the assessment framework described below. In contrast, the separation of reading, writing and speaking and listening in National Curriculum English (DCFS/QCA 2007), coupled with a hierarchical emphasis on prescribed print-based English Heritage texts, determines a greater level of structure and prescription.

NCEA (National Certificate of Educational Achievement)

Aligned with the New Zealand curriculum in 2011, the revised NCEA is assessed through successful completion of credit-bearing Achievement Standards by students aged 16–18 in Years 11–13. Each Standard is pitched at a level of difficulty from 1 to 3. Between 4 and 8 of these are teacher-assessed internally and at least 3 are externally assessed at each level. The number of Standards attempted varies from school to school and from student to student. At the time of data collection, the new NCEA was in its first year of alignment. Students in Years 12 and 13 were still studying under the old system.

Emerging issues

In analysing the data, some key issues have emerged which pertain to choices of texts and poets, distinctions between teaching and using poems, identity and development of voice through teacher modelling and students' writing, poetic forms and assessment of students' writing. These issues are explored below and form the basis of a detailed comparative analysis with the UK sample reported in Dymoke (2012a and 2012b).

Textual choices

A noticeable difference between the English and New Zealand curricular and examination systems is the range of genres and specific texts available for study. New Zealand teachers and students seemed much less restricted than their English counterparts in the choice of genres that they can discuss, compose or respond to in examinations. The NCEA offers guidance about ensuring that appropriate texts are chosen from within the very broadly labelled genres: visual, oral and written (extended and short). In addition, students are required to write about an unseen prose text, a poem and a non-fiction text in the 90851 level 1 externally assessed examination 'Show understanding of significant aspects of unfamiliar written text(s) through close reading, using supporting evidence'. This is the *only* occasion in Level 1 study where response to poetry is compulsory. In the majority of internally and externally assessed Standards, *teachers and students have free rein to choose which genres and texts they respond to or create in the classroom*. With such choice, however, comes responsibility and several teachers voiced the concern: 'what happens if I choose the wrong thing?'

There are no NCEA-prescribed authors or named texts. Even Shakespeare is no longer a prescribed author. Some teachers in Schools A, B and C and the wider sample were very unhappy about this change. They felt students needed to develop an awareness of the playwright's influence on literature and language. Nevertheless, the lack of prescription appears to enable schools, individual teachers and students to engage in textual work that is geared to students' interests, concerns and contexts. One teacher described the opportunity to engage his students with 'the multiplicity of voices and connections between them' as one of the pleasures of teaching poetry. An experienced teacher in School C stated:

> 'If we had a canon it would disadvantage our students because they are outside of the dominant culture... We can use texts which speak to our kids.'

Another colleague stressed that 'what connects' was important rather than 'which poets'. As a result, poets that the teachers elected to use included published work/performances by Pacific Island poets of Samoan heritage including Tusiata Avia, Selina Tusitala Marsh and Karlo Mila and Maori writers such as Apirana Taylor. Other popular twentieth-century and contemporary poets included New Zealand and Pacific Island poets Fleur Adcock, James K. Baxter, Dennis Glover, Ruth Dallas, Bub Bridger, Glenn Colquhoun, Lauris Edmond, Kevin Ireland, Hone Tuwhare and Albert Wendt and, from world literature, John Agard, Maya

Angelou, Patricia Beer, Billy Collins, Seamus Heaney, Claude McKay, Wilfred Owen and W. B. Yeats.

Although some teachers were beginning to use digital recordings from the New Zealand Electronic Poetry Centre[4], the majority of poems used were single-sheet photocopies. One teacher compiled her own anthologies. Nevertheless, across the sample, New Zealand students appeared to have minimal experience of reading single-authored collections or published poetry anthologies. In contrast, each GCSE examination board in England produces a poetry anthology that is the main source of poems for use with Year 10 and 11 students. As stipulated by national requirements, these anthologies contain a range of English, Welsh and Irish Literary Heritage poetry.

In the New Zealand system, without prescribed texts or dedicated examination anthologies, the wealth of emerging international voices can perhaps be more quickly integrated into a scheme of work than emerging poets in the United Kingdom could be. Student choice of texts is also an important element of the process. In guidance for 4-credit internally assessed level 1 Standard 91104 ('Analyse significant connections across texts, supported by evidence'), teachers are reminded that 'at least one text must be student selected' (NZQA 2012: 2). Students are also permitted to use newly composed texts *of any genre* in their responses. An example of this is a student's choice of 'The Facebook Sonnet' by Sherman Alexie. This was published in *The New Yorker* in May 2011 and written about in an internal paper in November 2011 alongside William Shakespeare's '*Sonnet 130*', Jane Austen's *Pride and Prejudice* and Lawrence Block's *Psyche's Dark Night* (NZQA 2012).

Poetry taught or poems used?

One of the most significant themes to emerge directly relates to the above discussion: the extent to which poetry is taught *as a discrete genre* for assessment purposes. In England, poetry is a 'taught' element of GCSE teaching and a compulsory location on the assessment journey. Selections of thematically linked poems are intensively studied in preparation for specific assessments including a 'controlled assessment' paper. Students are expected to be able to draw comparisons between the poems they have studied and, in some cases, with other types of texts. Experienced teachers explained that rather than the *genre of poetry* being 'taught' and 'studied' in Years 10 and 11, *poems* were 'used' in English lessons. Indeed, in all NZ schools I visited, a body of poetry as a distinct mode of expression was not 'taught' in-depth in preparation for Level 1

NCEA. Instead, poems were 'used', often as single entities, within units of work. Students were required to respond to the poem(s) in terms of thematic value and connections with other texts. For example, a poem might be used as part of a war unit alongside film texts and Michael Morpurgo's novel *Private Peaceful*. In one Year 11 class, the poem '*Still I Rise*' by Maya Angelou was used with her novel *I Know Why the Caged Bird Sings* and *To Kill a Mockingbird* by Harper Lee in order to explore the concept of extended metaphor. The poem enabled students to make connections between the prose texts. In this way, poetry potentially has a far less central or secure place in the New Zealand curriculum than in previous iterations of the Standards. As O'Neill had identified, it was not necessarily 'being taught for poetry's sake' (2006: 24).

Some teachers argued that, once fully implemented, the aligned NCEA Standards could lead to a considerably reduced textual diet for students. They commented on how students could 'double up' and use the same text for different Standards. The number of texts required for study had also been slimmed down. For example, a 4 credit level 1 paper 'Show understanding of specific aspect(s) of studied written text(s), using supporting evidence' now requires students to write about one or more short texts of their choice (such as a poem/song lyric, digital/online text or short story) in-depth rather than the two texts previously stipulated (NZQA 2012). However, other teachers thought the revised assessments might free up the time to teach other things that could be contextually more relevant to individual students.

In spite of this concern about reduction, the majority of teachers perceived that a dedicated poetry unit could be a 'forced experience' for learners. Such a unit might turn the spotlight on poetry in an artificial or even unnecessary way. In contrast, integrating a single poem or small groups of poems alongside prose and other multi-modal texts within thematic units of work, film was considered a more 'natural' approach that reflected the spirit of the revised curriculum. One teacher in school C said that poems provided 'intertextuality' within units of work. For her, they were the glue that could secure connections between other texts by providing opportunities for higher-level thinking and ways into discussion about a group of texts. Her rationale contrasted with that expressed by 9 of the 13 of teachers interviewed for whom inclusion of a poem or poems in thematic work 'remove[d] the fear of poetry'. In this way, teachers could make poetry 'accessible' and perhaps more familiar. One school B teacher, who had worked in UK and NZ schools, felt poetry was not covered adequately in Yr 11 in New Zealand. This meant that students were 'jittery . . . frightened of it but when they get it, it's the coolest thing'. She considered that they needed to 'get their fitness up for poetry' in order to be able to cope with the genre choices and challenges they could face in Level 2 and 3 of NCEA or undergraduate study.

The notion that poetry could be a frightening and inaccessible medium for students *and* their teachers has been explored previously (see Benton 1986, 1999; Hughes and Dymoke 2011). In New Zealand classrooms, a poem might induce less fear if it were juxtaposed against texts such as films or gaming texts or blog posts that students are perhaps more familiar with or personally inclined to encounter outside of school. A poem could, therefore, be more 'accessible' if students are able to arrive at an understanding of it *through their reading and discussion of other texts written in different forms.* It could be argued that, by making poetry 'accessible' through single poems, teachers are endeavouring to remove poetry from the 'pedestal' (Benton 1986: 6) on which it has long been located. If poetry is repositioned on a more equal footing with other, more frequently encountered, texts, could such a move be advantageous or detrimental to poetry and to its survival as a classroom text?

It is inappropriate to conclude that all New Zealand senior secondary teachers and students are afraid of poetry. Four of the interviewed teachers were passionate advocates of the genre. They wanted to make opportunities to integrate poems wherever feasible within senior secondary English. One teacher in school B relished the chance to 'look at something so small and perfectly formed . . . it is a great way to show how rich a text can be'. He wanted to ensure that students left school with some experience of the genre: 'kids don't read poetry and won't after they leave school. It is great to give them something to take away'. For this practitioner, teaching poetry was about so much more than using occasional poems or delivering a curriculum. His comments convey an ease with the genre coupled with an admiration for its linguistic potential. Within his educational philosophy, engagement with poetry is a fundamental right for students and something which could sustain them in adulthood. This philosophy both challenges and is challenged by an examination system in which poetry has a restricted space.

Identity, modelling and student voice

As is explored above, poems are used for thematic purposes within units of work. A key tenet of the cultural responsiveness agenda in New Zealand is the importance of identity and belonging as represented through language:

Ko te reo te tuakiri   Language is my identity.
Ko te reo tōku ahurei   Language is my uniqueness.
Ko te reo te ora.   Language is life. (Ministry of Education 2007: 18)

Identity was a common theme for Yr 9 and Yr 10 units of work. Units typically included activities linked to films, song lyrics, poems and short prose texts. A School C teacher explained that the principles of *Te Kotahitanga*[5] underpinned some of the department's text selections and poetry activities. 'The power of cultural interpretations of poetry' was identified by one group of teachers as a key reason for using poetry in the classroom.

Teacher modelling of writing was one way in which shared experience, exploration of identity and student voices could be developed. In School C, a small group of female Year 10 students talked about the poems and song lyrics they had read and written. Their teacher had read and discussed the poem 'My Puletasi' (written by a student from another NZ school) with them. The poem, about a young woman's feelings on wearing her traditional Samoan dress, had been used as a model for their teacher's poem about a special item of jewellery. She shared her draft with the class and, in doing so, shared something of her own identity through writing and discussion. This personal link was clearly significant to the students. It enabled the teacher to build trust with them. One said: 'the teacher made a poem about her pearls. . . [that] connects to us.' The poems and accounts they wrote included pieces on a dress made by a grandmother in Hong Kong, a girl's first rosary and a necklace worn in memory of a girl's dead sister. Their poems showed that they had been inspired to write personally and in detail about their chosen items.

English teachers at school B seemed to have a clear grasp of how the principles of *Te Kotahitanga* informed their practice, particularly in terms of developing especially Maori and Tongan students' confidence as communicators. Three staff members described their modelling of poetry. One used Glenn Colquhoun's 'The trick of standing upright here' (1999: 32) as 'a template' for her writing, deliberately attempting to place aspects of her culture and language in context. A teacher, who led the creative writing programme in school A, regularly participated in poetry writing activities with senior students and shared work in progress. Building confidence as writers and encouraging students to write from experience were priorities for many of the teachers. Lunchtime or regular off-timetable writing workshops were established features of some schools' provision. Students' writing, including poetry, was used in examination papers. Teachers encouraged senior students to seek audiences for their work beyond the classroom through publication and competition entries.

Given this encouragement, it was interesting that some students and teachers thought poetry was different or at odds with their everyday experiences beyond the classroom. Yr 10 students in school C told me 'We only do poems when we have to at school'. They did not associate the song lyrics they listened to inside and outside of school with poetry. For some teachers, reading poetry was purely a school-based activity. One experienced practitioner described reading poetry outside school as 'an affectation . . . a romantic notion . . . reading under a tree, wearing Laura Ashley and eating a crisp apple'. In contrast, one pre-service teacher wanted to refute the old-fashioned image of the poet/bard as 'a man in a rabbit skin suit playing a lute'. She wanted students to view poets as worldly people who wrote about everyday situations. The teachers' images connote poetry as unfashionable: the bard writer and the romantic reader are outsiders participating in activities that may bring them personal pleasure but appear unconventional to others. Like many educators before them, these teachers' contrasting views demonstrate the challenges that poetry faces if it is ever to be fully accepted as a popular form of communication rather than as a school subject. The views about poetry enshrined in the images could be explained by differences in taste, levels of classroom experience or by the teachers' poetry education. However, the need to make connections between poetry and everyday life and enable students to move towards a greater understanding of what drives people to write/perform/read poetry are crucial to the genre's development and its survival.

Poetic forms

Free verse poetry was the predominant form read and written. Students might write list poems or parallel poems using contrasting metaphors. One school B teacher was developing a slam[6] poetry option for a level 1 presentation assessment. There was also some very limited reading (but not writing) of sonnets. It was surprising that there was no emphasis on teaching and learning about a range of poetic forms: much depended on an individual teacher's preferences. In contrast in England, the GCSE anthologies encompass a variety of rhyming and free verse forms, including sonnet, villanelle, dramatic monologue and ghazal. Even within the restrictive GCSE framework, there are opportunities for students to develop an understanding of some of poetry's structural possibilities. The small range of poetic forms used by the sample underlines that theme is the prime driver for textual choices. Some practitioners thought that form was being 'neglected'. A School A teacher sensed that the new NCEA Standards promoted 'less of a grounding in poetic form, periods or literature and technical terminology'. For her, poetry now had to be 'fitted in with everything else'.

Free verse found poetry was especially popular and used across the NZ Year 9–12 classes – much more than might be the case in the United Kingdom. Writing found poetry involves selecting language from previously composed texts and 'rehous[ing] found language in poetry' (Green 2010: 113). This form perhaps enables teachers to knock the 'fear' out of poetry that teachers have identified above as a potential generic barrier. It makes poetry accessible by drawing on other text types and requiring its composers to use few rules in their re-composition. One school B teacher told her class: 'Poetry lies in buried places. . . We are taking something from a text and using it for poetry.' By emphasizing this act of borrowing, she seemed to be offering reassurance. In a world where cut and paste and mash-ups are everyday literacy experiences, this act could draw students into a collaborative process as 'produser(s)' (Bruns 2006) rather than requiring them to act as solitary authors waiting for the muse to strike.

I expected to find distinct Maori or Samoan forms taught in some NZ classes. Some experienced teachers said that a mihi[7] might possibly be taught, as part of an identity unit, but it would only be taught if the teacher felt confident about using the form and was able to research it fully in preparation. Teachers at an in-service event said that the appraisal system required them to demonstrate cultural responsiveness in their teaching. Some had previously set themselves appraisal targets to broaden their knowledge of poetry texts or to practise reading aloud texts by Pacific Island, Maori or Caribbean poets ready for performance in class. Green questions whether Pakeha poets should use Maori language and culture: is it trespassing to borrow Maori motifs/narratives or to speak in the place of the unspoken (Green and Ricketts 2010: 460)? When engaging with all cultural forms and artistic practices, sensitivity to origin, connotations and reasons for use are important considerations. The limited range of forms could be explained by lack of confidence about the genre, coupled with a desire not to offend. Conversely, it could be perceived as an excuse not to take creative risks that might lead to greater cultural understanding and inclusion, for fear of the impact that such risks might have on students' assessment outcomes.

Assessment of poetry writing

Difficulties in marking students' poetry were raised by many teachers. For some teachers, a lack of marked NCEA exemplars did not enable them to assess writing with sufficient certainty about what was required. Locke describes students as 'credit gatherers' (2010: 10) and teachers who are 'fixated by the need to produce results' (2010: 14). Although nothing quite so extreme was witnessed, several teachers in one department spoke of the 'risk' of submitting poetry for a 450-word internally assessed creative writing unit. They said that students' portfolios might include some drafts of poetry, but prose texts were much more likely to be chosen for submission for final assessment because they felt on safer ground.

Separate formal and creative writing Standards are only now available at Level 1 NCEA. From 2012, level 2 students are required to produce a selection of 'crafted and controlled writing'. Teachers who led Writing programmes for senior students were concerned of the impact that this reduction in assessment options would have. Given the comments above about assessing poetry, this change could give less confident teachers even greater cause to omit poetry writing from their examination teaching altogether. This issue is also of concern in England, where past and present GCSE specifications offer limited assessable opportunities for students' poetry and teachers can find it hard to make time for poetry writing in lessons.

Conclusion

This chapter can only provide a brief snapshot of emerging issues from New Zealand. It is evident that the sample NZ teachers feel they are experiencing pressures in their English teaching as newly aligned NCEA Standards are implemented and they come to terms with new tensions between assessment and creative opportunities. Some teachers fear poetry is being 'sidelined' or 'left out' and that lack of direct reference to poetry in NCEA achievement objectives could have a significant long-term impact. Other teachers are experiencing a freeing up of their teaching, which could give them space to explore how poetry could permeate other aspects of assessment (such as presentations).

Teachers showed how students could be encouraged to draw on their experiences outside the classroom in their poetry writing and they commented on how poems could introduce students to new experiences through language. Several practitioners shared the joy of the 'light bulb moment' when a student suddenly fully engaged with a poem for the first time. Nevertheless, there is concern that 'Poetry could be left out' of the new assessment regime. With greater exemplification of writing assessment and dissemination of effective intertextual use of poetry, this could be a very opportune time for poetry to join the front chorus line of texts in New Zealand classrooms rather than to rest as a seldom heard visiting soloist.

I would like to thank the teachers and students who welcomed me into their classrooms and my Poetry Matters colleagues whose invaluable feedback has helped to shape this chapter.

17

Digital Poetry, Power and Social Justice

Janette Hughes

Introduction

In my work with students on digital poetry production over the past 6 years, I have witnessed first-hand the power of the poem to give voice to those things that concern adolescents most. Students from 11 to 17 years old in a variety of classrooms in Ontario, Canada have composed compelling digital poems that speak to the importance of giving adolescents opportunities to think about who they are, what they care about and what they want to communicate to the world. In this chapter, I share examples of how some students have used digital poetry as a vehicle for expressing their own identities as individuals and as change agents to communicate their understandings of global issues.

Digital media, digital poetry and social justice

Contemporary Canadian poet Molly Peacock (1999) describes poetry as the 'fusion of three arts: music, storytelling, and painting' where the line represents the poem's music, the sentence explains the story and the image displays the 'vision' of the poet (p. 19). Because of its regular use of imagery, figurative language and melodic devices, poetry lends itself to the kinds of multimodal expression afforded through new digital media. A change in the materiality of text inevitably changes the way in which we read or receive a text and has important implications for the way in which we construct or write our own texts. When we communicate with others, we express ourselves in a variety of ways (through sounds, gestures, body language, the clothes we wear, etc.), but unless we are performing poems in some way, we have typically been limited to pen and paper technology when composing poetry. The materiality of digital media offers students who are growing up in a digital age new ways to read, write and perform poetry for wider audiences.

There is no question that we communicate more and more via screen (Kress 2003; Kress and Van Leeuwen 2001) so it is important to better understand how 'millennial' students (Gee 2002) use and interact with new media in the context of their writing. The objective of the research I have been conducting is to develop a conceptualization of the relationship between new media and students' writing of poetry while they are immersed in using new media. In particular, I am interested in the following two questions: (1) How might new (digital) media help us reconsider what poetry is and does in the classroom and (2) What is the relationship between digital media and adolescents' understanding of global issues while they are immersed in using digital media. Through my work with adolescents in five different classrooms, I examined the affordances offered by shifting modes of expression (which include the use of image, sound, gesture, colour, special effects).

Poetry has long been a powerful medium for social activism. Consider the work of Langston Hughes, Pablo Neruda and Robert Hass, to name only a few of the many poets who have used poetry to illuminate the need for change. In 1985, Audre Lorde insisted that she wanted her poems 'to engage, and to empower people to speak, to strengthen themselves into who they most want and need to be and then to act, to do what needs being done' (p. 36). She also argued that poetry is a

> vital necessity of our existence. It forms the quality of the light within which we predicate our hopes and dreams toward survival and change, first made into language, then into idea, then into more tangible action. Poetry is the way we help give name to the nameless so it can be thought. The farthest horizons of our hopes and fears are cobbled by our poems, carved from the rock experiences of our daily lives. (ibid)

We cannot assume, however, that students are applying a critical reading to a poem or are effecting change by writing about social justice issues. As Janks (2000) points out, teaching students to compose using different semiotic modes does not necessarily lead to critical reading or social action. Consider, for example, the smiling student in Figure 17.2 who is holding a sign that reads 'stop poverty' while wearing an expensive Abercrombie and Fitch t-shirt. The author of the poem could have considered what the whole image was conveying, rather than focusing on the writing on the sign and the accompanying text that reads, 'we can change the statistics'. Students need to practice doing critical readings of images, and sounds as well as print text, and first drafts of digital poems, such as the one in Figure 17.1, can be revisited with a critical eye.

Research design

This qualitative research makes use of a case study methodology which includes detailed field notes, transcribed interviews with students and teachers, and the digital and multimodal texts created by students. Individual students, and their digital texts, were considered as individual cases within each setting case. I coded the interview transcripts following traditional coding procedures (Strauss and Corbin 1990) and compared themes across the different research settings in order to identify recurring and overlapping thematic and structural patterns (Black 2007). The multimodal texts created by the students were analysed within a framework of semiotic meta-functions (Kress and Van Leeuwen 2001; Jewitt 2008; Burn 2008), which considers design and production as representational, interactive and textual. Because of the complex blending of multimodal data elements, I also used the digital visual literacy analysis method of developing a 'pictorial and textual representation of those elements' (Hull and Katz 2006: 41); that is, juxtaposing columns of the written text, the images from digital texts

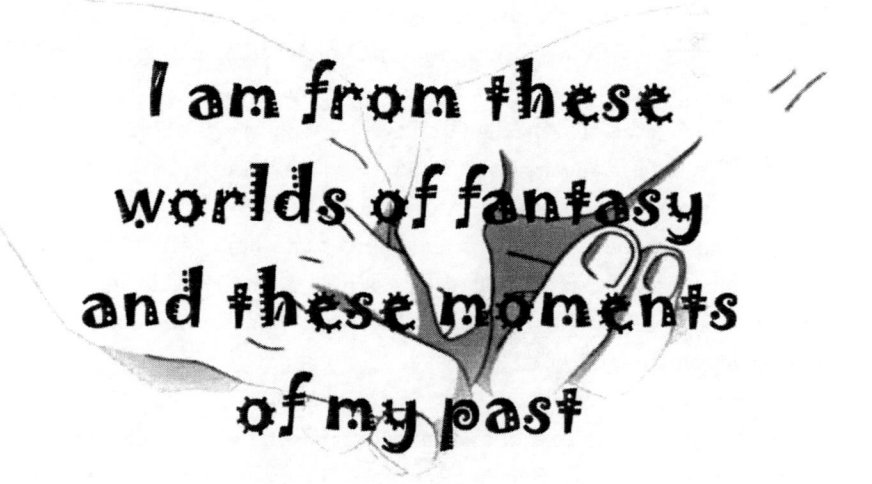

I am from these worlds of fantasy and these moments of my past

Figure 17.1 First draft of a digital poem.

and data from interviews to facilitate the 'qualitative analysis of patterns' (p. 41). In this chapter, I focus on the various modes of expression (i.e. visual image, gesture, movement) and how these work in concert to create meaning. In the authoring of the digital texts, I am particularly interested in moments that might be interpreted as 'turning points' (Bruner 1990) in the representation of identity and/or the conceptual understanding of adolescent issues.

A number of themes emerged as I explored digital poetry as a new literacy practice and examined how the creation of digital poetry has the potential to encourage student engagement, attention to the performative characteristics of poetry, including an increasing sense of audience, and to promote transformation as student writers position themselves as agents of change in poems based on social justice issues that concern them. As Lankshear and Knobel (2007) argue, new literacy practices include both 'new technical stuff' and 'new ethos stuff' that enable students to participate in literacy practices that 'involve different kinds of values, sensibilities, norms and procedures' compared with those that typify more traditional literacies (p. 7). The themes that I explore in this chapter can be examined through these two categories.

The new technical stuff

Multimodal remixing

Constantly emerging digital tools, both hardware (mobile devices, computers, Smartphones) and software (programs and applications that allow users to tap into text, image, sound, communication functions, etc.), are making the task of creating digital texts quite easy, regardless of how tech-savvy the user might be. Part of the reason creating digital texts is so popular with adolescents is that a reasonably high-quality text can be created without expertise in computer programming. Many adolescents are quite adept at 'remixing' – taking bits and pieces of various media from different sources and pulling them together to create a new digital text. The following example of grade 8 student, 'Vincent' (all names are pseudonyms), who creates a short digital poem about his own identity, illuminates this point.

Vincent was a 13-year-old newcomer to Canada. His class, located in a Toronto school in which 86 per cent of the student population were English Language Learners, participated in a digital poetry project that focused on student identity. In this particular class, the majority of the students were East Asian, primarily from Sri Lanka. Vincent had arrived in Canada from China with his parents approximately 3 years previously. He was the only Chinese student in the class. Vincent very rarely spoke in class, and when he did speak, it was in small groups, and done reluctantly. He was similarly reticent to share any of his work with the class, asking that it not be read aloud or posted. It was unclear to his teacher at this point in the autumn knew whether he was quiet because of his personality or because of something else. Any attempts at getting to know Vincent better had been met with some resistance.

The research assistant, classroom teacher and I worked with the students in the class on a Friday afternoon. We read George Ella Lyons' poem, 'Where I'm From' (1999) and talked about how her present identity was shaped by the people, place and things that surrounded her as she grew up. We also explored how the era into which she was born influenced her life. After the reading and discussion, and after viewing some examples of 'Where I'm From' digital poems, the students were given about 20 minutes to brainstorm some ideas for a poem of their own based on their childhood identities. We explained that they would be given more time the following week to work on a digital poem in the computer lab. Vincent came back to school on Monday morning with his poem completed (view Vincent's poem at http://faculty.uoit.ca/hughes/where-i-m-from.html).

Working on MovieMaker, Vincent created a digital poem that combined images (both still and moving) representing his earlier life in China and his love of Japanese anime. From a quick viewing of the digital poem, it is very evident that he is skilled with technology. Adding video was not a requirement for this assignment and to get these video segments, Vincent had to capture the video clips from YouTube and then edit them on MovieMaker, removing the sound track in order to accommodate his own sound track. No one at school showed him how to do this; he figured it out on his own. Vincent took images from what he calls his 'worlds of fantasy and reality' and merged them in a very sophisticated technological way to express himself. He draws on his past and present and gives us a glimpse into his out-of-school literacies, his love of anime and his cultural past, demonstrating the technological savvy that some of our students have.

Adolescents are engaged in forming and questioning their identities on many different levels (Anstey and Bull 2006; Cope and Kalantzis 2000; Weber and Mitchell 2008) and this is evident in Vincent's poem as well. He says that he 'slips from the world of fantasy to reality', and he says they are the same to him, but that he belongs in neither world. It is obvious that he is trying to figure out his place in his world (Figure 17.2). From his teacher's perspective, Vincent was

Figure 17.2 Communicating personal identity through digital poetry.

a very quiet student who normally didn't talk in class, but he created a powerful and personal performance of self in a mode that begs to be shared with others. In fact, when Vincent returned to school on Monday morning with his poem on a memory stick, he was anxious to share it with his teacher and with us, and readily agreed to allow us to share it via a data projector with the whole class. Vincent's teacher learnt more about him in this short poem than she had learnt in the 7 weeks he'd been in her class. Although getting to know her students better was not the primary goal of the project, the teacher was interested in seeing how the students might communicate their personal identities through digital poetry.

Multilinear authoring process

Multilinearity was evident in the way the students approached combining the various modes of expression. Creating poetry (and I would suggest, other forms of writing as well) in a digital environment requires a different kind of authorship and offers insights into how context shapes meaning. For example, approximately two-thirds of the students wrote the text of their poems first and then considered which images and soundtracks they needed to find to complement the text. The others worked with images first and wrote the text of the poem based on these visual images. Regardless of how they began the process, however, they all worked back and forth between the various modes available to them. They often began with some words and phrases they had brainstormed and then started to look for supporting visuals once they had a theme for the poem in mind. Those students who wrote the entire text of the poem first claimed that they were compelled to change the text to make it better suit the images they found. In the follow-up interviews, three students commented that it was more challenging to create a digital poem than a conventional print poem because it was difficult to find the 'right' image to convey what they wanted. It is not a simple task to join visual images with words. It requires that the creator possess a new or different set of skills, including visual artistry and imagination. It is certainly a more complex task to find or create images that move beyond the literal; however, part of our role as English educators is to help students develop visual literacy. We found it helpful, if not absolutely necessary, to work with the students in advance on their visual literacy skills by having them analyse, critique and reflect on visual images. Asking students to write a poem with pen and paper and then having them digitize it by adding images, sound and fancy fonts is not representative of a new literacy. That is just using technology as an add-on to what we've always done. It is the 'new ethos stuff' which includes things like collaboration, collective intelligence, open distribution and sharing with an audience that makes the creation of these digital poems a new literacy.

Personalized technology

Although the digital poetry projects were introduced at school, and students were given class time and access to computers to work on them, most of the students chose to do much of the creative work at home. It is interesting to note that for many of the students, their 'digital identities' exist in their homes, rather than at school. When asked why they chose to work at home on the digital poems, a common response was that it was 'easier' to do it at home because they were more comfortable with their own technology. With the advent of cloud computing and digital tools such as Google Docs, it has become more convenient for students to work back and forth between home and school without having to worry about compatibility issues or carrying a memory stick or external hard drive. Despite these advances in technology, the vast majority of students I have worked with still opted to work primarily at home on the digital poems. If we consider the typical environments for computers in schools, they tend to be labs where computers are lined up back to back in rows, giving a sense of mass production and institutionalization, which is hardly an environment that might inspire creativity (Lankshear and Knobel 2007; Richardson and Mancabelli 2011). The implications point to the need to move towards the use of personalized technologies in the classroom, rather than to rely on the computer lab model still in existence in many schools.

The new ethos stuff

Collaboration has long been a component of the writing process (Atwell 1998; Graves 1983). We encourage our students to share ideas, peer edit work, engage in writing conferences to offer feedback to friends, and publish and share their finished pieces. Despite this, the creative process is often seen as solitary and critics of screens (whether they be computers or hand-held gaming devices) often comment that they isolate students from each other and society (Hughes and Dymoke 2011; Peacock 1999). However, throughout the process of creating digital poems, our students collaborated in a variety of ways. They helped each other to take photos and many of them used images of their friends and family in their performances. They helped each other with technical problems and offered each other feedback through each stage of the process. Three boys worked together to perform their poems as songs – they wrote lyrics, performed the songs and edited the videos together and one student even collaborated with her mother to write a song to accompany her poem.

The transformational potential of poetry

Students performed in their worlds – they used clips from YouTube, and DVDs, drew on their knowledge of and passion for music videos, anime and video games.

One student wrote a poem about the life of a soldier in which he juxtaposes images from several online war games with real images of soldiers, past and present. He doesn't glorify war, as you might expect (as most war videogames do), but talks about the control the State has over a soldier's life – an interesting parallel to the control the gamer has over his characters in the virtual world. They wrote about personal concerns – the pressure on the dancer to stay thin, the loss of a friend to drink-driving, the perils of steroid use and the pressures of school and homework. They wrote about social justice issues – poverty, war, treatment of women, violence and weapons; in most cases, they put themselves into these poems using their images and they linked these issues to their lives and wrote about how to make change.

These poems are powerful not only because they can be shared so easily on YouTube or in other digital spaces, but also because they position adolescents as agents of change in their world. Keeping our goal of exploring the relationship between digital media and adolescents' understanding of global issues, while immersed in using digital media in mind, we prepared two groups of grade 6 students (11-year olds) to create digital poems based on their learning about First Nations people in Canada and the tragic legacy of residential schooling, by examining visual representations of First Nations people and the conditions in which some of them live, for example, in Attawapiskat, a northern Ontario community plagued by a housing and infrastructure crisis. While we wanted to encourage students to respond to the very real conditions facing First Nations people in Canada in an open and honest way in their poems, we also wanted to ensure that stereotypical notions of First Nations culture were not reinscribed and perpetuated. One of the things that we did involved exploring symbols associated with the Cree First Nation. The students participated in the *Project of Heart* (http://poh.jungle.ca/) which is an artistic organization dedicated to commemorating the lives of the thousands of First Nations children in Canada who were taken from their homes and who died as a result of being sent to residential schools. Our two grade 6 classes were assigned to Blue Quills, a former residential school in Alberta that has since been transformed into a First Nations College. The students decorated tiles using the symbols we viewed and discussed. When they were finished, a First Nations elder led a smudging ceremony, which promotes healing through cleansing the tiles of any negative energy. He also gave the students a first-hand account of life in residential schools and then the tiles were sent back to the Project of Heart organizers to be included in their tile gallery.

This kind of background preparation and visual scaffolding by the teacher helped students to move beyond using literal images and helped them to consider how their images, text on screen (font, colours and movement) and soundtracks were working together. Some of the students used soundtracks that they found on Creative Commons, but others wanted to create their own soundtracks. We brought a musician (Ian Parliament) in to work with some students to write music to accompany their digital poems. The students read their poems aloud to Ian and talked to him about what kind of music they envisioned that would complement the tone of their poems. After considerable discussion about tempo, whether to use major or minor chords, and what style/genre of music they preferred, Ian worked with the students to put the text of the poem into song. One of the poems that was set to music and sung by the three students was called 'Just By a Thread' (see Figure 17.3). It is included below and can be heard at http://faculty.uoit.ca/hughes/just-by-a-thread.html.

Just By a Thread

Water Flow.
Beating, abuse, loneliness.
I had to fight just to live.
Everyone deserves freedom.
I was taken away from it.
We are all connected, but were told to be different.
They destroyed our ways and wrecked the environment.

Figure 17.3 Image from 'Just By A Thread'.

Treated like puppets, with no rights.
Tragedy has no flow.
Hatred, blood, death.
Why?

When we asked the young authors how they felt adding music might have enhanced their poem, one of them responded:

> Since the poem already has a deep meaning, adding the music just emphasizes the meaning so that people can understand it and they won't just skip it – hear it once and then don't think about it. They actually take time and think about the poem . . . I think the music added to the poem because the music we had was deep and slow and this poem is telling us that change isn't really fast – it's not sudden – it takes a long while.

They also felt it was important to share the poem with classmates, family and others because it conveys an important message about how First Nations people were treated for over a century in Canada and this is not something that is typically found in their social studies textbooks.

Looking ahead

As we continue our work with adolescents composing digital poetry, we draw on our experiences in all of these classrooms. We note that students must be given opportunities to express themselves in a variety of ways, using all of the new technologies available to them at school and at home. In addition to the 'new technical stuff', we need to pay attention to the performative affordances of digital tools as students write for larger and more global audiences. After viewing more than 100 digital poems, and trying to determine what qualities or elements a 'good' digital poem has, we have found that the more effective poems are the ones that use more abstract images in conjunction with the text. Students need to see examples of digital poetry so that they can begin to imagine what they might be able to accomplish. The examples do not have to be exemplary; they just need to be given opportunities to discuss what works and what doesn't work when creating a digital poem, and start developing a critical lens for the digital poetry they create. By far, the biggest challenge is getting students to select images and music that move beyond the literal in order to get them thinking more figuratively, given that poetry itself employs figurative language using similes, metaphors, hyperbole and personification to make the reader/viewer see the familiar in a new way. We have found that this is best done by asking students to consider what message they want to convey and then to think about how each mode might contribute to that message. We ask them to be able to explain how each mode offers a different layer of meaning to the poem and we suggest that they use a chart adapted from Hull and Katz (2006) to help them, similar to the one shown in Table 17.1 below:

Table 17.1 Chart used to explore how each mode offers a different layer of meaning.

Linguistic (print)	Linguistic (verbal)	Visual (image)	Audio (sound)	Gestural (movement)	Special effects	Spatial

Conclusion

Through poetry writing, adolescents can give voice to those things that concern them most. As educators, we need to provide them with opportunities to think about who they are and what they want to represent to the world through not only what they say but also how they say it. Although creating awareness of problems in the world around us is an important first step, it is not enough. Students need to discover that 'change occurs only when individuals act to create it' (O'Neil 2010: 48). The performative potential of digital media facilitates exploration and creation of digital texts lending voice to the local and global issues that adolescents are most concerned about. These texts can, in turn, be shared with others as a way of engendering social change. Emancipatory actions can encourage students to write, read and re-write the world and the word, linking literacy to human agency and the power to 'effect social transformation' (Janks 2010: 161). I will close this chapter with the words of 13-year-old Irena (See Figure 17.4), who explains that, 'my purpose was to help people realize that it doesn't take a whole army of people to change or impact the world. I was focusing on the message that any small contribution is still a contribution and it can make a bigger effect than they think.'

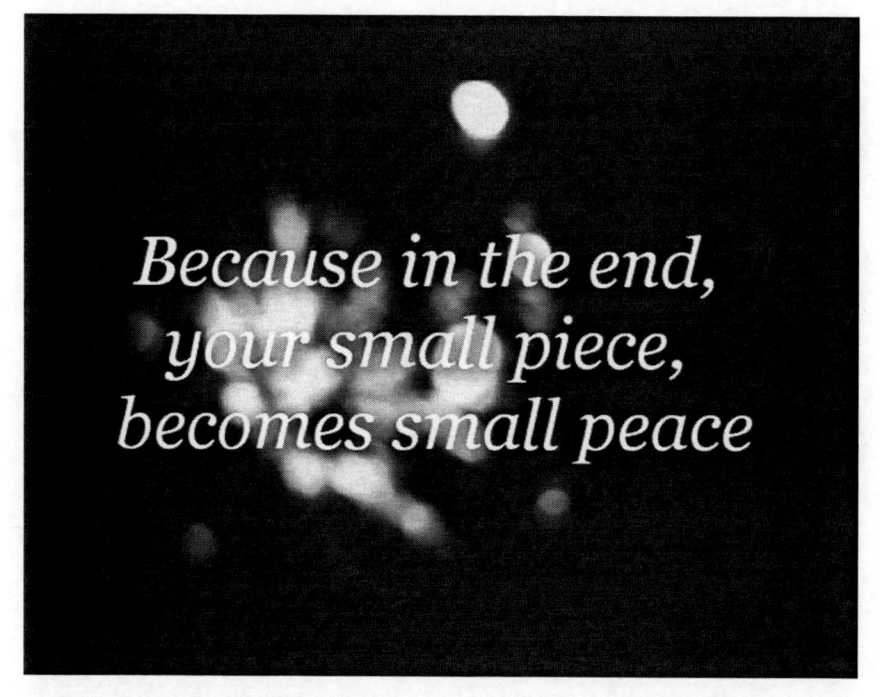

Because in the end, your small piece, becomes small peace

Figure 17.4 Irena's words.

18

Commentary: Poetry, Culture and Identity

Andrey Rosowsky

The three chapters in this section each address, in their own ways, the important nexus between poetry, culture and identity. Whether it is through the lens of getting young people to write poems drawing on their cultural and linguistic resources (Obied and Hughes) or whether it is through an examination of the tensions that exist between notions of the canon and the prescription of various forms – however defined – and national educational priorities (Dymoke), this nexus is always in the foreground of these writers' thoughts. Arjun Appadurai (1996) has shown us that the present moment of globalization is characterized by two major changes in socio-cultural processes – mass electronic communication and mass human movement. Each of these plays a crucial part in the three chapters in this section. The young people in Vicky Obied's chapter live in London, one of the most multilingual and multicultural communities on the planet, a very materialized outcome of Appadurai's vision of mass human movement; the young students in Ontario are inhabitants of their virtual and non-virtual worlds, belonging, as 'Vincent' says, in neither, as they explore their identities through digital technologies; and Sue Dymoke's references to the principles of Te Kotahitanga, and the attempts by teachers and students to reach out to the cultural and linguistic resources of the indigenous Maori heritage of New Zealand, are very much part of that shift in cultural paradigm where diversity and the valorization of cultural identity is part of the globalized context.

Obied provides us with a vivid exploration of young Londoners' identities through poetry, employing bi- and multilingual forms of language in a translanguaging mode. Her emphasis is on pupil voice and making connections between the lived realities of these young people and the forms of literary expression they can relate to. She also presents us with South London trainee teachers pitting themselves against the monolithic restrictions of the high-stakes testing regimes operating in UK schools presently and seeking to access those variegated sounds and shapes of linguistic origin against a backdrop of minority language shift and loss. These young people are helped by their trainee teachers to reach out to their primordial stock of cultural resources (song and verse) in order to forge intercultural understandings and negotiate identities within a multilingual reality that sits uncomfortably alongside a monolingual educational system. She makes the important point that it is these skills and this experience of negotiation and intercultural navigation, rather than performance in compartmentalized testing, which reflect more closely the social needs of citizens in postmodern contexts. We are moving from the 'what' of identity, of culture and of language to the 'how', and, in doing so, enter a more fluid, a more dynamic and a more negotiable set of circumstances, where essentializing notions of identity and culture give way to pluralities of identity, culture and ethnicity. She stresses how notions of identity are tied to feelings of social justice (this is linked to Hughes' 'agency' below) and poses the question can young people 'use poetry' (see Dymoke) as a way of negotiating their entry into and securing their place on the curriculum. She believes that when content and form (heritage languages) are drawn upon in the classroom (home to school), the disconnections usually felt and experienced are minimized. This may have significant impact on pupil engagement and attainment at school. We have known for a while (Gee 1990) that the disjuncture between home and school is not conducive to smooth transition to, and progress within, school. Conversely, we know that when home and school environments coincide culturally and linguistically, the opposite is usually true. The notion of 'linguistic repertoires' (Blommaert 2010) likewise acknowledges the resources that young people bring to their fluid lifestyles and life patterns in this late modern age with its affordances of mass digital communication and mass movement across the globe. We are far from the bounded world of fixed identities and monolingual dispositions. Rather such young people's propensities lie in their varied, permeable and flowing cultural and linguistic links. What Obied highlights very strongly in this chapter is how teachers are key agents in the promotion and recognition of these varied resources. In my own research (Rosowsky 2008), I have reported how I was dismayed, but perhaps not surprised, to discover that many teachers teaching children of diverse linguistic and cultural backgrounds knew very little of the languages spoken by their pupils (to the extent they did not know the name of any languages used at home nor were aware of how such languages might be supported, e.g. in complementary schooling). I have also had the experience shared by 'Luke' who found his pupils nonplussed and embarrassed by seeing their heritage languages in a written form with which they were unfamiliar. More recently, I have been disconcerted on a number of occasions to overhear teachers in staff rooms referring to 'cultural' poems (in the UK AQA GCSE Anthology referred to by Dymoke in her chapter), and, by doing so, reinforcing the essentializing and stereotypical perspectives such a choice of material was, with the best of intentions, designed to resist. This experience is to the shame and discredit of us all and is the direct result of accepting (consciously or not) the essentializing and monolingual hegemony that often prevails in our established school systems, at least in the United Kingdom.

In a similar fashion to Obied, Janette Hughes shares with us her work with young multilingual and multicultural Canadians as they negotiate their identities through their varied and rich linguistic and cultural resources. Through poetry they draw upon not only their shared heritage in terms of language and culture, but also their identities as living and breathing young teens interacting and engaging with the affordances of their age, the digital age. The home-school divide is again referred to in this chapter as we learn of 'Vincent' and his taciturn school persona being transformed dramatically by the deployment of his digital and linguistic resources to create a bold statement of his identities. The plurality he recognizes in himself is unabashed and unrepentant. Here is a young person at ease with the notion of layered and permeable identities, finding himself at home in the liminal world of 'flow' and negotiation. This is far away from the understanding of identity promulgated by the founders of Indian Residential Schools, with their fixed, bounded and unitary notion of culture and language, which 'Vincent' and his peers were introduced to by their skilful and compassionate teachers. The power of poetry to inspire and galvanize is here apparent as young Canadians participate in the nationwide movement to address past wrongs of their country's history. Here, they are 'agents of change' and share in that same aspiration for social justice with Obied's young multilingual Londoners. The 'transmediation' of these young people and their teachers is yet another example from that range of 'trans-modal' processes which we all use in our different ways to negotiate our way across and through the varied and variegated flows of culture, language and identity that characterize the age we live in. Sharing in the same dynamic as translanguaging, or translingualism (Creese and Blackledge 2010), these young people operate not within, and with, different modes and codes, but across and through them, stressing their fluidity rather than the autonomous and fixed nature of their borders. As with the findings of Obied, the disconnection between home and school also characterizes the experience of these young Canadians because, as yet, it is the home, rather than the school, where such digital affordances have most resonance, and where they are most linked in with identity.

Sue Dymoke provides a fascinating account of the search to recognize cultural identity in two settings, the United Kingdom and New Zealand. The New Zealand context for her chapter reveals how, beyond any discussion of the relevance of teaching 'form', poetry is seen as a vehicle for the expression of what is important and personal to those involved, readers and writers. The 'bicultural heritage' of its citizens is reflected in its bilingual curriculum and, more importantly it would appear, its policy recognition of indigenous diversity through the principles of *Te Kotahitanga*. Fishman (1991) reminds us wisely that official recognition of minority languages in official documents and institutions is only part of the solution to arresting language and cultural shift. Alongside such well-meaning processes, there must also be accompanying efforts to promote the language inter-generationally. My own research (Rosowsky 2011) has looked at how engagement in poetry and song in traditional languages may contribute to the maintenance of said languages among young people. It will be interesting to learn of the use of such forms in New Zealand and other contexts to bolster language maintenance particularly among the young, who gravitate to majority forms and modes more readily than their elders. What is emerging, at least in the communities I work with, is the potentiality of majority and minority languages working together in translingual ways to create poetry and song. The role of teachers, as with those in Hughes and Obied's studies, is also a key consideration. Dymoke expected to find distinct Maori or Samoan forms being taught but found teachers a little uncertain about how this might happen. It reinforces the idea that teachers' own knowledge about diversity is every bit as crucial as their positive attitudes and we must always be vigilant of promoting a romanticized view of diversity and multilingualism. All three authors, therefore, in their ways, stress and advocate the primacy of identity and culture in the creative and imaginative process involved in poetry reading and writing. All three leave us with an optimistic and vivid vision of the potentiality of young people to negotiate and navigate their way through the multiple flows of their cultural, linguistic and creative resources and repertoires.

19

Afterword

Myra Barrs with Morag Styles

This book asks us to think seriously about poetry education in all its aspects. It is an investigation of the factors that influence the teaching of poetry – from the experience and the attitudes of teachers, to the pressures of national curricula and exams. It asks how students – and teachers – can develop as readers and writers of poetry and how this development can be supported. Themes emerge and, in the spaces between the articles, new possibilities are generated.

What is a poem?

One of the questions that arises in this book is: what is a poem and how do we recognize one? Unsurprisingly, this question finds no answer. The multiplicity and variety of poetry would mock any attempt to give an easy answer. When asked by Boswell 'Sir, what is poetry?', Dr Johnson replied: 'Why Sir, it is much easier to say what it is not. We all *know* what light is, but it is not easy to *tell* what it is' (Boswell 1776: 38). Attempts to reduce this question to a matter of formal description are usually doomed; one of the big problems of poetry education is that it is the easily identifiable formal features of poems that often become the focus of attention, and that assume disproportionate importance in the minds of both teachers and students.

Because of this, undue emphasis is often placed on types of poetry (limericks, cinquains, tankas) which can be pinned down by a set of descriptors, or on imagery (simile, metaphor, personification), or on stanza forms (couplet, quatrain), or on rhyme schemes or metrical patterns. More time tends to be spent on the aspects of poetry that are thought to be teachable (e.g. rhyme) than on the aspects that are more subtle and less easily generalized about (e.g. rhythm).

Formalism

This formalist approach to poetry teaching was absolutely central to the National Literacy Strategy, and the influence of that initiative is still evident now, both in curricular assumptions and in teaching approaches. Like the writing curriculum, the Strategy's poetry curriculum was shaped by genre-based linguistics; form was paramount and poems were often studied in genre categories. Approximately 35 different poetic forms were referred to in the Strategy documents, including ballads, haikus and sonnets, and the other forms referred to above. But to start with form in teaching poetry is to start in the wrong place – poetry too quickly becomes regarded as a sort of crossword puzzle instead of as a way of singing/a kind of music.

Form can be liberating, as Don Paterson suggests in his illuminating study of the sonnet:

> 'The sonnet isn't some arbitrary construct that poets pit themselves against out of a perverse sense of craftsmanlike duty – it's a box for their dreams and represents one of the most characteristic shapes human thought can take. Poets write sonnets because it makes poems easier to write.' (1999)

But form can also be horribly constricting as in Roger McGough demonstrates in his haiku 'The only problem' (in Astley 2002: 18).

Poetic judgement

Formalist approaches are limited and show little awareness of the less teachable features of poems – for instance, line breaks, which are used by the makers of all kinds of poetry. Line breaks signal a little pause, a breath, a missed beat. Crucially, they emphasize meaning – where the line break comes has significance – and they may also introduce hesitation or ambiguity. The line break is a poet's basic tool which is very little discussed in classrooms, perhaps because there are no fixed rules involved; deciding where a line break should go is very much a question of poetic judgement.

The American poet Dana Gioia describes very clearly how basic line breaks are to the effect of a poem. He says:

> There should be a reason why every line ends where it does. Line breaks are not neutral. Lineation is the most basic and essential organizing principle of

verse. A reader or auditor need not understand the principle behind each line break intellectually, but he or she must intuitively feel its appropriateness and authority. (Gioia 2009)

But to 'intuitively feel' the principle behind a line break we need to have read a great deal of poetry. There is nothing mystical about this process of developing a feeling for the poetic decisions that shape a poem, and there are no short cuts to this kind of knowledge. Through broadening and deepening our experience as readers of poetry, we come to *know* what a poem is. This is something far too complex to be reducible to knowledge of a set of formal features which can be directly and explicitly taught.

A framework of knowledge and experience

A well-known quotation from Chapter 4 of the Bullock Report, in which we hear the unmistakable accents of James Britton, applies to all learning, including the learning of poetry:

> 'In order to accept what is offered when we are told something, we have to have somewhere to put it; and having somewhere to put it means that the framework of past knowledge and experience into which it must fit is adequate as a means of interpreting and apprehending it. Something approximating to "finding out for ourselves" needs therefore to take place if we are to be successfully told.' (1975: 50, section 4.9).

A poetic education has, above all, to enable learners to develop a framework of knowledge and experience into which their encounters with new poems and new aspects of poetry can fit. So, the central question for poetry education is: how are students, or teachers, to acquire the level of knowledge and experience of poetry they need in order to develop as readers and writers of poetry? A good place to start might be with Joy Alexander's advice to student teachers which contains her three basic principles for teaching poetry:

> 'You learn to read poetry by reading poetry'.
> 'Poets write poems so as to direct us to read poems the way they intended'.
> 'Find as many ways as possible to get young people to read poetry for themselves'.

Reading aloud, being read to, performing poems, making one's own anthologies – these are all good ways of being immersed in poetry. Other possible starting points suggest themselves throughout this book, but one point seems inescapably clear: the effective poetic education of *students* is deeply dependent on the effective poetic education of *teachers*. It is, therefore, a matter of concern that several of the chapters in this book suggest that poetry is an area where many teachers feel lacking in knowledge and experience.

Poetry and the teacher

This is not surprising given the fact that for nearly 20 years teachers in England have been working in a system which has increasingly laid down both what is to be taught and how it is to be taught – leaving less and less room for teachers' own ideas and initiative. The top-down and overdetailed national curriculum and national strategies have chipped away at teachers' professional confidence. Several contributions to this book provide evidence that many teachers feel deskilled in teaching poetry, although others show that teachers can find deep satisfaction and a sense of personal autonomy in teaching poetry.

Student teachers' 'poetry journeys'

Fiona Collins and Alison Kelly offer a clear analysis of the national scene and of how reductionist and didactic approaches to the English curriculum have put undue emphasis on poetic form and on assessment, and therefore constrained student teachers' options in teaching poetry. In their study of student teachers' attitudes to poetry, they found that only 6 respondents out of 49 recalled consistently positive 'poetry journeys'; there was a higher proportion of positive memories from their primary education than from their secondary schooling. Throughout schooling, most students reported that *teachers* had been a paramount factor in their enjoyment of poetry.

Four of these six students were followed into their teaching practice, and here – despite these student teachers' willingness to embark on teaching poetry – they did not always find a strong enough 'community of practice' with the class teacher to enable them to develop their work in this area. One student did find such a community with a teacher who loved poetry and was willing to give her free rein in choosing and discussing poetry with the class. But another student was only able to teach a single poetry lesson by choosing poems that would link in with RSPB week. Collins and Kelly also comment that whilst on school practice many student teachers encounter the tensions in their identities between being a learner and a teacher.

But the 'tensions... between being a learner and a teacher' are not experienced only by student teachers. Most teachers have to be prepared to be learners in areas where they lack knowledge and experience, but it is not always easy for them to hold these roles in balance. As teachers they are often expected to be universal experts, and as learners they have to acknowledge inexperience and uncertainty, to be tentative and try things out, and to be prepared to make mistakes. We have been working lately in an education system which views teachers as technicians, which assumes that teaching should be fast-paced and instructional. We need a *truly educational* education system, one where it is understood that teachers should also be learners, and where there is much more space for enthusiasm and imagination.

Subject leaders: Responding and assessing

Andrew Lambirth et al explore another aspect of the teacher's role in the poetry curriculum: responding to children's writing of poetry. Unfortunately, given the times that we all live in, 'respond' too quickly turns into 'respond and assess', and the authors move into a review of how the National Curriculum, national assessment and the framework for Assessing Pupil's Progress (APP) used in England have impacted on the teaching of poetry. In all these cases, the assessment criteria for writing, as they point out, are oriented towards prose forms. The National Literacy Strategy, with its focus on the technical elements of poetry, did nothing to encourage creative poetry teaching approaches. In such a system – in one of the most telling quotations used in this book –

> Many teachers work bureaucratically when they should work artistically (Freire 1985: 79).

The authors studied primary subject leaders' attitudes towards 'responding to and assessing' children's poetry. They found that poetry was not used by any of the subject leaders to assess children's writing progress, instead teachers focused on genres which fitted more easily into the Assessing Pupil Progress assessment framework. The knock-on effect of this was that poetry was less regularly taught. (Similarly, Sue Dymoke, in her account of the study of poetry in New Zealand, found that poetry was not usually offered as part of writing assessment because it was a 'risk'. This created a real danger that 'Poetry could be left out').

Most subject leaders were reluctant to assess poetry and regarded the development of a set of criteria for such assessment as being potentially counterproductive. They tended to see poetry as a 'special case' because of being 'from the heart' or an expression of 'the child's voice'. The authors point out that the limitations of this view of poetry writing as primarily self-expression: Benton suggests that protecting what is considered to be the child's self-expression and viewing it as 'sacrosanct' leaves little room for intervention and consequently limits the writer's capacity to communicate.

Perhaps one problem in this whole area is the too ready elision of 'respond' and 'assess'. It doesn't need to be like this. If teachers could only unhook these two terms they might be better able to find positive ways of responding to students' writing that would help to improve it – without rushing to assess it. Responding and intervening are essential to teaching, they are basic to the teaching-learning dialogue. We need to rediscover formative assessment, not in the sense of testing ever more frequently, but in the original sense of describing and analysing what students can do and discussing with them what they need to work on.

'A pool of freedom around a rock'

But other chapters provide more hopeful insights into teachers' attitudes to poetry. Anthony Wilson suggests that the metaphors that teachers use when they discuss the teaching of poetry can reveal fundamental beliefs about writing poetry. He finds that the overarching metaphor, in the responses of 33 teachers to a questionnaire-survey, is the idea of freedom – freedom to play and experiment, freedom to bring emotion into learning, freedom from curricular restrictions.

What is so moving about this chapter is the insight into teachers' deepest personal feelings about an aspect of their teaching that they view as 'a joyous lifeline in a target driven job'. The metaphors they use reveal their commitment and their passion:

> 'reading, discipline and crafting leading to the writer playing in a kind of ocean, a pool of freedom around a rock.'
> 'seeing the subject through a microscope and a telescope simultaneously'.
> 'a form of writing which embodies a fragment of the soul'.
> 'a dialogue with oneself which also expresses and speaks to something shared'.

'I now teach from a reader's point of view'

Teresa Cremin's chapter on Exploring Teachers' Positions and Practices is a case study of what happens when one teacher is encouraged through a UKLA project to widen her practice in teaching poetry and to document the changes in her classroom. She expands her knowledge of modern poetry for children and also returns to the 'music and pleasure' of poets like Christina Rossetti and Robert Louis Stevenson. She notices things about her own reading – how she sub-vocalizes when she reads, how she has 'a sense of felt, physical engagement with some poems'. She shares her growing experiences of poetry reading with her class, reading and rereading poetry to children at least three times a week. She rediscovers her passion for poetry, with surprising results:

> . . . it has allowed me into my teaching again – to share something of my own love of literature and particularly poetry.

There is a sadness in this remark, which suggests that for some reason this teacher has felt excluded from her own teaching in the past. Perhaps many teachers who have been asked to teach from a preordained script have come to feel that they are no longer in charge of their teaching.

The effect of her changing practice on her pupils is striking. They are able to talk to an interviewer about what she is reading:

> Jonah: 'Silver' by Walter de la Mare – we've heard it on a tape too, she remembers her dad reading it to her when she was a child.
> Troy: She's also reading Christina Rossetti's poems – like 'Hurt no living thing' – it's about animals and Mrs Longing has been talking about how Christina Rossetti likes nature so she writes about it. You can choose what you write about if you are a poet.
> Gurjit: Also she's been reading Sheree Fitch, she's a new poet and she's still alive although lots of poets are dead.

These three 'initially reluctant' readers listed among their favourite poets Eleanor Farjeon, Robert Louis Stevenson, Wes Magee, Edward Lear, Tony Mitton, John Agard, Christina Rossetti, Sheree Fitch and Gervase Phinn.

We are impressed throughout this case study by the clarity of the process by which this teacher's rediscovery of the 'music and pleasure' of poetry leads to a personal change, and how this leads to a change in her relationship with children, which in turn leads to a changed relationship between the children and poetry. What this chapter powerfully conveys is the necessarily personal nature of teaching and learning. No research in which the researcher is an outside observer can quite match the drama of seeing a teacher tracking her own personal and professional development in this way, and observing the impact of her changed practice on children.

'It must give pleasure'

Gary Snapper suggests that for many advanced literature students, poetry education has led to negative feelings. At the GCSE level, they have studied prescribed poems in order to 'write highly formulaic answers to often highly formulaic questions on exam papers under intense time pressure'. As a consequence, they are often left with negative feelings:

> I enjoy reading it but not analysing it.

Routines of teaching poetry for examinations have become 'reductive de-aestheticised approaches' which can 'disable the text'.

He concludes that the way in which poetry is introduced in schools needs to be rethought:

> we need to make room for types of learning and reflection that are currently undervalued. . . . .(students) need to become aware of the sensual aesthetic qualities of poetry as well as to analyse its meanings . . . . they need to hear and watch poetry, and read and perform it, in order to experience its sounds and textures. They need to be re-connected to the singing and storytelling origins of poetry.

Snapper talks about students being 're-connected', as if an original connection has been lost. That original connection was surely in nursery rhymes and playground rhymes, in rhyming games, in rhythm and dance, in play.

Perhaps the most important thing that we can take from many of the chapters in this book is that the teaching of poetry needs always to keep in touch with the sensual aesthetic qualities of poetry – ideas of 'progression' which imply that developing as a poetry reader and writer always means moving towards a more abstract focus on form and meaning will leave behind the heart of the experience. We all need to be re-connected, all the time, to the basics of poetry – sound, rhythm, pattern, music, play and pleasure. 'It must give pleasure', says Wallace Stevens, in his 'Notes towards a Supreme Fiction' (1965).

The American poet Edward Hirsch describes walking once through a museum in Athens and coming across a tall-stemmed wine cup from ancient Greece inscribed with a line of Sappho:

'Mere air, these words, but delicious to hear.'

He comments:

I paused for a long time to drink in the strange truth that all the sublimity of poetry comes down in the end to mere air and nothing more, to the sound of these words and no others, which are nonetheless delicious and enchanting to hear. (Hirsch 2006)

Like wine, poetry needs to be tasted, held in the mouth and savoured.

Writing poetry

Along with the pleasures of reading, we need – teachers as well as students –to experience the pleasures of writing. The ESRC seminars gave its members such experiences and with them the familiar frustrations that come from writing to order – the blank paper, the blank mind, the slow stirring of an idea . . . . But we also experienced the pleasure of making, of getting back in the kitchen, getting our hands in the dough. 'Poetry is like bread,' wrote Pablo Neruda, 'it should be shared by all, by scholars and by peasants, by all our vast, incredible, extraordinary family of humanity' (2010).

Making is central to poetic experience; and with that comes the *messiness* of making. Don Paterson observes that

Academics . . . often make the crucial error of failing to understand that the poem ends up on the page as a result of a messy and unique process, not a single operation. (1999)

Learning how to tangle with language, the pleasures and frustrations of making, must be part of coming to know poetry.

As in teaching drama, where 'teacher-in-role' is such a powerful way of sharing in and leading children's learning, so in the poetry classroom teachers will be most effective if they can become poetry learners alongside their students so as to see from the inside what the dilemmas are, experience the discoveries and lead a community in shared learning.

Interdependence and interaction

Wherever we start – with children reading and reflecting on poetry, with students making their own poems, with the pleasures of giving poetry a voice by reading it aloud – we always arrive at the need to integrate all these modes in an adequate poetry curriculum so that they can influence and nourish each other.

One of the main things that we know about language development and literacy development is that the different language modes develop through interaction – interaction with people and interaction between the modes. When language is divided into categories, as it was in the National Curriculum and the National Literacy Strategy in the United Kingdom, there is always a danger, despite our best efforts, that we shall forget or neglect these most basic interrelationships. Speaking always depends on listening, in the teaching of poetry as in the learning of language. There is always a reader in the writer. And it's through talk *about* reading and writing that we share our experiences and perceptions of what it is that is being said and what works in this way of saying. Gary Snapper refers to Richard Andrews' observation that our ideas of teaching poetry in school need to 'embrace the multi-modality of poetry'.

Performance

Performance is a key way in, because it takes poetry off the page and makes it into living sound. It allows us to 'taste' the poem, and to live it. As Denise Levertov declares, the essence of the poetic imagination is a savouring and 'chewing' of experience, bringing 'all that lives to the imagination's tongue' (Levertov 1964). Performing a poem is one of the most enjoyable ways of finding out how it tastes, how it works, how it hangs together, how rhythm, word music, the patterning of language and sound all combine to express feelings and meanings.

In the poetry seminar series which gave rise to this book, we listened to and viewed recordings of students' performances of poems. Though something of the atmosphere of these performances comes over in the accounts published here, the full zest and individuality of those readings cannot be completely conveyed on the page. They clearly showed students experiencing poetry as a kind of music, which it is, and coming to feel completely at home with it. Performing their own poems so stirred the 5th grade New York students in Janine Certo's class that they took to organizing poetry readings in the family rooms of each other's houses. It was no longer a school thing, it was cool.

Transformative pedagogy

How is poetry going to matter to modern students? Sasha Matthewman suggests that poetry can raise environmental consciousness; it can help children to develop a deeper knowledge and respect for nature and their own environment. This chapter begins to articulate some very new ideas that sent us hurrying off to read Jonathan Bate's *The Song of the Earth*. Matthewman calls his book a 'groundbreaking ecocritical study of nature poetry' in which Bate offers 'nuanced re-readings of romantic poetry locating authors and texts within their historical, geographical and environmental contexts'.

Bate's thesis is far-reaching. He is interested in the romantic poets, and in rereading them to show that, far from being aesthetes, promoting an appreciation of 'beauty in nature' like that of the day trippers pouring into the Lake District at the beginnings of 'picturesque tourism', they are much more like ecological critics. In the poem 'Lines Written Above Tintern Abbey', Wordsworth ignores the abbey, which was the focus of the guidebooks, and instead focuses on the landscape above it, its woods and copses, its 'plots of cottage ground' and orchards. His mind dwells on the 'round ocean and the living air/and the blue sky' and on the 'motion and the spirit' that 'rolls through all things', and holds all life together. Bate suggests that this vision is 'Wordsworth's distinctive version of the Gaia principle' (2000).

Matthewman takes her class of 30 PGCE student teachers on a field trip to Tintern Abbey, as an 'experiment in ecocritical pedagogy'. The students read and discuss the poem, relate it to their own experience of the landscape and discuss critical questions related to the picturesque. They write their modern takes on the picturesque scene, with its inevitable cast of tourists. They also follow a sculpture trail through the forest during which they are asked to focus and write about one sculpture and also about one particular wildflower that they find. Matthewman comments that the students' poems suggest that 'there is something very powerful to be learned from the close observation and shared experience of environment'.

This is perhaps not a very new realization, but it is a very convincing one. It matters a great deal that poetry should not just be something dreamed up at a desk, or as a linguistic game. It matters that poetry should become for students a way of seeing the world around us, whether urban or rural. It matters that poetry should be about something real, and important to the writer. Matthewman suggests that teaching nature poetry is as much about encouraging environmental awareness as it is about poetic education, and in this sense may be a 'transformative pedagogy'. Perhaps we need to aspire to a transformative pedagogy in all poetry teaching.

Poetry teaching should create change – changes in awareness, changes in sensibility, changes in our sense of language and changes in our thinking. For poetry itself creates change. Wallace Stevens shows us how things 'are changed upon the blue guitar' (Stevens 1965: 52).

Or as James Berry puts it:

> Poetry is a form of music that stirs connections. It's the human experience in discovery. It opens up ideas that you didn't know existed until you tried to put them into words. Writing poetry is a way of striving to see as deeply as possible, as widely as possible, as accurately as possible. (2011: 14)

Notes

Chapter 4

1 See Hennessy and McNamara (2011) for further discussion. I do not suggest here, however, that the British examination system is entirely to blame for teachers' choice of reductive pedagogical strategies: there is plenty of evidence that such pedagogies in literature teaching remain even when there is no examination. Protherough (1986) writes: 'Examinations can act as a convenient scapegoat for teachers who, in their heart of hearts, like the security of familiar "academic" pressures' (p. 148). There is also plenty of evidence that such pedagogies are strong internationally.

Chapter 9

1 In most Primary Schools in the United Kingdom, a teacher is given subject leadership responsibility for literacy. The role includes overseeing the resources, documentation, monitoring and staff development for literacy in the school. They are sometimes referred to as Literacy Strand Coordinators or Literacy Leaders, Literacy Managers or Literacy Subject Leaders.

Chapter 13

1 Lochhead, Liz. (1985) *True Confessions and New Clichés*. Edinburgh: Polygon.
2 Hutchby, Ian and Robin Wooffitt. (1998) *Conversation Analysis*. Cambridge: Polity Press.
3 AQA. (2008) *2008 Examiner Standardisation GCSE English Specification A Paper 2 Tier H, Script 5*. Manchester: AQA.

Chapter 14

1. The Poetry Archive website is available at www.poetryarchive.org.
2. Joy Alexander cites Ruth Finnegan (2005) 'The How of Literature,' *Oral Tradition*, 20(2), 164–87 in her use of this term.

Chapter 16

1. In England, Wales and Northern Ireland, there are four examination boards. Scotland has a separate examination system.
2. Decile ratings from 1 to 10 (10 is highest) are based on the proportion of students from low socio-economic communities.
3. Aged 14–18.
4. www.nzepc.auckland.ac.nz/.
5. An initiative, aimed at raising achievement of Maori students and building respect through recognition of cultural perspectives (see Bishop and Berryman 2006).
6. A poetry slam is a competitive event in which poets perform original work to an audience that serves as the judge.
7. A structured form of Maori greeting used in a welcome ceremony.

References

Alexander, J. (2000) 'Orality and Modern Culture: "Listening" in the English Classroom', *Changing English*, 7(2), 167–76.
— (2008) 'Listening – the Cinderella Component of English,' *English in Education*, 42(3), 219–33.
— (2010) 'The affordances of orality for young people's experience of poetry,' in M. Styles, L. Joy, and D. Whitley (eds), *Poetry and Childhood*. London: Trentham, pp. 211–18.
Anderson, J., and Obied, V. (2011) 'Languages, Literacies and Learning: From Monocultural to Intercultural Perspectives,' *National Association for Language Development in the Curriculum (NALDIC) Quarterly*, 8(3), 16–26. Spring 2011. NALDIC.
Andrews, R. (1991) *The Problem with Poetry*. Milton Keynes: Open University Press.
Anstey, M., and Bull, G. (2006) *Teaching and Learning Multiliteracies: Changing Times, Changing Literacies*. Newark, DE: International Reading Association.
Appadurai, A. (1996) *Modernity at Large: Cultural Dimensions of Globalization*. Minneapolis: University of Minnesota Press.
AQA. (2008) *2008 Examiner Standardisation GCSE English Specification A Paper 2 Tier H, Script 5*. Manchester: AQA.
Armstrong, S. L., Davis, H. S., Paulson, E. J. (2011) 'The Subjectivity Problem: Improving Triangulation Approaches in Metaphor Analysis', *International Journal of Qualitative Methods*, 2(2), 151–63.
Askew, M., Brown, M., Rhodes, V., Wiliam, D. and Johnson, D. (1997) *Effective Teachers of Numeracy*. London, King's College: University of London.
Assaf, L. C. (2008) 'The Professional Identity of a Reading Teacher: Responding to High Stakes Assessment', *Teachers and Teaching: Theory and Practice*, 14(3), 239–52.
Astley, N. (2002) *Staying Alive: Real Poems for Unreal Times*. Tarset, Northumberland: Bloodaxe Books.
Atwell, N. (1998) *In the Middle: New Understandings About Writing, Reading, and Learning*. Portsmouth, NH: Boynton/Cook Publishers Inc.
Aubrey, C. (1997) *Mathematics Teaching in the Early Years: An Investigation of Teachers' Subject Knowledge*. Falmer: London.
Bakhtin, M. (1981) *The Dialogic Imagination*. Texas: University of Texas Press.
— (1986) *Speech Genres and Other Late Essays*. (V. W. McGee, Trans.). Austin, TX: University of Texas Press.
Ball, S. J. (1990) *Politics and Policy-Making in Education: Explorations in Policy Sociology*. Routledge: London.

Barton, D. (2007) *Literacy: An Introduction to the Ecology of Written Language*. Oxford: Blackwell.
Bate, J. (2000) *The Song of the Earth*. London, Basingstoke and Oxford: Picador.
Beard, R. (2000) 'Research and the National Literacy Strategy', *Oxford Review of Education*, 26, 3/4, The Relevance of Educational Research (Sep.–Dec. 2000), 421–36.
Benton, M. (1978) 'Poetry for Children: A Neglected Art', *Children's Literature in Education*, 9(3), 111–26.
Benton, P. (1984) 'Teaching Poetry: The Rhetoric and the Reality', *Oxford Review of Education*, 1(3), 319–27.
— (1986) *Pupil, Teacher, Poem*. Sevenoaks: Hodder and Stoughton Educational.
— (1999) 'Unweaving the Rainbow', *Oxford Review of Education*, 25(4), 521–31.
— (2000) 'The Conveyor Belt Curriculum? Poetry Teaching in the Secondary School II', *Oxford Review of Education*, 26(1), 81–93.
Bereiter, C., and Scardamalia, M. (1987) *The Psychology of Written Composition*. Hillsdale, NJ: Erlbaum Associates.
Berninger, V. W., Fuller, F., and Whittaker, D. (1996) 'A Process Model of Writing Development Across the Life Span', *Educational Psychology Review*, 8(3), 193–218.
Berry, J. (2011) 'Thinking about poetry', in *A Story I Am In: Selected Poems*. Tarset, Northumberland: Bloodaxe Books.
Bianchi, C. (2005) Bombing of Poems. In *Performances: Research at Goldsmiths*. http://www.gold.ac.uk/media/performances.pdf (accessed 29/05/12).
Bishop, R., and Berryman, M. (2006) *Culture Speaks*. Wellington, New Zealand: Huia Publishers.
Bisplinghoff, B. S. (2002) 'Under the Wings of Writers: A Teacher Who Reads to Find Her Way', *The Reading Teacher*, 56(3), 242–52.
Black, R. (2007) 'Digital Design: English Language Learners and Reader Reviews in Online Fiction' in M. Knobel, and C. Lankshear' (eds), *A New Literacies Sampler*. New York: Peter Lang.
Blake, J., and Shortis, T. (2010) *Who's Prepared to Teach School English? The Degree Level Qualifications and Preparedness of Initial Teacher Trainees in English*. London: The Committee for Linguistics in Education (CLIE).
Blamey, M., Fitter, R., and Fitter, A. (2003) *Wildflowers of Britain and Ireland*. London: A&C Black.
Blommaert, J. (2010) *The Sociolinguistics of Globalisation*. Cambridge: Cambridge University Press.
Bluett, J. (2011) *Survey of Poetry Experience 2011*. http://teachersandpoetry.pbworks.com/w/browse/#view = ViewFolder&param = Poetry%20Matters%20Student%20Survey (accessed 26/10/12).
Boal, A. (1995) *The Rainbow of Desire: The Boal Method of Theatre and Therapy*. New York: Routledge.
Booktrust. (2010) *The Motion Report: Poetry and Young People*. London: Booktrust.

Boswell, J. (1776) *James Boswell's Life of Samuel Johnson 1766–1776.* (1994 edition) M. Waingrow (ed.). Edinburgh: Edinburgh University Press.

Brownjohn, S. (1980) *Does It Have to Rhyme? Teaching Children to Write Poetry.* London: Hodder and Stoughton.

— (1990) *What Rhymes with 'Secret'?* London: Hodder and Stoughton.

— (1994) *To Rhyme or Not to Rhyme?* London, England: Hodder and Stoughton.

Bruner, J. S. (1986) *Actual Minds, Possible Worlds.* Cambridge, MA: Harvard University Press.

— (1990) *Acts of Meaning.* Cambridge, MA: Harvard University Press.

Bruns, A. (2006) 'Towards produsage: Futures for user-led content production', in F. Sudweeks, H. Hrachovec, and C. Ess (eds), *Proceedings: Cultural Attitudes towards Communication and Technology.* Perth, Australia: Murdoch University, pp. 275–84.

Bullock Report. (1975) *A Language for Life.* London: HMSO.

Burn, A. (2008) 'The Case of Rebellion: Researching Multimodal Texts' in J. Coiro, M. Knobel, C. Lankshear, and D. Leu (eds), *Handbook of Research on New Literacies* (pp. 151–78). NY: Lawrence Erlbaum Associates.

Butterfield, E. C., Hacker, D. J., and Albertson, L. R. (1996) 'Environmental, Cognitive and Metacognitive Influences on Text Revision', *Educational Psychology Review*, 8(3), 239–97.

Calder, A. (2011) *The Settlers Plot: How Stories Take Place in New Zealand.* Auckland: Auckland University Press.

Cameron, D. (2001) *Working with Spoken Discourse.* London: Sage.

Carver, R. (1986) 'Eagles', in *Where Water Comes Together with Other Water.* New York: Vintage Books.

Certo, J. L., Apol, L., Wibbens, E., and Yoon, S. (2010) 'Poetry writing PK-12: Current research and implications for practice and future research' in G. Troia, R. Shankland, and A. Heintz (eds), *Putting Writing Research into Practice: Applications for Teacher Professional Development.* New York: Guilford Press.

Certo, J. (2011) Posterous posting, 17/01/11. ESRC Poetry Matters Seminar Series, 2011–12. http://poetrymatters.posterous.com/.

Chambers, A. (1979) 'General comments', in Wain, J., A. Tucker, and A. Chambers, *The Signal Poetry Award*, May 1979. Thimble Press: Stroud, pp. 63–79.

Chapman, M. L. (1999) 'Situated, Social, Active: Rewriting Genre in the Elementary Classroom', *Written Communication*, 16(4), 469–90.

Charmaz, K. (2006) *Constructing Grounded Theory.* London: Sage Publications.

Children, Schools and Families Committee. (2010) *From Baker to Balls: The Foundations of the Education System Ninth Report of Session 2009–10.* http://www.publications.parliament.uk (accessed 7/9/2012).

Coe, M. (2006) *Our Thoughts Are Bees: Writers Working with Schools.* London: Wordplay Press.

Coffey, A., and Atkinson, P. (1996) *Making Sense of Qualitative Data Analysis: Complementary Strategies.* Thousand Oaks, CA: Sage.

Coleridge, S. T. (1995) 'The Rime of the Ancient Mariner', in J. Green (ed.), *Key Poets: Classic Poetry for National Curriculum Key Stages 3 and 4*. Harmondsworth, Middlesex: Penguin.

Collins, B. (1988) *The Apple That Astonished Paris*. Arkansas, Fayetteville: University of Arkansas Press.

Collins, F. M., and Kelly, A. (2009) 'A Poem a Day: Exploring student teachers knowledge about and attitudes towards poetry', Paper presented at *Poetry and Childhood* International Conference, British Library, April 2009.

Colquhoun, G. (1999) 'The trick of standing upright here', in *The Art of Walking Upright*. Aotearoa New Zealand: Steele Roberts.

Commeyras, M., Bisplinghoff, B. S., and Olson, J. (2003) *Teachers as Readers: Perspectives on the Importance of Reading in Teachers' Classrooms and Lives*. Newark, DE: International Reading Association.

Cook, G. (2000) *Language Play, Language Learning*. Oxford: Oxford University Press.

Cookson, P. (2000) *The Works: Every Kind of Poem You Will Ever Need for the Literacy Hour*. London: Macmillan.

Cooney, S. (2000) *Studies in Verse/The Nature of Poetry: Bad Poetry*. http://homepages.wmich.edu/~cooneys/poems/bad/index.html (accessed 7/9/12).

Cope, B., and Kalantzis, M. (1993) *The Powers of Literacy: A Genre Approach to Teaching Writing*. Pittsburgh: University of Pittsburgh Press.

— (eds) (2000) *Multiliteracies: Literacy Learning and the Design of Social Futures*. London/New York: Routledge/Falmer.

Cox, B. (1991) *Cox on Cox: An English Curriculum for the 1990's*. London: Hodder and Stoughton Educational.

Creese, A., and Blackledge, A. (2010) 'Translanguaging in the Bilingual Classroom: A Pedagogy for Learning and Teaching?' *The Modern Language Journal*, 94, 103–15.

Cremin, T., Bearne, E., Mottram, M., and Goodwin, P. (2008a) 'Primary Teachers as Readers', *English in Education*, 42(1), 1–16.

— (2008b) 'Exploring Teachers Knowledge of Children's Literature', *Cambridge Journal of Education*, 38(4), 449–64.

Cremin, T., Mottram, M., Collins, F., Powell, S., and Safford, K. (2009) 'Teachers as Readers: Building Communities of Readers', *Literacy*, 43(1), 11–19.

Cresswell, J. W. (2002) *Research Design: Qualitative, Quantitative, and Mixed Methods Approaches*. London: Sage.

Crimmel, H. (2003) *Teaching in the Field: Working with Students in the Outdoor Classroom*. Salt Lake City: University of Utah Press.

Cropley, A. J. (2001) *Creativity in Education and Learning: A Guide for Teachers and Educators*. London: Kogan Page.

Crossley-Holland, K. (2000) 'Different – but oh how like!', in G. Cliff-Hodges, M. Drummond, and M. Styles (eds), *Tales, Tellers and Texts*. London/New York: Cassell, pp. 15–26.

Crystal, D. (1998) *Language Play*. Harmondsworth: Penguin.

Csiksentmihalyi, M. (2002) *Flow: The Psychology of Happiness*. London: Rider.
Cummins, J. (2000) *Language, Power and Pedagogy: Bilingual Children in the Crossfire*. Clevedon: Multilingual Matters.
— (2006) 'Identity texts: The imaginative construction of self through multiliteracies pedagogy', in O. Garcia, T. Skutnabb-Kangas, M. Torres-Guzman (eds), *Imagining Multilingual Schools: Languages in Education and Glocalization*. Clevedon: Multilingual Matters, pp. 51–68.
Datta, M. (2007) *Bilinguality and Literacy* (Second Edition). London/New York: Continuum.
Day, C., Kington, A., Stobart, G., and Sammons, P. (2006) 'The Personal and Professional Selves of Teachers: Stable and Unstable Identities', *British Educational Research Journal*, 32(4), 601–16.
Dias, P., and Hayhoe, M. (1988) *Developing Response to Poetry*. Buckingham: Open University Press.
Department for Children, Families and Schools & Qualifications and Curriculum Authority (DCFS & QCA). (2007) *The National Curriculum: English*. London: DCFS.
Department for Education and Employment & Qualifications and Curriculum Authority (DfEE & QCA). (1999) *English: The National Curriculum for England (Key Stages 1–4)*. London: The Stationery Office.
Department for Education and Employment (DfEE). (1998) *The National Literacy Strategy: Framework for Teaching*. Sudbury: DfEE Publications.
Department for Education and Employment (DfEE). (2000) *Grammar for Writing*. London: DfEE.
Department for Education and Skills (DfES). (2006) *Primary National Strategy: Framework for Literacy and Mathematics*. Nottingham: DfES Publications.
— (2009) *Primary National Strategy*. http://webarchive.nationalarchives.gov.uk/20110809091832/http://www.teachingandlearningresources.org.uk/primary (accessed 5/2/13).
Department of Education and Science (DES). (1975) *A Language for Life* (The Bullock Report). London: HMSO.
Department of Education and Science (DES). (1989) *English in the National Curriculum*. London: HMSO.
Dickenson, T. (2003) *Wildflowers: An Easy Guide by Habitat and Colour*. Dartington: Green Books.
Donoghue, D. (1981) *Ferocious Alphabets*. London: Faber and Faber.
Dooley, C. M. (2005) 'One Teacher's Resistance to the Pressures of Test Mentality', *Language Arts*, 82(3), 177–85.
Dreher, M. (2003) Motivating Teachers to Read, *The Reading Teacher*, 56(4), 338–40.
Duffy, C. A. (1992) as cited in Fraser, A. (1992) (ed.) *The Pleasure of Reading*. London: Bloomsbury.
Duke, N. K. (2000) '3.6 Minutes Per Day: The Scarcity of Informational Text in First Grade', *Reading Research Quarterly*, 35(2), 202–24.

Dunn, J., Warburton, N., Styles, M. (1987) *In Tune with Yourself.* Cambridge: Cambridge University Press.

Dymoke, S. (2001) 'Taking Poetry off its Pedestal: The Place of Poetry Writing in an Assessment-Driven Curriculum', *English in Education*, 35(3), 32–41.

— (2002) 'The Dead Hand of the Exam: The Impact of the NEAB Anthology on Poetry Teaching at GCSE', *Changing English*, 9(1), 85–92.

— (2003) *Drafting and Assessing Poetry: A Guide for Teachers*. London: Paul Chapman.

— (2007) 'Pre-service poetry teaching: Can the pursuit of 'quality' also embrace creativity?' Paper presented at AERA conference, April 2007, Chicago.

— (2011) 'Creativity in English teaching and learning', in J. Davison, C. Daly and J. Moss (eds), *Debates in English Teaching*. London: Routledge, pp. 142–56.

— (2012a) 'Poetry Is an Unfamiliar Text: Locating Poetry in Secondary English Classrooms in New Zealand and England During a Period of Curriculum Change', *Changing English*, 19(4), 395–410.

— (2012b) 'Opportunities or Constraints? Where Is the Space for Culturally Responsive Poetry Teaching within High Stakes Testing Regimes at 16+in Aotearoa New Zealand and England?' *English Teaching: Practice and Critique*, 11(4), 19–35.

Dymoke, S., and Hughes, J. (2009) 'Using a Poetry Wiki: How Can the Medium Support Pre-Service Teachers of English in their Professional Learning about Writing Poetry and Teaching Poetry Writing in a Digital Age?' *English Teaching: Practice and Critique*, 8(3), 91–106.

Dyson, A. (2003) *The Brothers and Sisters Learn to Write*. New York: Teachers College Press.

Dyson, A., Gallannaugh, F., and Millward, A. (2003) 'Making Space in the Standards Agenda: Developing Inclusive Practices in Schools', *European Educational Research Journal*, 2(2), 228–44.

Ellis, V., Fox, C., and Street, B. (2007) *Rethinking English in Schools*. London: Continuum.

Elster, C., and Hanauer, D. (2002) 'Voicing Texts, Voices Around Texts: Reading Poems in Elementary School Classrooms', *Research in the Teaching of English*, 37(1), 89–134.

English, E., Hargreaves, L., and Hislam, J. (2002) 'Pedagogical Dilemmas in the National Literacy Strategy: Primary Teacher's Perceptions, Reflections and Classroom Behaviour', *Cambridge Journal of Education*, 32(1), 9–26.

Erickson, F. (2003) 'Some notes on the musicality of speech', in D. Tannen and J. Alatis (eds), *Lingusitcs, Language and the Real World: Discourse and Beyond*. Washington DC: Georgetown University Press, pp. 11–35.

Faust, M., and Dressman, M. (2009) 'The Other Tradition: Populist Perspectives on Teaching Poetry Published in English Journal, 1912–2005', *English Education*, 41, 114–34.

Finnegan, R. H. (2005) 'The How of Literature', *Oral Tradition*, 20(2), 164–87.
Fisher, M. (2003) 'Open Mics and Open Minds: Spoken Word Poetry in African Diaspora Participatory Literacy Communities', *Harvard Educational Review*, 73(3), 362–89.
Fishman, J. A. (1991) *Reversing Language Shift: Theoretical and Empirical Foundations of Assistance to Threatened Languages*. Clevedon, UK: Multilingual Matters.
Fowler, A. (1982) *Kinds of Literature: An Introduction to the Theory of Genres and Modes*. Cambridge, MA: Harvard University Press.
Fraser, A. (ed.) (1992) *The Pleasure of Reading*. London: Bloomsbury.
Fraser, D. (2006) 'The Creative Potential of Metaphorical Writing in the Literacy Classroom', *English Teaching: Practice and Critique*, 5(2), 93–108.
Freire, P. (1985) *The Politics of Education*. London: Macmillan.
Freire, P., and Macedo, D. (1987) *Literacy: Reading the Word and the World*. London: Routledge and Kegan Paul Ltd.
Friedrich, P. (1979) *Language, Context, and the Imagination*. Palo Alto: Stanford University Press.
Gannon, G., and Davies, C. (2007) 'For the Love of the Word: English Teaching, Affect and Writing', *Changing English*, 14(1), 87–98.
Garcia, O. (2009) *Bilingual Education in the 21st Century – A Global Perspective*. Chichester: Wiley-Blackwell.
Garrard, G. (2010) 'Problems and Prospects in Ecocritical Pedagogy', *Environmental Education Research*, 16(2), 233–45.
Gee, J. P. (1990) *Social Linguistics and Literacies: Ideology in Discourses*. Hampshire: The Falmer Press.
— (2002) 'Millennials and bobos, blue's clues and sesame street: A story for our times', in D. E. Alvermann (ed.), *Adolescents and Literacies in a Digital World*. New York: Peter Lang, pp. 51–67.
Gibbons, P. (2009) *English Learners, Academic Literacy, and Thinking*. Portsmouth, NH: Heinemann.
Gioia, D. (2009) *Thirteen Ways of Thinking about the Poetic Line*. http://www.danagioia.net/essays/e13ways.htm (accessed 25/10/12).
Goodwyn, A. (2001) 'Second Tier Professionals: English teachers in England', *Language Studies in Language and Literature*, 1, 149–61.
— (2004) *English Teaching and the Moving Image*. London: RoutledgeFalmer.
Gordon, J. (2004) 'Verbal Energy: Attending to Poetry', *English in Education*, 38(1), 92–103.
Grainger, T., Goouch, K., and Lambirth, A. (2005) *Creativity and Writing: Developing Voice and Verve in the Classroom*. London: Routledge.
Graves, D. (1983) *Writing: Teachers and Children at Work*. Portsmouth, NH: Heinemann.
Green, P., and Ricketts, H. (eds) (2010) *99 Ways into New Zealand Poetry*. Auckland, New Zealand: Vintage, pp. 451–61.

Hall, K. (2002) 'Co-Constructing Subjectivities and Knowledge in Literacy Class: An Ethnographic- Sociocultural Perspective', *Language and Education*, 16(3), 178–94.

Hall, L., Johnson, A., Juzwik, M., Stanton, E., Wortham, F., and Mosley, M. (2010) 'Teacher Identity in the Context of Literacy Teaching: Three Explorations of Classroom Positioning and Interaction in Secondary Schools', *Teaching and Teacher Education*, 26, 234–43.

Hayes, J. R., and Flower, L. S. (1980) 'The Dynamics of Composing', in Gregg, L. W., and Steinberg, E. R. (eds), *Cognitive Processes in Writing*. New Jersey: Lawrence Erlbaum Associates, Hillsdale, pp. 31–50.

Heaney, S. (1981) *Preoccupations: Selected Prose* 1968–1978. New York, US: Farrar, Straus and Giroux.

— (1989) 'Influences: The power of T. S. Eliot', *Boston Review*. October, http://bostonreview.net/BR14.5/heaney.html (accessed 23/10/12).

— (1998) 'Death of a Naturalist', in *Opened Ground: Poems 1966–1996*. London: Faber and Faber.

Hennessy, J. (2011) 'Dissecting the bird to articulate the song' Exploring the nature of teaching and learning poetry in the Irish leaving certificate classroom. *Unpublished PhD thesis*. Department of Education and Professional studies, University of Limerick, Ireland.

Hennessy, J., and McNamara, P. (2011) 'Packaging Poetry? Pupils' Perspectives of their Learning Experience within the Post-Primary Poetry Classroom', *English in Education*, 45(3), 206–23.

Henry, J. (2001) 'Warning to Cool the Test Frenzy', *Times Educational Supplement*, November 2nd, No. 4453, 8.

Hirsch, E. (1999) *How to Read a Poem and Fall in Love with Poetry*. San Diego, CA: Harvest Book, Harcourt, Inc.

— (2006) 'Mere Air, These Words, but Delicious to Hear'. http://www.poetryfoundation.org/learning/article/177210 (accessed 25/10/12).

Holbrook, D. (1967) *The Exploring Word: Creative Disciplines in the Education of Teachers of English*. Cambridge: Cambridge University Press.

Holliday, A. (2011) *Intercultural Communication and Ideology*. London: Sage.

Hornberger, N. (2010) 'Language and education: A Limpopo lens', in N. Hornberger, and S. McKay (eds), *Sociolinguistics and Education*. Bristol: Multilingual Matters, pp. 549–64.

Hughes, T. (1967a) *Poetry in the Making*. London: Faber and Faber Ltd.

— (1967b) 'The Thought-Fox', in *Poetry in the Making*. London: Faber and Faber Ltd.

Hughes, J., and Dymoke, S. (2011) ' "Wiki-Ed Poetry": Transforming Pre-Service Teachers' Preconceptions About Poetry and Poetry Teaching', *Journal of Adolescent & Adult Literacy*, 55(1), 46–56.

Hull, G. A., and Katz, M. (2006) 'Creating an Agentive Self: Case Studies of Digital Storytelling', *Research in the Teaching of English*, 41(1), 43–81.

Hunt, C. (2006) 'Travels with a Turtle: Metaphors and the Making of a Professional Identity', *Reflective Practice* 7(3), 315–32.

Hutchby, I., and Wooffitt, R. (1998) *Conversation Analysis*. Cambridge: Polity Press.

Hymes, D. H. (1996) *Ethnography, Linguistics, Narrative Inequality: Toward an Understanding of Voice*. London: Taylor & Francis.

HyperRESEARCH. Copyright © 1988–2007. Researchware, Inc.

Jackson, D. (1979) 'Process in Action: A Sixth Form Approach to Seamus Heaney', *English in Education*, 13(3), 23–32.

Jakobson, R. (1987) *Language in Literature*. Cambridge, MA: The Belknap Press of Harvard University Press.

Janks, H. (2010) *Literacy and Power*. New York: Routledge.

— (2000) 'Domination, Access, Diversity and Design: A Synthesis for Critical Literacy Education', *Educational Review*, 52(2), 175–86. doi:10.1080/713664035.

Jewitt, C. (2008) *Technology, Literacy, Learning: A Multimodal Approach*. New York: Routledge.

Jocson, K. M. (2005) ' "Taking it to the Mic": Pedagogy of June Jordan's Poetry for the People and Partnership with an Urban High School', *English Education*, 37(2), 132–48.

Kellogg, R. T. (1994) *The Psychology of Writing*. Oxford: Oxford University Press.

Kingman, J. (1988) *Report of the Committee of Inquiry into the Teaching of English Language*. London: HMSO. retrieved from: http://www.educationengland.org.uk/documents/kingman/index.html.

Koch, K. (1970) *Wishes, Lies, and Dreams: Teaching Children to Write Poetry*. New York: Chelsea House.

— (1973) *Rose Where Did You Get that Red? Teaching Great Poetry to Children*. New York: Random House.

Kress, G. (2003) *Literacy in the New Media Age*. London: Routledge.

Kress, G., and Van Leeuwen, T. (2001) *Multimodal Discourse: The Modes and Media of Contemporary Communication*. London: Arnold.

Kress, G., Jewitt, C., Bourne, J., Franks, A., Hardcastle, J., Jones, K., and Reid, E. (2004) *English in Urban Classrooms*. London: RoutledgeFalmer.

Lakoff, G., and Johnson, M. (1980) *Metaphors We Live By*. Chicago, IL: University of Chicago Press.

Lambirth, A., Smith, S., and Steele, S. (2012) ' "Poetry Is Happening But I Don't Exactly Know How": Literacy Subject Leaders' Perceptions of Poetry in their Primary Schools', *Literacy*, 46(2), 73–80.

Lankshear, C., and Knobel, M. (2007) 'Sampling "the New" in New Literacies', in M. Knobel, and C. Lankshear (eds), *A New Literacies Sampler*. New York: Peter Lang, pp. 1–24.

Lantolf, J., and Appel, G. (1994) *Vygotskian Approaches to Second Language Research*. Norwood, NJ: Ablex.

Lave, J., and Wenger, E. (1991) *Situated Learning: Legitimate Peripheral Participation*. Cambridge: Cambridge University Press.

Lawrence, D. H. (1929) 'Preface to "Chariot of the sun" by Harry Crosby', in E. D. Macdonald (ed.), *Phoenix*. London: Heinemann.

Leavis, F. R. (1986) *Valuation in Criticism and Other Essays.* Cambridge: Cambridge University Press.

Lensmire, T. (1994) *When Children Write: Critical Re-Visions of the Writing Workshop.* New York: Teachers College Press.

Lewis, C. S. (1992) *An Experiment in Criticism.* Canto imprint, Cambridge: Cambridge University Press.

Levertov, D. (1964) *O Taste and See.* New York: New Directions.

Lewis C. S., and Tillyard, E. M. W. (1939) *The Personal Heresy.* London: Oxford University Press.

Lochhead, L. (1985) *True Confessions and New Clichés.* Edinburgh: Polygon.

Locke, T. (2008) 'English in a Surveillance Regime: Tightening the Noose in New Zealand', *Changing English*, 15(3), 293–310.

— (2009) 'The disappearance of enjoyment: How literature went wandering in the literacy woods and got lost', in J. Manuel, P. Brock, D. Carter, and W. Sawyer (eds), *Imagination, Innovation, Creativity: Re-Visioning English in Education*. Putney, NSW: Phoenix Education, pp. 123–38.

— (2010) 'Reading, writing and speaking poetry', in D. Wyse, R., Andrews, and J. Hoffman (eds), *The Routledge International Handbook of English, Language and Literacy Teaching*. London: Routledge, pp. 367–78.

Lorde, A. (1985) *Sister Outsider: Essays and Speeches.* Berkeley, CA: Crossing Press.

Lyons, G. E. (1999) 'Where I'm From', in *Where I'm From, Where Poems Come From*. Spring, Texas: Absey and Co. http://www.georgeellalyon.com/where.html (accessed 27/10/12).

Marshall, B. (2000) *English Teachers – The Unofficial Guide: Researching the Philosophies of English Teachers.* London: RoutledgeFalmer.

Martin, T. (2003) 'Minimum and Maximum Entitlements: Literature at Key Stage 2', *Reading, Literacy and Language*, 37(1), 14–18.

Martlew, M. (1983) *The Psychology of Written Language: Developmental and Educational Perspectives.* London: Wiley.

Matthewman, S. (2007) 'But What About the Fish? Teaching Ted Hughes' Pike with Environmental Bite', *English in Education*, 41(3), 66–77.

— (2011) *Teaching Secondary English as if the Planet Matters.* Abingdon: Routledge.

McClenaghan, D. (2003) 'Writing Poetry – and Beyond', *English Teaching: Practice and Critique*, 2(2), 96–102.

McCormick, K. (1994) *The Culture of Reading and the Teaching of English.* Manchester University Press.

McGough, R. (2002) 'The Only Problem', in N. Astley (ed.), *Staying Alive*. Tarset, Northumberland: Bloodaxe Books.

McPake, J., Hélot, C., Anderson, A., and Obied, V. (2010) *Professional Development for Staff Working in Multilingual Schools.* Strasbourg: Council of Europe. http://www.

coe.int/t/dg4/linguistic/Source/Source2010_ForumGeneva/5-FormationProfStaff_en.pdf (accessed 29/05/12).

McRae, J. (1996) 'Representational language learning: From language awareness to text awareness', in R. Carter, and J. McRae (eds), *Language, Literature and the Learner*. London/New York: Longman, pp. 16–40.

Medwell, J., Wray, D., Poulson, L., and Fox, R. (1998) *Effective Teachers of Literacy: Final Report on a Research Project*. Exeter: University of Exeter.

Miles, M. B., and Huberman, M. A. (1994) *Qualitative Data Analysis: An Expanded Sourcebook* (Second Edition). Thousand Oaks, CA: Sage.

— (2002) *The Qualitative Researcher's Companion*. Thousand Oaks, CA: Sage Publications.

Miller, C. R. (1984) 'Genre as Social Action', *Quarterly Journal of Speech*, 70(May), 151–67.

Mills, K. A. (2009) 'Multiliteracies: Interrogating Competing Discourses', *Language and Education*, 23(2), 103–16.

Ministry of Education. (2007) *The New Zealand Curriculum*. Wellington: Learning Media Limited.

— (2012) *What Has Changed in the English Curriculum?* http://seniorsecondary.tki.org.nz/English/What-has-changed (accessed 15/9/12).

Mission, R., and Sumara, D. (2006) 'Reclaiming the "Creative" in the English/Literacy Classroom', *English Teaching: Practice and Critique*, 5(2), 1–5.

Morgan, W. (2006) ' "Poetry Makes Nothing Happen": Creative Writing and the English Classroom', *English Teaching: Practice and Critique*, 5(2), 17–33.

Moss, G. (2000) 'Raising Boys' Attainment in Reading: Some Principles for Intervention', *Reading*, 34(3), 101–6.

Motion, A. (2010) 'What Every Child Wants, What Every Child Needs', Speech given at the North of England Education Conference, York, England. 8th January 2010.

Murray, L. (1997) 'On Being Subject Matter'. http://www.duffyandsnellgrove.com.au/TeachersNotes/notes/Murraytn.html (accessed 23/10/12).

Myhill, D. A. (2005) 'Testing Times: The Impact of Prior Knowledge on Written Genres Produced in Examination Settings', *Assessment in Education*, 13(3), 289–300.

— (2011a) 'Grammar for designers: How grammar supports the development of writing', in S. Ellis, E. McCartney, and J. Bourne (eds), *Insight and Impact: Applied Linguistics and the Primary School*. Cambridge: Cambridge University Press, pp. 81–92.

— (2011b) 'The ordeal of deliberate choice': Metalinguistic development in secondary writers' in Berninger, V. (ed.), *Past, Present, and Future Contributions of Cognitive Writing Research to Cognitive Psychology*. New York: Psychology Press/Taylor Francis Group, pp. 247–74.

Myhill, D. A., Jones, S. M., Lines, H., and Watson A. (2012) 'Re-Thinking Grammar: The Impact of Embedded Grammar Teaching on Students' Writing and Students' Metalinguistic Understanding', *Research Papers in Education*, 27(2), 139–66.

Neruda, P. (2010) M. Eisner, (ed.), *The Essential Neruda: Selected Poems*. Tarset, Northumberland: Bloodaxe Books.

Netland, J. T. (1993) 'Reading and Resistance: The Hermeneutic Subtext of *The Rime of the Ancient Mariner*', *Christianity and Literature*, 43(1), 37–58.

Norton, B. (2010) 'Language and Identity', in N. Hornberger, and S. McKay (eds), *Sociolinguistics and Education*. Bristol: Multilingual Matters, pp. 349–69.

NZQA. (2012) *Assessment Guidance*. http://www.nzqa.govt.nz/ncea/assessment/search.do?query=English&view=exams&level=02 (accessed 6/3/12).

Obied, V. (2007) "Why Did I Do Nothing?' Poetry and the Experiences of Bilingual Pupils in a Mainstream Inner-City Secondary School. *English in Education*, 41(3), 37–52.

— (2010) 'Can One-Parent Families or Divorced Families Produce Two-Language Children? An Investigation into How Portuguese-English Bilingual Children Acquire Biliteracy within Diverse Family Structures', *Pedagogy, Culture & Society*, 18(2), 227–43.

Ofsted. (2007) *Poetry in Schools: A Survey of Practice, 2006/07*. London: Ofsted.

— (2012) *Moving English Forward: Action to Raise Standards in English*. London: Ofsted.

Oliver, M. (1994) *A Poetry Handbook*. San Diego, CA: Harcourt Brace.

O'Neill, H. (2006) 'Once Preferred, Now Peripheral: Poetry and the National Assessment for Year 11 Students in New Zealand Post-Primary Schools', *English Teaching Practice and Critique*, 5(3), 93–126.

O'Neil, K. (2010) 'Once Upon Today: Teaching for Social Justice with Postmodern Picturebooks', *Children's Literature in Education*, 41, 40–51.

Ong, W. J. (1982) *Orality and Literacy: The Technologising of the Word*. London: Routledge.

Paterson, D. (ed.) (1999) 'Introduction', in *101 Sonnets: From Shakespeare to Heaney*. London: Faber and Faber.

Peacock, M. (1999) *How to Read a Poem … and Start a Poetry Circle*. Toronto: McClelland and Stewart Inc.

Peel, R. (2000) 'Beliefs about "English" in England', in R. Peel, A. Patterson, and K. Gerlach (eds), *Questions of English: Ethics, Aesthetics, Rhetoric and the Formation of the Subject in England, Australia and the United States*. London: Routledge/Falmer, pp. 116–88.

Pinsky, R. (1998) *The Sounds of Poetry: A Brief Guide*. New York: Farrar, Strauss and Giroux.

Pirrie, J. (1987) *On Common Ground*. London: Hodder.

— (1994) *On Common Ground: A Programme for Teaching Poetry* (Second Edition). Godalming: World Wide Fund For Nature.

Poulson, L. (2001) 'Paradigm Lost? Subject Knowledge, Primary Teachers and Education Policy', *British Journal of Educational Studies*, 49(1), 40–55.

Powell, S. (2009) 'Live Poetry, Live Poetry: Poetry Live! The Anthology, and Poetry at GCSE', *English Drama Media*, 13, 9–13.

Protherough, R. (1986) *Teaching Literature for Examinations*. Milton Keynes: Open University Press.

Public Broadcasting Service (PBS). (2001) *Interview with Billy Collins*. www.pbs.org.newshour (accessed 28/6/12).

Rassool, N. (2004) 'Sustaining Linguistic Diversity within the Global Cultural Economy: Issues of Language Rights and Linguistic Possibilities', *Comparative Education*, 40, 199–214.

Ray, R. (1999) 'The Diversity of Poetry: How Trainee Teachers' Perceptions Affect their Attitude to Poetry Teaching', *The Curriculum Journal*, 10(3), 403–18.

Regan, S. (2001) 'Poetry, Please', *English Subject Centre Newsletter*, 2, 7–9.

Rich, A. (1993) *Essay on Poetic Theory: Someone Is Writing a Poem*. http://www.poetryfoundation.org/learning/essay/239326 (accessed 21/3/12).

Richardson, W., and Mancabelli, R. (2011) *Personal Learning Networks Using the Power of Connections to Transform Education*. Bloomington, IN.: Solution Tree Press.

Robinson, K. with Aronica, L. (2009) *The Element: How Finding Your Passion Changes Everything*. London: Viking.

Rosen, M. (1997) 'Making Poetry Matter', in M. Barrs, and M. Rosen (eds), *A Year with Poetry*. London: Centre for Literacy in Primary Education.

— (1989) *Did I Hear You Write?* London: André Deutsch.

— (1982) *I See a Voice*. London: Hutchinson and Co.

Rosmarin, A. (1985) *The Power of Genre*. Minneapolis, MN: University of Minnesota Press.

Rosowsky, A. (2008) *Heavenly Readings: Liturgical Literacy in a Multilingual Context*. Clevedon: Multilingual Matters.

— (2011) ' "Heavenly Singing": The Practice of Naat and Nasheed and its Possible Contribution to Reversing Language Shift Among Young Muslim Multilinguals in the UK', *International Journal of Sociology of Language*, 212, 135–48.

Rummel, M. K., and Quintero, P. (1997) *Teachers'/Reading Teachers' Lives*. Albany, NY: State University of New York Press.

Rymes, B. (2010) 'Classroom discourse analysis: A focus on communicative repertoires', in N. Hornberger, and S. McKay (eds), *Sociolinguistics and Education*. Bristol: Multilingual Matters, pp. 528–48.

Sainsbury, M. (2009) 'Developing Writing in a High-Stakes Environment', in R. Beard, D. Myhill, J. Riley, and M. Nystrand (eds), *The Sage Handbook of Writing Development*. London: Sage, pp. 545–60.

Sansom, P. (1994) *Writing Poems*. Tarset: Bloodaxe Books.

Schechner, R. (1988) *Performance Theory*. London: Routledge.

— (2003) *Performance Theory*. London: Routledge.

Schwalb, N. (2006) 'East of the River: Crossing Borders through Poetry in Middle Schools', *English Journal*, 96(1), 40–5.

Sedgwick, F. (2003) *Teaching Poetry*. London: Continuum.

Sharples, M. (1999) *How We Write: Writing as Creative Design*. London: Routledge.

Shattuck, R. (1999) *Candor and Perversion: Literature, Education and the Arts*. New York: WW Norton.

Showalter, E. (2003) *Teaching Literature*. Oxford: Blackwell.

Shulman, L. S. (1986) 'Those Who Understand: Knowledge Growth in Teaching', *Educational Researcher*, 15(2), 4–14.
Skelton, S. (2006) 'Finding a Place for Poetry in the Classroom Every Day', *English Journal*, 96(1), 25–9.
Sleeter, C., and Cornbleth, C. (2011) *Teaching with Vision: Culturally Responsive Teaching in Standards-Based Classrooms*. New York: Teachers College Press.
Snapper, G. (2009a) 'Editorial', *English Drama Media*, issue 13, 2–3.
— (2009b) 'Beyond English Literature A Level: The Silence of the Seminar?', *English in Education*, 43(3), 193–210.
— (2011) 'From School to University and Back Again: Travels between Sixth Form and HE English', *English Drama Media*, 21, 43–50.
Spiro, J. (2007) 'Teaching Poetry: Writing Poetry – Teaching as a Writer', *English in Education*, 41(3), 78–93.
— (2009) 'Creating Space: Where I Stand', *Educational Journal of Living Theories*, 1(2), 140-71.
— (2011) 'Reader response and the formulation of literary judgement', in J. Swann, R. Pope, and R. Carter (eds), *Creativity in Language and Literature: The State of the Art*. London: Palgrave Macmillan, pp. 231–44.
— (2013) 'Learner and writer voices: Learners as writers and the search for authorial voice', in D. Disney (ed.), *After Babel*. Pennsylvania: John Benjamins.
Stables, A. (2002) 'Poetic Experience: Found or Made?' *English in Education*, 36(3), 28–35.
— (2010) 'The Song of the Earth: A Pragmatic Rejoinder', *Educational Philosophy and Theory*, 42(7), 796–807.
Stevens, W. (1965) *Selected Poems*. London: Faber and Faber.
Stibbs, A. (2000) 'Can You (Almost) Read a Poem Backwards and View A Painting Upside Down? Restoring Aesthetics to Poetry Teaching', *Journal of Aesthetic Education*, 34(2), 37–47.
Strauss, A., and Corbin, J. (1990) *Basics of Qualitative Research: Grounded Theory Procedures and Techniques*. Newbury Park, CA: Sage.
Street, B. (ed.) (1993) *Cross-Cultural Approaches to Literacy*. Cambridge: Cambridge University Press.
— (1995) *Social Literacies: Critical Approaches to Literacy in Development, Ethnography and Education*. London: Longman.
Styles, M. (1992) 'Just a kind of music: Children as poets', in M. Styles, E. Bearne, and V. Watson (eds), *After Alice: Exploring Children's Literature*. London: Cassell, pp. 73–88.
Sumara, D. J., and Davis, B. A. (2006) 'Correspondence, Coherence, Complexity: Theories of Learning and their Influences on Processes of Literary Composition', *English Teaching: Practice and Critique*, 5(2), 34–55.
Swanson, D. R. (1978) 'Toward a Psychology of Metaphor', *Critical Inquiry*, 5(1), 163–6.
Task Group on Assessment and Testing. (1987) *A Report*. London: Department of Education and Science and The Welsh Office. http://www.educationengland.org.uk/documents/pdfs/1988-TGAT-report.pdf (accessed 7/9/12).

Thompson, L. (ed.) (1996) *The Teaching of Poetry: European Perspectives*. London: Cassell.

Training and Development Agency (TDA). (2008) *Results of the Newly Qualified Teacher Survey 2008*. http://extra.shu.ac.uk/nqtstudy/downloads/nqt_survey_results_2008_1_exec_sum.pdf (accessed 29/05/12).

Troman, G. (2008) 'Primary Teacher Identity, Commitment and Career in Performative School Cultures', *British Educational Research Journal*, 34(5), 619–33.

Vygotsky, L. S. (1962) *Thought and Language*. Cambridge, MA: MIT Press.

— (1978) *Mind in Society: The Development of Higher Mental Processes*. Cambridge, MA: Harvard University Press.

Weber, J., and Horner, K. (2012) *Introducing Multilingualism*. London/New York: Routledge.

Weber, S., and Mitchell, C. (2008) 'Imagining, keyboarding, and posting identities: Young people and new media technologies', in D. Buckingham (ed.), *Media. Youth, Identity, and Digital Media*. Cambridge, MA: The MIT Press, pp. 25–48.

Weinstein, S. (2009) *Feel these Words: Writing in the Lives of Urban Youth*. New York: SUNY Press.

— (2010) 'A Unified Poet Alliance: The Personal and Social Outcomes of Youth Spoken Word Poetry Programming', *International Journal of Education & the Arts*, 11(2), 1–24.

Wells, R., and Swain, C. (2008) *Teachers as Readers: Pick a Poem*. Project Report for Medway Local Authority.

Wilson, A. C. (2005a) 'The Best Forms in the Best Order? Current Poetry Writing Pedagogy at KS2', *English in Education*, 39(3), 19–31.

— (2005b) 'Signs of Progress': Reconceptualising Response to Children's Poetry Writing', *Changing English*, 12(2), 227–42.

— (2007) 'Finding a Voice? Do Literary Forms Work Creatively in Teaching Poetry Writing?' *Cambridge Journal of Education*, 37(3), 441–57.

— (2009) 'Creativity and constraint: Developing as a writer of poetry', in R. Beard, D. Myhill, M. Nystrand, and J. Riley (eds), *The Sage Handbook of Writing Development*. London: Sage, pp. 387–401.

— (2010) 'Teachers' Conceptualisations of the Intuitive and the Intentional in Poetry Composition', *English Teaching: Practice and Critique*, 9(3), 53–74.

Wilson, A. C., and Myhill, D. A. (2012) 'Ways with Words: Teachers' personal epistemologies of the role of metalanguage in the teaching of poetry writing', *Language and Education*. 26(6), 553–68.

Wordsworth, W. (1984) 'Lines Written a Few Miles above Tintern Abbey on Revisiting the Banks of the Wye during a Tour, July 13, 1798', in S. Gill (ed.), *William Wordsworth*. Oxford: Oxford University Press.

Yandell, J. (2008) 'Exploring Multicultural Literature: The Text, the Classroom and the World Outside', *Changing English*, 15(1), 25–40.

Yates, C. (2007) 'Writing Like Writers in the Classroom: Free Writing and Formal Constraint', *English in Education*, 41(3), 6–19.

Zuzovsky, R. (1994) Conceptualizing Teachers' Knowledge About Teaching: An Advanced Course in Teacher Education, *Studies in Educational Evaluation*, 20, 387–408.

Index

A poem a day   25
Adcock, F.   158
adjectives   58, 75, 98
Advanced Level (A- level) English   31–41, 45, 122, 199
affordances   168, 177
Agard, J.   17, 26, 158, 190
Ahlberg, A.   10, 28–9
Alexander, J.   4, 118, 124, 139–40, 186, 198
alliteration   51, 128
Anderson, J.   144, 149
Andrews, R.   1, 33–4, 61, 87–8, 92, 193
Angelou, M.   158–60
Anstey, M.   171
anthologies   34, 78, 83, 122, 147, 159, 163, 182
Appol, L.   109
Armstrong, S. L.   63
Assaf, L. C.   11
Assessing Pupils' Progress (APP)   87, 90, 188
assessment   3, 5, 22–4, 34, 67–8, 84–7, 90–2, 96, 98, 129, 154–66, 187
   assessment, controlled   159
   assessment tools   90–1
Assessment Qualifications Alliance (AQA)   197
attention   4, 117
attitudes   149
   attitudes to poetry   20–30
Auden, W. H.   56
auditory imagination   119, 122–3
Austen, J.   159
Avia, T.   158

backwash effect   86, 91
Bakhtin, M.   106, 147
Ball, S. J.   68
ballad   117–18, 184
Barrs, M.   6

Bate, J.   71–3, 77, 194
Baxter, J.   158
Beard, R.   68
Beer, P.   159
Benton, M.   62
Benton, P.   2, 23–4, 52, 61–2, 88, 93, 100, 154, 161, 189
Bereiter, C.   2
Berninger, V. W.   51
Berry, J.   195
Bevan, C.   15, 17
Bianchi, C.   144
bilingual   180, 183
   poetry   149
   students   150
Bishop, R.   198
Bisplinghoff, B. S.   10
Blake, J.   144
Blake, W.   26, 38
Blamey, M.   82
Block, L.   159
Bloom, V.   10
Bloomaert, J.   181
Bluett, J.   35
Boal, A.   107
Boswell, J.   184
Bridger, B.   158
Britton, J.   186
Brownjohn, S.   61, 65, 75–6
Bruchac, J.   110
Bruner, J. S.   62, 170
Bruns, A.   164
Bullock Report (1975)   21, 23
Burn, A.   169
Butterfield, E. C.   51
Byron, G.   72

Calder, A.   72
Cameron, D.   146
Canada   5, 140
Carver, R.   81

case studies   14, 26–30, 44, 77–82, 169, 190
Certo, J.   4, 30, 105, 138–9, 193
Chambers, A.   22
Chapman, M. L.   108
Charmaz, K.   155
Children's poetry   10
cinquain 184
Clare, J.   73
classroom observation   155
coding   64, 89–90, 107, 155, 169
Coe, M.   76
Coffey, A.   13
cognitive skills   51
Coleridge, S. T.   5, 116–18, 140
Collins, B.   31, 40, 121, 159
Collins, F. M.   3, 24, 44, 186
Colquhoun, G.   158, 162
Commeyras, M.   2, 11
community   99, 101, 106, 109, 114–15, 138, 145–6, 175
community of practice   29, 60, 97, 187
composing   108, 154, 167–79
composition   50
conceptualization (of poetry)   87
concrete poetry   53, 57
confidence   29, 33, 42, 50, 52, 96, 99, 121, 125, 162, 164–5, 187–8
Cook, G.   101
Cookson, P.   22
Cooney, S.   84
conversation analysis   130–1, 134, 140
Cope, B.   108, 171
Cope, W.   10
Cox, B.   65
creating   156
creative/creativity   5, 49, 52, 64–6, 164, 174, 183
   abilities   86
   writing movement   87, 101
Creese, A.   182
Cremin, T.   2–3, 9–10, 13, 19, 24, 42–4, 88, 190
Cresswell, J. W.   90
Cropley, A. J.   64
Crossley-Holland, K.   144
Crystal, D.   101
Csiksentmihalyi, M.   101
cultural anxiety   30

cultural boundaries   146
cultural identity   145, 180
cultural memory   44–5
culturally responsive   155
culture   2, 24, 26, 30, 33–4, 36, 38, 41, 61–2, 148, 180–3
transformative poetry cultures   5, 141–83
Cummings, E. E.   75
Cummins, J.   144, 149
curriculum   1–2, 22, 39, 52, 61–4, 67–70, 86, 91, 93, 96, 98, 105, 118, 121, 123, 139, 145–6, 148, 152, 154–66

Dahl, R.   10
Dallas, R.   158
Datta, M.   144
Day, C.   21
design   49–50
Dias, P.   1
Dickenson, T.   79
difficulty   34, 93
digital poetry   5, 167–79
digital recordings   159
Dignan, D.   81–2
Dooley, C. M.   11
Donoghue, D.   118–20
drafting   65, 76
drafts   107, 162
dramatic monologue   163
Dreher, M.   11
Duffy, C. A.   10, 20–1, 26, 28, 38
Duke, N. K.   106
Dunn, J.   87, 92
Dymoke, S.   2, 5, 24, 30, 35, 37–8, 50, 52, 59, 62, 84, 86–7, 91, 120, 154, 157, 180–3, 188
Dyson, A.   67, 114

echo   128, 130, 133, 135–6, 140
eco-critical   71–83
Economic and Social Research Council (ESRC)   1–2, 6
ecopoetry   71–3
Edmond, L.   158
elementary schools   105–6, 108
Eliot, T. S.   122–4
Ellis, V.   2
Elster, C.   105–6

empowerment   50, 52, 126, 149
en-performancing   119–20, 122
English as an Additional Language (EAL)   5, 143–53
environment   72, 194
experiential approach   74
experiment   65, 69, 150, 189

Farjeon, E.   10, 17, 190
Faust, M.   154
fear of poetry   160–1, 165
feedback   52, 59, 76, 80, 94, 174
Ferlinghetti, L.   131–2
fieldwork   77–82
Fine, A.   17
Finnegan, R. H.   119–20, 198
First Nations people   175–7
Fisher, M.   107
Fishman, J. A.   183
Fitch, S.   14, 17–18, 190
form   10, 16, 20–3, 34, 38–40, 42, 44–5, 49–50, 65, 92, 97, 113, 115, 157, 163–4, 180–5, 187
found poetry   164
Fowler, A.   106
Fraser, D.   62
free verse   163–4
free writing   61
Freire, P.   153

Gannon, G.   10
Garcia, O.   151
Garrard, G.   73
Gee, J. P.   168, 181
gender   129
General Certificate of Secondary Education (GCSE)   23, 31–2, 35–8, 122, 154, 159, 163, 165, 182
genre   12, 49, 72, 76, 90–1, 93, 105–8, 114, 121, 132, 145, 151, 158–9, 161, 163–4, 176, 184–5, 188, 192
ghazal   163
Gibbons, P.   149
Gilpin, W.   77–8
Gioia, D.   185–6
Glover, D.   158
Goodwyn, A.   65
Gordon, J.   4, 39, 140
Grainger, T.   10

grammar   53–4, 75
Grammar for Writing   87
Graves, D.   108
Green, P.   164
grounded theory   155

haiku   50, 121, 184
Hall, K.   11
Harris, J.   109
Hass, R.   168
Hayes, J. R.   5, 51, 52
Heaney, S.   73, 122–3, 159
heard poetry   127–37
hearing   116–26, 192
Hennessy, J.   154, 197
Hirsch, E.   124, 192
Holbrook, D.   117
Holliday, A.   147
Hopkins, G. M.   74
Hornberger, N.   146
Hughes, J.   5, 62, 161, 174, 180
Hughes, L.   168
Hughes, T.   10, 61, 65, 74, 77
Hull, G. A.   169–70, 178
Hutchby, I.   197
hyperbole   177
Hymes, D. H.   106

iambic pentameter   50
identity   9, 11, 19, 114, 148, 153, 157, 161–3, 167, 170–2, 180–3
improving a poem   54, 58
inclusive education   143–53
intercultural practices   143–53
interdisciplinary learning   77
intertextuality   110, 139, 160, 166
interviews   12, 53–5, 59, 89–91, 107, 110–14, 146, 155, 169
intonation   129, 132, 136
Ireland, K.   158

Jackson, D.   39
Jakobson, R.   106
Janks, H.   168, 178
Jewitt, C.   169
Jocson, K. M.   107

Kay, J.   10
Keats, J.   72

Kellogg, R. T. 2, 51
Kelly, A. 3, 24, 44
kennings 58
Kingman Report (1988) 86, 91
knowledge 145, 186–7, 194
  subject knowledge 9–10, 19, 24, 28, 30, 33, 37, 43, 88–9, 94, 120
Koch, K. 61
Kress, G. 154, 168–9

Lakoff, G. 63
Lambirth, A. 2–3, 86, 96, 98–9, 101, 188
Langford, W. 109
language 22, 34, 49–54, 58, 62, 75, 86, 97, 101, 106, 144–5, 147, 161, 163, 166, 181–2, 192
  development 146, 193
  games 75
  play 98, 145
Lankshear, C. 170, 174
Lantolf, J. 106
Lave, J. 29
Lawrence, D. H. 4
layout 49, 57, 128
Lear, E. 10, 17, 190
learners 9, 11, 61–2, 66, 96–7, 99, 101, 126, 143–53, 160, 170, 184, 186, 188, 192
learning 12–13, 20–1, 25, 29, 37, 40, 44–5, 53, 59, 62, 64, 71, 77, 83, 89–90, 97–9, 106, 120, 127–9, 139, 144, 157, 163, 175, 186, 189, 191–3
Leavis, F. R. 123–4
Lee, H. 160
Lensmire, T. 114
Levertov, D. 193
Lewis C. S. 126
limerick 121, 184
line break 184–6
line length 49, 57, 97
listening 4, 37, 103–40, 156, 193
literacy 150, 173, 197
  lessons 10
  pedagogy 106
  subject leaders 89–91, 197
literary analysis 32, 45, 121
  criticism 40
  study 3, 31–2
  theory 39–40

Lochhead, L. 129–30, 132–5, 197
Locke, T. 1, 68, 154, 165
Lorde, A. 168
Lyons, G. E. 171
lyrical poetry 34
lyrics 38, 163

McClenaghan, D. 61
McCormick, K. 39
Magee, W. 17, 190
McGough, R. 10, 185
McKay, C. 159
Maori 156, 158, 164, 180, 183, 198
McPake, P. 146
McRae, J. 144, 151
Mare, W. de la 18
Marsh, S. T. 158
Martin, T. 19
Martlew, M. 51
Matthewman, S. 4, 71, 75, 97, 99, 194
meaning 3, 5, 31, 35, 38–9, 41, 50–3, 55–6, 59, 63, 72, 97–8, 117, 122–4, 128, 136, 147–8, 152–3, 170, 173, 178, 185, 191
meaning making 84, 105–8, 120, 138, 156
Medwell, J. 89
metacognition 51
metalanguage 128
metalinguistic understanding 3, 49–60
metaphor 61–70, 96, 121, 152, 177, 184, 189
metre 128
mihi 164
Mila, K. 158
Miles, M. B. 63, 90, 107
Miller, C. R. 106
Milligan, S. 10
Mills, K. A. 148
Milne, A. A. 10
Mission, R. 62
Mitton, T. 17, 190
model (of learning) 64
modelling 157, 161–2
models 74–5, 81, 97
Morgan, W. 62
Morpurgo, M. 160
Moss, G. 12
Motion, A. 23–4, 30, 33

multi-modal 34, 49, 119, 138, 167
multi-modality 153
Murray, L. 124
music 15, 38, 57, 120, 122, 167, 177, 190–1, 193
musicality 144, 152
Myhill, D. 3, 49, 51–3, 96–7, 101, 154

National Certificate of Educational Achievement (NCEA) 154–66
National Curriculum 22, 36, 87, 187, 193
National Literacy Strategy 22, 75, 92, 185, 188, 193
National Strategy 13, 22, 187
nature poetry 4, 71, 73, 80–2, 194
Neruda, P. 168, 192
Netland, J. T. 116
New Zealand 5, 72, 154–66, 180, 183, 188
New Zealand National Curriculum 154–66
New Zealand Qualifications Authority (NZQA) 159–60
Nicholls, G. 10
Norton, B. 148
Nvivo 54

O'Neill, H. 154, 160
Obied, V. 5, 61–2, 144, 150, 152, 180–3
Office for Standards in Education (Ofsted) (2007 *Poetry in Schools*) 1–2, 10, 22, 24, 33, 42, 68, 86–8, 91–2, 154
Oliver, M. 109
Ong, W. J. 120
onomatopoeia 121
oral 156, 158
  response 129, 151
orality 76, 118, 126
Owen, W. 27, 151, 159

Pacific poets 158, 164
Pakeha 72, 156
Paterson, D. 185, 192
Peacock, M. 167, 174
pedagogy 1–5, 13, 24–5, 30, 36, 39, 44–5, 53, 62, 64, 71–3, 77, 89, 91, 94, 97, 99–101, 116, 120–1, 128–9, 140, 143–53, 194–5, 197
  environmental 73
  of place 79

Peel, R. 9
performance 45, 105, 138–9, 172, 193
performing 4, 37, 105–15, 140, 163, 167, 186
personal expression 88, 93
  personal growth 65–6, 87, 98
  personal voice 62, 65, 152
personification 177, 184
Phinn, G. 14, 17, 190
Pinsky, R. 123
Pirrie, J. 61, 65, 74
Plath, S. 28
play 18, 22, 27, 35, 56, 58, 60, 65–6, 69, 115, 137, 189, 191
pleasure 31, 99, 163, 190, 192
Poem a Day 25, 27
poetic structure 54–9, 74–5
Poetry Aloud 140
Poetry Archive 139, 198
Poetry By Heart 140
Poetry Jam 109, 112–14
Poetry Live! 36–7, 139
Poetry Matters 1–2, 5–6, 166
Poetry Out Loud 140
Point Evidence Explanation (PEE) 132, 138
portfolios 12, 105, 112, 165
Postgraduate Certificate of Education (PGCE) 77–83, 97, 194 *see also* student teachers
Poulson, L. 88–9
Powell, S. 23, 36
presenting 156
Primary National Strategy 13
primary teaching 10–30, 42–4, 63–4, 85–9, 94, 99, 129, 147, 187–8, 199
problem (with poetry) 33, 43
problem (of poetry education) 184
professional development 43, 191
progress 22, 66, 86–91, 98, 151, 188, 191
Project of Heart 175–7
prose 21, 52, 55, 59, 67, 99, 158
Protherough, R. 197
Pullinger, D. 44
punctuation 49, 51, 58, 123, 128
puns 53
puzzle of poetry 36, 55, 185

questionnaire 25–7, 29, 63–4, 149
quotations 127, 131–2, 135–6

rap 148
Rassool, N. 150
Ray, R. 2, 24, 27
readers of poetry 117–18, 186, 190, 193
　epi-readers 118, 120
　graphi- readers 118
reading 1, 7–45, 74, 76, 79, 106, 109, 115, 118–19, 121, 139, 154, 156, 158, 161, 163, 168–9, 183, 190, 193
　aloud 15, 18, 56, 121, 123–6, 164, 186
　for pleasure 9–11, 13, 15–17
　habits 9
　histories 15
　Reading Teacher studies 11
recitation 29
Regan, S. 32
resistance 31–41
response to poetry 2–4, 39, 84–95, 98, 117, 127, 140
revision 107, 115
rhyme 28–9, 54–7, 59, 75, 119, 128, 145, 184, 191
rhythm 16, 34, 38, 49, 54–7, 59, 71–3, 119, 121–3, 145, 184, 191, 193
Rich, A. 49–50
riddles 53
risk 65, 69, 126, 164–5, 189
Risper, R. 109
Robinson, K. 101
Romantic poetry 71, 194
Romantic tradition 87
Romantic view of poetry writing 52, 163
Rosen, M. 10, 26, 28–9, 61, 65, 76, 85, 87, 96
Rosmarin, A. 106
Rosowsky, A. 181, 183
Rossetti, C. 10, 14–15, 17–18, 190
rules 49–50, 54–5, 67, 145, 164, 185
Rummel, M. K. 11
Rymes, B. 144

Sainsbury, M. 68
Samoan 158, 162, 164, 183
Schechner, R. 106–7
Schwalb, N. 61–2
secondary English teaching 10, 21, 27, 29, 33, 52, 131–2, 144, 154–66
Shakespeare, W. 39, 158, 159

Sharples, M. 2, 49, 100
Shattuck, R. 122
Sherman, A. 159
Showalter, E. 32
Shulman, L. S. 88–9, 94
simile 121, 177, 184
singing 38, 41, 191
Skelton, S. 61
slam poetry 138, 163, 198
Sleeter, C. 155
Snapper, G. 3, 22–3, 32, 43–5, 191, 193
social justice 5, 167–79
social literacy practices 115, 155
sociocultural theory 62
song 55, 71, 73, 110, 119–20, 145–7, 160–3, 174, 176, 183
sonnet 49, 121, 163, 184–5
sound 73, 120
speaking 103–40, 156, 193
Spiro, J. 100–1
Stables, A. 52–3, 60, 71, 73, 100
standards 67, 91, 96, 159
　US Common Core Standards 106
　Standard Assessment Tasks (SATs) 86
Stevens, W. 191, 195
Stevenson, R. L. 10, 14–15, 17, 190
Stibbs, A. 39
storytelling 38, 41
Strauss, A. 13, 64, 169
Street, B. 115, 155
student choice 158–9, 161
student teachers 77–83, 122, 146–53, 156, 180–1, 187, 194 *see also* Postgraduate Certificate of Education (PGCE)
Styles, M. 6, 61
Sullivan, J. 110
Sumara, D. J. 62
Swenson, M. 74
syllables 50, 57

talking about poetry 101, 116, 138, 153, 190
tanka 49, 184
Taylor, A. 158
Te Kotahitanga 162–3, 180, 183
teacher training 20–30
Teachers as Readers 10–13, 24
testing 2, 88

thinking about poetry   40, 49, 53–5, 58–9, 64–9, 82, 92–3, 160, 177, 195
Thompson, L.   1, 154
transcription   130–1
transition   27
Troman, G.   87, 91
Tuwhare, H.   158

undergraduate teaching   20–32, 39–44
United Kingdom Literacy Association (UKLA)   9–10, 42
United States curriculum   105

verse   16, 34, 38, 44, 49–50, 55, 59, 123, 181, 186
villanelle   163
virtual worlds   180
visual   120, 156, 158, 173
   visual scaffolding   176
visiting poet(s)   28, 76, 109
vocabulary   54, 59, 79, 92, 151
voice   110, 114–26, 139, 157–8, 180, 189, 193
   personal voice   62, 65, 152
   poetic voice   76
Vygotsky, L. S.   62, 106–7

Walker, M.   110
war poetry   151–2

Weber, J.   148
Weber, S.   171
Weinstein, S.   107
Wendt, A.   158
Whitman, W.   75
wild flowers   79–82, 97, 194
Williams, W. C.   123
Wilson, A.   2–3, 10, 50, 52, 54, 61, 65–8, 75–6, 84, 86, 88, 91, 96, 98, 101, 189
word choice   54
word games   75
Wordsworth, W.   72, 77–9, 97, 119–20, 194
Wragg, T.   88
writers   16, 50–1, 61, 74, 76, 86–8, 92, 95, 97–101, 140, 158, 162, 170, 180, 183–4, 186
writing   1–4, 20, 34, 37, 47–101, 105–15, 127, 138, 144, 148, 153, 156, 161–3, 165, 183, 192, 195
writing workshop   74, 77, 80, 82, 98

Yates, C.   61
Yandell, J.   154
Yeats, W. B.   159

Zephaniah, B.   10, 24
Zuzovsky, R.   63